Also by Tom Gorman

Big League Business Thinking: The Heavy Hitter's Guide
to Top Managerial Performance (*with Paul C. Miller*)

Multipreneuring

(mŭl•ti•pre•ñeur′•ing) 1. *v.* Using a variety of skills and a series of careers to succeed. 2. *n.* The hottest career strategy for success in the 1990s—and beyond.

Tom Gorman

A FIRESIDE BOOK

Published by Simon & Schuster

FIRESIDE
Rockefeller Center
1230 Avenue of the Americas
New York, NY 10020

FIRESIDE and colophon are registered trademarks
of Simon & Schuster Inc.

Designed by Abby Kagan/King Kong Cody Design

Manufactured in the United States of America

1   3   5   7   9   10   8   6   4   2

Library of Congress Cataloging-in-Publication Data

Gorman, Tom.
Multipreneuring / Tom Gorman.
p. cm.
Includes index.
1. Creative ability in business.   2. Industrial
management.
3. Success in business.   I. Title.
HD53.G67   1996
650.1—dc20   96-3788
                                                        CIP

ISBN 0-684-81180-4

To Phyllis, Danny, and Matt

Contents

Introduction   9

Part One
The Multipreneurial Response to Change

1. Adapting to the New Marketplace   17

Part Two
The Principles of Multipreneuring

2. Add Value Constantly   43
3. Manage Risk Aggressively   65
4. Work Productively and Flexibly   90
5. Learn Continually   112

Part Three
The Practices of Multipreneuring

6. Act Like a Producer   135
7. Market Hard, Sell Soft   159
8. Exploit Technology   184
9. Take Care of Business   206

Part Four
The Transition to Multipreneuring

10. Making the Transition   233

    Acknowledgments   259
    Index   263

Introduction

Imagine, if you will, that you are not independently wealthy, but that you are certain of your ability to generate a high income. Imagine that you can leave your current employer or line of work, even leave your current industry, and continue earning this income as you move on to a new situation. Imagine that you have total confidence in your ability to locate and even create income-generating situations. Imagine that you are contacted regularly by people who want to hire you, but you often turn them down because they cannot afford you or you are too busy to take on new assignments.

Now imagine that you are never bored with your work. Instead you are excited by the economic opportunity you see everywhere. You wake up in the morning energized by the possibilities you see around you. You are an opportunity seeker and a creator of value. You are a profitable economic entity, taking inputs, working with them, and getting results such that people know in their hearts that you are worth every penny they pay you.

Imagine that you have moved beyond the cycle of employment, unemployment, job searches, and employment. You have moved beyond the adolescent corporate rituals of recruitment/indoctrination/hazing and membership/betrayal/ostracism. Instead your work-life consists of open, mature, adult-adult business relationships founded upon mutual need and value for value.

Imagine the accompanying sense of self-respect. Imagine saying to the next person who tries to flummox or exploit you, "Frankly, I don't see that as fair, and I'm disappointed that you would suggest it," *and* imagine that you are telling them this, not as you are walking out the door, not as they hand you your final check, not after you've given them ten years of your time and talent, but rather as you sit across from them the very first time they try to flummox or exploit you. And imagine that they respect you for telling them this as you move on to address the next topic of discussion.

If you cannot imagine any of this, you are reading the right book. If you can only imagine this, you are reading the right book. Because multipreneuring can make this imagined state of affairs a reality for you. All it takes on your part is a willingness to face reality and a deep desire to change.

Others have done it, and their experiences are the essence of this book. Years of secondary research, scores of formal interviews, hundreds of informal conversations, and two decades of my own experience have demonstrated that the multipreneurial approach to career management can be learned. There has never been a better time to start learning it. And, like it or not, an approach like this has become a necessity in the radically changed workplace of today—and tomorrow.

This is a book about how to manage your career in a way that will work for you in the newly restructured corporate world. Life in the managerial and professional ranks has undergone true structural change. The social contract between employer and employee has changed. The skills that you need in order to get a job have changed. Even the idea of what "to get a job" means has changed, and so has the attitude and the very identity that you must bring to the workplace. I call this attitude the multipreneurial attitude and this identity that of the multipreneur.

What is multipreneuring? It begins with the idea that each of us is an economic unit. So each of us—as either internal staff or external contractor—must add value to our work in excess of the amount we are paid. Our economy will be in flux for years to come, so each of us must develop and sell a portfolio of high-level skills useful in generating revenue, cutting costs, or improving processes in a variety of settings. *That* is multipreneuring. Companies are fostering new ways of getting work done—telecommuting, job sharing, and outsourcing—and are forming strategic alliances that result in virtual, modular, and networked corporations. So we must adapt to new ways of working and managing. *That* is multipreneuring. And since companies are becoming too flat to offer traditional paths to advancement and are relinquishing the role of provider of social goods in fat benefit plans, each of us must develop the flexibility, maturity, discipline, and courage to create our own career path and to become our own benefits managers. *That* is multipreneuring.

I've coined the word "multipreneuring" from the Latin *multi* meaning "many" or "more than one" and the English word "entrepreneur," which stems from the French verb *entreprendre*, which means "to undertake." So multipreneuring literally means "more than one undertaking." The play on the word "entrepreneur" is obvious: to succeed in business today, and even in many non-business fields, you have to be something of an entrepreneur, that is "one who organizes, manages, and assumes the risks of a business enterprise." This is largely what multipreneurs do. They organize their resources, manage their careers, and assume sensible risks. But multipreneuring entails more than just acting entrepreneurially.

Multipreneuring entails actually having multiple skills, so that you can develop multiple sources of income and multiple careers, either simultaneously or serially. Multipreneuring enables you to manage risks—financial risks, professional risks, emotional risks, and creative risks—rather than deny them or be disabled by them. Multipreneuring represents a continual process of learning new skills, new strategies, new fields, new businesses, and new markets and of developing new contacts, customers, and friends. Essentially, multipreneuring entails understanding the principles and practices that will enable you to prosper in times of massive economic change, like, for example, the times we live in now.

To become a multipreneur you must realize that your economic value depends upon your ability to make or save money for others and your ability to add value to processes. Your economic value will not depend upon your position, seniority, or connections. You must therefore train yourself to see opportunities where others see problems, dislocations, and barriers. You must choose your assignments on the basis of the skills you can learn as well as those you can apply. You must develop your interpersonal and technological skills to a high level so that you can make things happen rather than hope they will happen.

You must grasp the truest nature of what it means to live in a free country that is moving from corporate feudalism to individual capitalism. The new factors of production—knowledge and technology—are available on an almost laughably open basis. Access to distribution channels and even to funding is openly available. It is all there for you to take and use to express your concept of how it should be done in the marketplace. What "it" is depends entirely upon you.

In this book you will meet people who are multipreneurs. They are positive examples of how to achieve business success today. Some have left long-term corporate life—either walking or feet first—and have found a new way of working. Others never really labored in the corporate vineyard, at least as full-time employees, for any length of time. They are not traditional freelancers, although some of them (like myself) have freelanced. They are not traditional entrepreneurs, although many of them have started and operated businesses. They are among the fleet of foot in today's economy (in fact, one multipreneur founded a chain of athletic shoe stores called Fleet Feet). They are among the most flexible, creative, successful careerists in the country.

I know that these are difficult times for many people, including many who never dreamed that their careers could fall into such seeming disarray or end so unceremoniously. Many people never thought that downward mobility could lie so close at hand. But if you have a decent education, or access to one, and work experience, wherever you acquired it, you have the ability to become a multipreneur. If you have been truly privileged and hold an undergraduate and perhaps a graduate degree, have significant work experience, and possess analytical, technical, and interpersonal skills, then you are extremely well positioned to become a multipreneur.

This is a threatening time for those who lack the right career management approach. But with this book you will learn how to develop an approach that will make this a time of opportunity, a time to achieve high levels of function, income, and independence. In this book you will learn how some of the most successful and agile businesspeople in our economy have prospered despite the chaotic career conditions around us. With this book you will, in your own way, learn to become a multipreneur.

part one

The Multipreneurial
Response to Change

1

Adapting to the New Marketplace

You may currently be employed full-time, working part-time, hustling as an independent contractor, or running your own business. Or you may aspire to one of these situations. Perhaps, as a victim of white-collar unemployment, you would at the moment be happy to have just about any means of earning a living. Whatever your career goals, you are pursuing them in a marketplace that has changed radically in recent years and shows no sign of stabilizing. I call those most adept at prospering in this environment "multipreneurs." This chapter lays out the characteristics of this restructured marketplace and introduces the principles and practices of multipreneuring.

What's Really Going on at the Office

You are no doubt familiar with the evolutionary process that Charles Darwin called survival of the fittest: in nature, species come into being, enjoy a life span, and then die off as they outlive their usefulness in the ecosystem. In this process, species that cannot adapt to the earth's changing environment are replaced by new ones better suited to it. Given that some species must die to give way to new species, evolution has also been called a process of "creative destruction."

Economists recognize creative destruction as a feature of capitalism. In a capitalist system, products, processes, technologies, and industries come into being, enjoy a life span, and then die, only to be replaced by new ones. Some of these economic phenomena, like the California Gold Rush, die naturally. But more often they are killed off by new developments, the way the telephone killed the telegraph.

Creative destruction also occurs in the business cycle: economic expansions peak when demand outstrips supply and productive capacity reaches its limit, frustrating growth, then inflation heats up—and recession comes along to clear a platform for new growth. Creative destruction in an economy can at times be so widespread that the process amounts to structural, rather than cyclical, change. Such structural change can signal the emergence of an entirely new economy. This occurred when the Industrial Revolution began overshadowing agrarian economies in Europe and North America. It is also occurring now as we continue to move from the Industrial Age into the Information Age and from corporate feudalism toward individual capitalism. In times of structural change, the environment demands that we adapt: as in nature, the game in the economy becomes survival of the fittest.

In evolution, those most fit to survive do so through some particular characteristic or set of abilities. The fastest fish elude predators. The strongest elk win battles for reproductive rights. The camels best able to store water can traverse the driest deserts. The giraffes with the longest necks can reach food unavailable to others. It is a pitiless process in which individuals lacking the qualities necessary to survival are weeded out of the population. Fortunately, human beings can adapt. And we have been doing exactly that during the restructuring of our economy, which began in earnest in the early 1990s.

In the late 1980s I realized that certain types of businesspeople not only were adept at dealing with change and dislocation, but actually thrived on it. I remember thinking that they must have possessed some special characteristics because they exhibited none of the symptoms of those who were not thriving, none of the fear, dependence, lethargy, and worry. Rather they were optimistic, independent, energetic, and enthusiastic about their business and career prospects. (I also realized that I was among this group.) I've since studied those best able to survive and prosper in the new economy. In this book you will learn what characteristics—and actions—lead to survival and prosperity in these changed economic times.

Clearly, creative destruction in our economy and its industries has destroyed many careers. Maybe it has affected yours. Perhaps you have been fired or laid off. Perhaps your career has run aground or has been adrift. You may be reaching an age at which you see your professional and financial dreams receding to the vanishing point. Or maybe you are just beginning your career and finding none of the security, on the one hand, or challenge, on the other, that you seek. If you are in any of these situations, it may be hard for you to grasp that creative destruction will clear a platform for new growth and new opportunity for our economy and for you as an individual. But while this may be hard to grasp, it is important that you grasp it. Because you can and will share in the new growth and new opportunity that creative destruction gives rise to *if* you understand the nature of the current economy—and then act on that understanding.

The New Marketplace

The corporations that dominated the U.S. economy for most of this century were built by former military men working from a military model. Thus the companies they created comprised divisions and officers and orders. In this model the chief executive officer or division head, with the assistance of his senior staff, defined an objective. The amassing of capital assets paralleled the amassing of military matériel. The chain of command ensured that movement of the matériel was in the direction of the objective—for example, increased market share. And the battle for market share occurred through price wars, positioning, rifle-shot or shotgun marketing strategies, and so on.

The employees forming the armies that the CEO deployed were akin to feudal knights in service to lords, artifacts of a medieval military model. The unwritten employment contract went like this:

> In return for guarding our fortress and fields and doing battle
> against our enemies, we will pay you and we will care for you

and yours. If you become ill, we will ensure that someone treats your illness. If you cannot work, we will see that you have an income. We will help you save for your old age and give you a pension. We will also reward you for loyalty: as you remain with us, we will increase your earnings in recognition of your years of service.

It was a good system. It worked well when U.S. companies had the vast, rapidly growing U.S. market to themselves and the business requirements of the Industrial Age prevailed. But today the U.S. market is not the world's largest by all definitions, and many nations have surpassed our economic growth rate. We obviously no longer have this market to ourselves. Also, the business requirements of the Industrial Age—from the amount and type of productive capital a company needs to the number and types of people it should have on the payroll—no longer apply. We as a society are shedding the feudal-knight, Industrial Age employment system in favor of a free-agent, Information Age system and for a new unwritten employment contract that now states:

If you make us money or save us money or otherwise continually prove your economic value to us, we will give you money, and maybe even a full-time job with benefits, for some period of time. But if you do not, we will not employ you at all.

In this system, all expenses are viewed as variable, so all employees are, for practical purposes, "free lances" (freelancers) or potential freelancers—even the damn CEO. Now you and I know that, technically, the salaries and benefits of white-collar employees have always been variable expenses, just like those of blue-collar workers. But until recently, only blue-collar workers endured the layoffs inherent in uneven production cycles driven by uneven demand. When it came to white-collar workers, management held to the feudal employment contract, rarely treating managers and professionals as a variable expense but rather acting as if they were a fixed cost.

This was not as crazy, or as unfair to blue-collar workers, as it sounds. The logic was that although the production line may be down, we still need managers, planners, and analysts because we are always managing, planning, and analyzing. However, senior management allowed managers to build unmanageable empires. They allowed planners to write plans that nobody used. They allowed analysts to analyze issues far afield of the core business. They also allowed past contributions, personal relationships, paternalistic tendencies, and feudal loyalties to outweigh economic considerations. Note the use of the past tense in the foregoing statements. Today, economic considerations rule. When all expenses are variable, we are all, functionally, freelancers rather than knights in service to a single lord.

In this environment, the very concept of "a job" (let alone "a career") changes. Your working relationships become more transaction based than relationship based. You become a service provider paid for work actually performed rather than a productive asset carried on the books. You must therefore sell your services in an open market. Your services must be competitively priced, and your economic value to the organization must be obvious. You may have to provide your own office space or equipment and develop a recognizable business identity. This way of working clearly differs from showing up at the office every day and putting in your eight to ten hours.

People wonder about the durability of this new economy. Are these changes real and permanent? Or are we simply going through a period of adjustment? There is a difference of opinion. For example, the president of a Chicago-based outplacement firm sees it as temporary: "Most people cannot live that way. Most people want the security and predictability of a full-time job at a single employer. Most people are not built to be able to keep going from one job to another as permanent freelancers." The flaw in this logic is the assumption that business will accommodate the needs of the workers. Historically it is the workers who have had to adjust to the needs of business.

The majority of the professionals I've spoken with in the executive recruitment and outplacement businesses believe that the new career climate amounts to a permanent or at least long-term feature of our society. They believe that it will certainly be with us into the next decade or longer. Richard Plazza, president of the Executive Source, an interim human resources executive service in New York City, sees the trend continuing "probably for the rest of this decade, because it makes good business sense." Unlike the Chicago-based outplacement pro, he believes that people will want more flexibility in their worklives: "People at the executive and manager level bring a lot to the table, but they don't have to be on site all the time—nor do they want to be." Charles Cates, president of EnterChange, an Atlanta-based outplacement firm, says that he "can't see companies going back to being dinosaurs. They're going to stay fit and trim after going through all this trouble to get that way." Jory Marino, a senior recruiter at New York's Sullivan & Company, an executive search firm, goes even farther: "I think that we'll all look back on the 1990s as a time when radical change took place, just as it did during the Great Depression and after World War II. There has been a basic change in the way companies relate to employees, and they're not going to change back."

As with most inevitable change, the most positive way of dealing with this situation is to somehow embrace it. But many people may not be ready to do that, which is the reason for this book. Multipreneuring comes naturally to some of us, but for many of us this kind of career change comes down to making a virtue of a necessity. Yet change we must, because the environment has changed, and it is demanding that we adapt. Let's take a closer look at the changes and start learning about the most adaptive responses.

Characteristics of the New Marketplace

In both natural evolution and economic evolution, the characteristics of the environment dictate the correct adaptive response. The characteristics of the new marketplace have become clear, and among them these six are key:

- Intense competition and rapid change
- Economic rationalization
- Transaction-based relationships
- Organizational metamorphoses

- Technology shift
- Individual capitalism

Each of these characteristics demands an adaptive response. As we discuss each characteristic, we'll identify the related adaptive response.

Intense Competition and Rapid Change

Business has never been as competitive as it is today. That's a cliché, right? Perhaps, but it is nonetheless true. Why would business be more competitive now than it was a hundred years ago or fifty or twenty-five years ago? There are several reasons. First, until recently most nations were successful in keeping domestic producers—and workers—protected from foreign competition. But this entire century has been a period of ever freer trade. Second, not only do competitors have easier access to the U.S. market, but they have never before been so numerous. Nations such as Mexico, Japan, and Korea, which in the 1960s had few factories for producing quality consumer durables, have driven some U.S. producers out of business. Third, the market for labor, including managerial and professional labor, has gone global. White-collar workers now compete against foreign managers and professionals for jobs, just as their blue-collar counterparts have competed for years. Finally, our society's open access to education, technology, and funding, and the ease of starting a business, has fostered intense internal competition. These factors make it possible for an Apple, Compaq, or Microsoft—in about ten years from a standing start—to oppose an established giant like IBM. Throw in deregulation, and you have MCI and Sprint taking serious share from AT&T over just a few years.

It is also a cliché to say that rapid change permeates society. But the fact is that change in business has become so rapid that even outfits with the resources of an IBM or an AT&T can neither anticipate it nor address it quickly enough. The U.S. automobile industry, for example, took fifteen to twenty years to address the Japanese cost and quality challenge and in the interim lost billions of dollars in annual revenues and profits.

To adapt to this level of competition and change, you need a strong professional identity. This identity should ideally be informed by the principles of multipreneuring: adding value constantly, managing risk aggressively, working productively and flexibly, and learning continually. The issue of identity will be addressed later in this chapter, and the principles of multipreneuring will be covered in part 2 of this book.

Economic Rationalization

Economic rationalization—in which every expense must be financially justifiable—represents a driver as well as a characteristic of the new economy. The early 1990s added a recession on top of the intense competitive pressures on companies. At that time, management placed all processes, products, and people under a financial magnifying glass. They were looking for answers to basic questions: Should we be making this product or performing this function? If so, how can we make it or do it more cheaply? If not, how can we get rid of it? And who are all these people who can afford to dress so well? What are they doing for us? Are they making money for us? The answers to these questions often led to discontinued operations, downsizing, outsourcing, and layoffs. Even the most senior executives and their salaries were scrutinized—and many were eliminated.

Traditional considerations that had influenced decisions about employees—seniority, loyalty, connections, and past achievements—gave way to economic considerations. Of course, smaller companies have always had to keep a tight rein on expenses, so they had less tendency to become bloated and were thus less subject to white-collar layoffs. But large companies realized that they were spending a lot of money they didn't really have to spend, so they downsized and substituted new ways of getting work done, all because managers and shareholders began asking tough questions—questions that determined the economic rationale for a decision.

To adapt to this intense focus on economic considerations in business, you must add value constantly. To do this you must adopt a focus similar to that of a company: you must ask the right questions. What is your true value to the firm? Is your contribution measurable in dollars? If so, is your contribution a multiple of what you are paid? If not, what is the economic rationale for your being there? If that rationale is absent, what can you do about it? How can you add value in excess of what you are paid? Other questions focus on your own long-term economic viability: What, exactly, is your competitive advantage in the marketplace? Are you fully exploiting this advantage? Is your current work situation increasing your market value? Is it helping you learn new skills?

Later we will look at ways to answer these questions so that you can analyze your current situation and any employment opportunities and assignments that come your way. Note that all of these questions apply, whether you are a full-time employee, an independent contractor, or anything in between.

Transaction-Based Relationships

Transaction-based relationships have come about because the economic rationale now dictates hiring and purchase decisions. In the restructured marketplace, concepts such as lifetime employment and brand loyalty have become downright quaint. The parties to a transaction now tend to see that transaction as a discrete event holding a potential loss or gain. Customers want the quickest delivery, the best quality, or the lowest price that they can get, given their needs at that moment. Suppliers want the most revenue, the highest profitability, and the greatest use of productive assets. Why? Because the goal is to achieve profitability on every economic event: every hire, every product, every sale, every purchase, every relationship. Also, given the pace of change, few people really know what their needs will be in the future. Next time, fast delivery might not be as important, or perhaps the customer will pay more for better quality. Since the elements determining the transaction may differ, so might the parties to that transaction.

This is not to imply that business relationships as we have known them are disappearing—but they are changing. Human beings are social animals. People like to do business with people they like. So the distinction is not between transactions and relationships, but between transaction-based relationships and relationship-based transactions. Transaction-based relationships tend to be shorter term and focused more on business considerations. Relationship-based transactions are entered into—or, for that matter, not entered into—

because of the relationship between the parties. (If you've ever had car repairs done by your brother-in-law, you know what I mean.)

Traditionally in business, many transactions would take place because of the relationship between the parties, and this is still often the case. For example, a company would get its trade financing services from its lead bank just because that bank was its lead bank. But today the company would be far more likely to get trade financing services from the bank that does the best job on trade financing—in terms of accuracy, timeliness, and cost—whether or not that bank is its lead bank. In a transaction-based relationship, each party wants the best deal it can get, more or less independent of the relationship.

To adapt to this transaction orientation, you must learn how to sell and market yourself in the new economy. This entails understanding your market and your products and services, positioning yourself accordingly, placing sensible bets, and always delivering on your promises.

Organizational Metamorphoses

If the reengineering wave proved anything, it is that businesses adapt to structural change by devising new business structures. Various models of the company best suited to the new economy have emerged, and they all represent a departure from the hierarchical, feudal-military corporations that dominated the twentieth century. They are flatter and more flexible. They strive for rapid response capabilities rather than long-range productive capacity. They dedicate themselves to developing and applying knowledge and technology rather than to conquering territory. They are more collegial and team oriented and less prone to command-and-control management.

According to Dallas-based consultant Joanne Pratt, who specializes in helping companies get the most out of technology, they tend to be constructed of a core of full-time employees who are essential to the basic business. Around this core there is a ring of employees that can get wider or narrower as the needs of the business dictate.* This ring includes part-time employees, independent contractors, just-in-

---

* This idea was also presented in *The Age of Unreason* by Charles Handy (Harvard Business Review Press, 1989).

time workers, supplier-partners, joint-venture partners, partners in strategic alliances, and so on. Those in the core engage those in the ring on a transaction basis, based upon their ability to deliver quality products and services in rapid response mode at a competitive price.

If you are in the core, you may well have the role of manager. But what is the role of a manager without a hierarchical command structure and an army of full-time employees to control? Management is the art and science of getting things done through others. If you are in the core of a company, how do you get things done through others when they are out in the ring? If you are out in the ring, you will also have to get things done through others, and sometimes those others will be in the core. How do you "manage your boss" when he or she is not even really your boss? How do you get things done through other departments when you—and perhaps they—are not even in the same organization? Isn't getting things done through others difficult enough when everyone's in the same company?

These questions will be explored, but for now understand that the new economy places new demands on managers. With less hierarchy, the manager's role can hardly be limited to communicating up and down the chain of command. (One may well ask, "What chain of command?") Indeed, the manager's role has changed. A manager is now more often charged with getting the job done through whatever means are necessary, and often he or she must do this without the traditional structures and motivational tools.

To adapt to this, you must realize that the role of the manager, either inside or outside an organization, now resembles that of a producer. I use the term "producer" as it is used in film, television, video game, conference, or book production. The producer organizes the factors of production—the money, the materials, the talent, the technicians, the distribution channels—and pulls them all together to bring a product or service to market profitably. The new organizational structures, because they have scattered both responsibility and the factors of production, have created an environment in which large returns accrue to those who can intermediate among these factors and the markets. In other words, those who can "make it happen" can make lots of money. Today it is useful to think of the effective manager as a producer-intermediary rather than as an executive who simply gives orders or delegates.

Technology Shift

As you've heard, we're now in the Information Age, the Age of the Smart Machine, the Age of the Knowledge Worker. This is not just the stuff of magazine covers. Rather, technology is driving most of the new opportunities in business. This is the case even in manufacturing, where the day is not far off when production managers will reprogram instead of retool. Technology has fostered entire industries—personal computers, software, cable TV, video games, wireless telecommunications, robotics, and biotechnology—and has permanently changed others, such as financial services and health care.

I call the technological element of today's marketplace the technology *shift* because technological developments often shift the competitive advantage, the market focus, or the production dynamics of an industry or business—or individual.

To adapt to technology shift, you must be familiar enough with technology to recognize and exploit opportunities. This does not mean that you must become a "techie." If you are not interested in technology, the effort expended to become a techie would likely be a painful waste of time. But we have reached the point in our economic evolution where to be successful, you must know about the technologies that impact your business and you must have some level of computer literacy. This may involve learning the technology itself and certainly involves understanding the impact of technology. Here's an example to illustrate this point, provided by consultant Joanne Pratt. In the nineteenth century the Industrial Age heralded a shift away from home-based agricultural and crafts businesses toward large, centralized production facilities because people had to go where the tools were. The tools were at the factory. In this century the mainframe computer gave a boost to the urban office building. The tools were still centralized in the office, and employees still had to go to where the tools were. The personal computer made the Information Age a reality, because it gave everyone inexpensive, decentralized access to information and the ability to create and manipulate it. With today's laptop and notebook computers, it is no longer necessary to go to the office. The tools can now be taken anywhere. The office-in-a-bag is a reality.

Yet most of us still go to the office. Why? Because the technology shift in this area has outpaced the shift in management methods. Managers still think in terms suited to the production line at the factory, believing that if employees are sitting at their workstations, work is getting done. Such managers unnecessarily resist new work processes, such as telecommuting. However, now even the most traditional manager needs to understand that technology has rendered the old, surveillance-style management techniques obsolete. New ways of managing and measuring productivity are needed, and everyone needs to understand how technology affects business.

Individual Capitalism

A major movement away from corporate feudalism and toward individual capitalism has evolved, and the elements just discussed are both causes and symptoms of this. This does not mean, however, that the United States is about to become a nation of cottage industries or that the workforce will be completely made up of actual freelancers. Large companies will still dominate many areas of business. There are still tremendous advantages conferred by large size in businesses like manufacturing and distribution, as well as in many technology- and knowledge-based businesses such as financial services, health care, telecommunications, and print publishing. Yet even large organizations now must often turn to the individual capitalist, and not just to keep their costs down, but for knowledge, skill, and creativity.

The individual armed with information, brainpower, and a personal computer has unprecedented leverage in the marketplace today, because of the strong technology and knowledge component in so many rapidly growing businesses. In the Industrial Age, when the extractive, transportation, and manufacturing industries grew most rapidly, the capital requirements of those businesses yielded little leverage to the individual. Also, the slower pace of change created fewer new opportunities to be exploited by smaller intermediaries. Today the individual has the leverage—due to access to the knowledge and technologies now so important to business—to enable him or her to truly practice individual capitalism, inside or outside a large organization.

That's the positive side: opportunities abound. On the negative side, however, organizations of all sizes want employees who do not expect to be "taken care of" by the company. That is one of the reasons many companies favor hiring independent contractors for work formerly performed by staffers. As noted, companies have abandoned the paternalistic posture they held in the past. Companies now expect employees to manage their own careers and plan their own financial futures rather than to work in anticipation of constant promotions and the pension plan. Of course, if you are either permanently or temporarily self-employed, the responsibility of taking care of yourself is squarely upon you.

To adapt to this situation, you must run your career as a business. You must think—and act—in terms of short- and long-range plans for your front-office and back-office operations, financial management, and benefits management. You must, inside or outside of an organization, have certain business resources in place and run your career with growth and profitability as the goals.

Let's quickly review the characteristics of the new marketplace and the corresponding multipreneurial response:

Characteristic of the New Marketplace	Adaptive Multipreneurial Response
Intense competition and rapid change	Develop a new sense of identity and a new set of principles
Economic rationalization	Add value constantly
Transaction-based relationships	Acquire sales and marketing skills
Organizational metamorphoses	Act like a producer
Technology shift	Exploit technology
Individual capitalism	Run your career as a business

Successful multipreneurs develop each of these adaptive responses to at least some degree. To become a multipreneur, you must do the same. This book is devoted to helping you develop these responses. It will do so by presenting the principles and practices of multipreneuring as embodied by actual multipreneurs.

A New Approach to Career Management

In this book you will learn a new approach to career management that will help you respond adaptively to the new economy. Ideally you will come to view yourself as an economic unit capable of adding value to goods and services in a variety of settings. This translates to having a core skill or area of expertise (which you may already have) and supplementing it with a portfolio of high-level business skills: producer-intermediary skills, marketing and sales skills, technology skills, and the skills needed to run your career as a business.

As you'll soon see, this adaptive response, the multipreneurial response, will not be as foreign as you might expect. You have a backlog of knowledge, skills, and experience to apply to this new way of earning a living. For example, in the area of producer-intermediary skills, you can draw upon any supervisory or management experience, project management experience, or budgeting or purchasing experience you may have. In marketing and sales skills, even if you have never been an account rep, you have probably performed a needs analysis or written a proposal or conducted a presentation of some kind. For the skills needed to exploit technology, you can reference any contact you've had with information technology, computers, and technologists. To run your career as a business, you can draw upon the knowledge gained from virtually any analytical, planning, and financial management tasks you've accomplished. Since the multipreneurial response is a process of adaptation, it represents a transition, rather than a departure, from your present position and past careers.

While the term "multipreneuring" is new, the strategy isn't. (Author-statesman-printer-merchant-scientist Benjamin Franklin was a multipreneur.) What is new—and notable—is the number of people who are going to have to adopt this approach to making a living. Lifetime employment at a single, paternalistic employer is no longer an option for most of us. Yet neither do we want to be professional quick-change artists, continually assuming and dropping professional identities. Multipreneuring represents a way of coming to terms with the rootlessness of the new economy. It is this widespread rootlessness that is new.

Multipreneurs You'll Meet

In this book you will meet people whom I've broadly classified as multipreneurs. Some worked in large organizations and then found life-after-corporate-death; some never worked for a large organization as full-time employees at all. Here is a sample of the multipreneurs you'll meet:

> Courtney Nelthropp, after twenty-two years with IBM, worked a year and a half with a small software firm and then purchased a Sir Speedy franchise in Stamford, Connecticut, with a partner in graphic arts. Courtney's philosophy represents a practical blueprint of how to think about any service business.

> Sally Edwards, a world-class triathlete from Sacramento, California, had no business experience when she began the retail chain Fleet Feet in the late 1970s. Sally is now developing sports-related applications for heart-rate monitors and owns a company in the high-tech snowshoe business. She has also written eight books. Sally is typical of the multipreneur who can undertake projects—and launch entire businesses—because she thinks she can and then follows through.

> David Rye has been (in chronological order) an engineer with Boeing, a partner in a computer services company, a senior executive of a nationwide medical laboratory, and a systems analyst. He began moonlighting to start his

business, Western Publishing, while employed at IBM in the 1980s. With Western Publishing he now supports himself and his family in Boulder, Colorado. He also teaches at the University of Colorado and at Denver Metropolitan College, more to keep on his toes and to stay in touch with younger people than for the money.

Atlanta-based market research consultant Ray Shu left his managerial position in marketing at Coca-Cola in the early 1990s and worked out of his home for several months. He soon found that he missed the camaraderie and social structure that he had at Coke, so he moved his one-man operation to an Executive Suites office services complex. There, among other independent operators, he found the social dimension he had missed when working out of his home.

Hall McKinley, an IBM alumnus, has had four high-level positions since he left Big Blue in 1986. He may be in his fifth or sixth position as you read this. Hall is not an interim executive per se but has been drawn to companies offering challenging situations and has become expert at the job search in the restructured corporate world.

Michèle Van Buren, training program designer, multi-image producer, and communications consultant, nurtured an idea for ten years before discovering that she could make a living at it. Setting out to sell orientation programs to corporations that were relocating their employees, she instead found that the companies that sell relocation services were the market she could best serve.

These people, and others, have much in common in terms of their attitudes toward work and their approaches to the marketplace. That's no coincidence. Prior to beginning my research, I identified five criteria to gauge a multipreneur (each multipreneur had to meet at least four):

- Independence from a single employer, as demonstrated by holding, consecutively or concurrently, at least three moneymaking positions in the past five years, as either employees or independent contractors
- Ability to learn and apply multiple skills, as demonstrated by success in more than one profession or technical discipline
- Flexibility and adaptability, as demonstrated by success—as defined by the individual—in a variety of settings
- Proactivity, as demonstrated by the ability to start a major project and see it through independently
- Self-insight, as demonstrated by the ability to articulate their thoughts and feelings about their careers

Throughout this book I have drawn upon the views and experiences of these multipreneurs to illustrate various aspects of successful adaptation to today's marketplace. In addition to their experiences, I've drawn upon my own careers as (1) manager of fast-food restaurants, (2) past-due bill collector, (3) credit analyst, (4) commercial lender, (5) marketing analyst, (6) executive recruiter, (7) product developer, (8) manager of product development, (9) manager of a thirty-five-person product group, (10) software salesman, (11) freelance business writer, (12) corporate trainer, (13) marketing consultant, (14) editor, and (15) book author.

Given that I have held fifteen positions in a little over twenty years (and that's not including any of the nine part-time jobs I had during my high school and college years), you may well ask if I ever stuck with anything. The answer is, yes: positions (2), (3), (4), and (5) were all in banking, spanning six years at Bankers Trust and Manufacturers Hanover Trust in New York City, during three years of which I earned an MBA. As an executive recruiter (6), I was on the hunt for bankers for two years and saw this as an extension of my banking experience. Positions (7), (8), and (9) were at Dun & Bradstreet over a four-and-a-half-year career. At D&B I moved into the information and publishing business, where I have been ever since. Then I left D&B voluntarily and entered position (10)—at a start-up software firm that collapsed within a year. I was in positions (11), (12), and (13) on my own simultaneously for five years. Then I was hired by one of my clients, DRI/McGraw-Hill, an economic forecasting and consulting firm, where—as of this writing—I am employed in position (14) as an editor, and (15), I write books on the side as an independent author. Concurrently I am contemplating a book-packaging business, but that is in the research and planning stages.

I have not met with success in every endeavor I have tried. But I have in most of them. I have always been able to find, create, or generate interesting work that paid well. Most important, though, is that I have learned from the failures and setbacks and have seriously investigated and contemplated what works and what does not work in terms of career management in our economy. So my personal experiences have motivated me to write this book as much as the people I have met and the career chaos I see around us today.

Building a New Professional Identity

Each of us has a professional identity. If your life is in balance, there are also other aspects of your total identity, other roles such as spouse, parent, friend, son or daughter, citizen, skier, surfer, dancer, and so on. However, if you have been in the workforce for a while, your professional identity accounts for a big part of who you are. This is understandable. You spend most of your waking hours working, and work is a major source of your daily social interactions. It is how you earn your livelihood and support yourself and perhaps others. In other words, it is natural to draw a big chunk of your total identity from your profession.

Fortunately—and unfortunately—it has been fairly easy for most Americans to form a professional identity. When you graduate from school and join a company, that company hands you a ready-made identity, and you readily adopt it either because you really wanted it or because you were lacking one and there it was. You start describing yourself in terms of your work. If you work for a well-known company, you proudly mention its name. If it is not well known, you also mention its industry and business. You describe yourself to others, and to yourself, in terms of your function in that company.

But what happens if you wind up losing that identity because your company downsizes, restructures, or is acquired? What do you do? The answer used to be, "I'll take most of my professional identity and go across the street." However, now the companies across the street are likely to be downsizing, restructuring, or getting acquired.

So the ready-made professional identity cuts both ways. It is clearly defined and offers a sense of security, but as hundreds of thousands have experienced—and all of us have seen—the company can tell you to leave or economic or industry developments can erode it. People who have been fired or laid off often find the effect on their professional identities the most difficult aspect of the experience, giving rise to self-doubt, depression, and what one multipreneur calls "a kind of surrogate death."

The identity of multipreneur can be your portable, self-contained professional identity. Since it relies on internal constructs rather than external structures, no one can take it away from you. It also positions you to change as conditions change. However, no one can hand it to you—you must create it yourself. The way to start creating it is to start taking note of how you think about yourself professionally.

Start with a Broad Definition

To become a multipreneur you must think broadly about who you are. Your professional identity is basically a definition: it is the way you define yourself in terms of your work. Like any definition, it can be narrow or broad, limiting or inclusive. I suggest that you start using a broad, inclusive definition of your professional identity.

Multipreneurs use such definitions. Often, even if they appear to be "businessmen" or "businesswomen," they actually think of themselves as teachers, communicators, or problem solvers, who can do those things in various settings. Hall McKinley, a planning and operating executive, sees himself as a teacher. So does Sally Edwards, who works at adapting technology to the needs of amateur athletes. Craig Hickman, editor of *Utah Business* magazine, business consultant, and author, describes himself as a conceptual thinker. Business consultant Emmett Murphy sees himself as a "hunter-gatherer." For the past fifteen years, regardless of my job, employer, or client, I have thought of myself as a communicator.

Most people define their professional selves far too narrowly. They tell themselves and others, "I'm a middle manager," "I'm a salesman," "I'm an engineer," "I'm an attorney." They will often narrow this even further: "I'm a production manager in an auto plant," "I'm an insurance salesman," "I'm an aerospace engineer," "I'm a patent attorney." They then can narrow this still further by linking that identity to a single company or by adding qualifiers such as "who has never done anything else" or "who is too old to learn a new field."

Such narrow definitions stem from total acceptance of an off-the-shelf professional identity. This can be rooted in a yearning for status or security or in a more fundamental search for identity or meaning. However, a narrow definition of your professional identity carries a downside not unlike that which an industry or company can face when it defines itself too narrowly. The railroads, for instance, were hobbled by too narrow a definition of their industry, and this hurt them when airplanes came along. Peter Drucker has pointed out that railroad people saw themselves as being in the railroad business and that if they had seen themselves as being in transportation, they would have purchased aircraft and become diversified carriers. This argues for a broad, inclusive, and fundamental definition of what you do for a living.

In case you have a tough time with this process, here are some ideas for redefining several broad job definitions even more broadly:

manager   = coach, thinker, planner, politician
salesperson = teacher, communicator, persuader, facilitator
attorney   = conceptualizer, writer, advocate
engineer   = designer, problem solver, builder
accountant = reporter, investigator, analyst

Of course, a broad, inclusive definition of your professional self is only a beginning, but it is a fundamental step in becoming a multi-preneur.

A person who has goals and who can locate others with complementary goals, work independently and as part of a team, move across professional cultures, develop a portfolio of skills applicable in various settings, and tap the resources needed to get the job done is a multipreneur. This person progresses by finding increasingly challenging assignments and by achieving ever higher levels of freedom, function, and financial reward.

How We'll Get There

This book is structured around the key elements of multipreneuring.

Part 1, "The Multipreneurial Response to Change," gave you an overview of the new marketplace and of the best adaptive responses, and started you on the road to developing a professional identity independent of employers.

Part 2, "The Principles of Multipreneuring," examines the matters of adding value, managing risk, working productively and flexibly, and learning continually. These four principles represent the foundation of multipreneuring.

Part 3, "The Practices of Multipreneuring," explores the multipreneur's portfolio of high-level business skills: producer-intermediary skills, marketing and sales skills, and technological skills. The skill of "taking care of business" will enable you to execute many of the functions, such as benefits management, formerly performed by your full-time, long-term employers.

Part 4, "The Transition to Multipreneuring," addresses the matter of crafting ways of moving successfully toward the multipreneurial lifestyle and covers the job search skills needed in the new economy.

In essence this is a manual for surviving and prospering in the new economy. This book does not assume that you want to get out of corporate life and stay out, nor does it assume that you want to get or hold on to a traditional, full-time, permanent position. Rather it assumes that you want to have engaging, productive, high-paying work regardless of what happens in the economy, in your industry, or in the companies that employ you. Multipreneurs have proven they can do this, and you can join their ranks.

Redefining Yourself

Let's start crafting a new definition of who you are professionally. One of the best ways of thinking about this is to ask yourself some fundamental questions:

What do you spend most of your time actually doing (talking on the phone, writing reports, making calculations)?

What kind of thinker are you? Is your strength in dealing with data, things, issues, or people? Do you excel at thinking about facts, tangibles, intangibles, or people?*

Are you a designer/builder/rebuilder? A teacher/communicator/presenter? A persuader/positioner/politician? A go-between/agent/broker/market maker? A problem solver? A technician? An analyst? A strategist?

Think across situations and settings. In what situations have you been most successful?

Your definition should be basic and broad. Ask yourself how you would explain your work to a ten-year-old. What do you physically do with your head and hands and voice and body? How do you bring about the results you get? What results can you point to in terms of how the world is different for your having been at work? Is something being built, shipped, installed? Is someone capitalizing upon an opportunity or avoiding trouble of some kind? Are people smarter for having dealt with you?

Also think broadly about your industry and your place in it, just as many companies do. Banks think of themselves as being in financial services; many financial services firms think of themselves as being in the even broader business of risk management.

Work at this until you have a broad, inclusive definition of your professional self.

* For more on this subject see *Big League Business Thinking* by Paul Miller with Tom Gorman (Prentice-Hall, 1994).

....

part two

The Principles of Multipreneuring

2

Add Value Constantly

If you add value constantly, you will always have work. If you do not, you will not. It's that simple. In the corporate-feudal economy, adding value was often secondary to career moves designed to extend your influence or improve your image. Back then such career moves made sense. Now, however, the best career move you can make is to add value to everything you touch.

What is value added? The definition depends on who does the defining. Financial managers define it by measures of profit or return on capital. Economists define value added as the value of the outputs minus the value of the inputs. I define it by the following formula:

$$\text{Value-Added} = \text{Your \$ Contribution} - \text{\$ You Are Paid}$$

Thus I use the term "value added" to mean money that your employers or clients either make or save by having you work for them, minus the amount they pay you. Clearly this is in keeping with the economic rationale driving the new economy. You may recall that adding value constantly represents the best adaptive response to the economic rationale.

The above value added formula represents both an analytical tool and a way of thinking. As an analytical tool it can, unfortunately, be imprecise because your dollar contribution can be extremely difficult to measure. (On the other hand, the dollars you are paid are all too easily counted.) As a way of thinking, however, the formula is quite powerful. If you really believe that you must contribute—in dollars earned or saved—more than you are paid, your approach to work changes. You come to see that you must do more for the organization than just show up. You realize that any sense of entitlement you might have regarding your job is utterly false—your employers and clients do not believe that you are entitled to a hell of a lot, unless you are making or saving them a hell of a lot.

Think for a moment about the sense of entitlement many of us feel. It is easy—especially if you are intelligent, educated, articulate, well dressed, and reasonably attractive and possess some skill or expertise—to think that somebody, literally, owes you a living. Why? Because that's the way it's supposed to work. And that's the way it used to work. The passing of that way of work has come as a shock to many of us. If anyone in this country thinks the sense of entitlement is strong among welfare and food stamp recipients, they should check in with someone who has spent ten, twenty, or thirty years working fifty weeks a year, forty hours a week. Why shouldn't they feel entitled to a salary, benefits, and security? The answer is "economics," a discipline also known as "the dismal science." The economics of continued employment have changed, and they are quite simple: add value or else.

You may feel that you deserve a certain lifestyle. But from the economic standpoint you "deserve" it if, and only if, you have the nonsalary, nonwage income—that is, income from interest, dividends, rents, royalties, and residuals—to support your lifestyle. If you don't, unfortunately, you are just a working stiff. And these days a working stiff must add value in order to keep working.

Cold Calculation

Let's look at the valued added formula as an analytical tool. The dollars you are paid (the third value in the formula) is a pretty straightforward number. Look at your gross pay for a period or for a project. But look out for hidden costs you create for your employer or client. Benefits, if you are an employee, are an obvious example and should be included in the calculation. If you are an independent contractor, include expenses you pass on to your clients, such as travel and lodging. If you are an employee, and in some cases even if you are not, be aware that you create overhead costs in the form of office space, heat and light, air-conditioning, telephones, office supplies, management attention, and perhaps support staff. While these overhead costs do not have to be included in your calculation, you should be aware of them. Management certainly is.

Calculating your dollar contribution (the second value in the formula) is often difficult because your actual contribution can be tough to isolate. It can also be tough to measure in dollars since most of us who are on staff work on only one phase of a larger operation or project. Suppose, for example, that you are the telecommunications industry analyst for a small consulting firm. You might figure things this way: "Last year, we sold $750,000 worth of industry analysis to telecom outfits and to those that deal with them. Meanwhile, I got an $80,000 base salary, a $20,000 bonus, and another $25,000 in benefits. Thus, I received $125,000 in total compensation while the company grossed $750,000. So my value added was $625,000 (= $750,000 − $125,000), five times my salary!"

But you're forgetting something. What about the account managers who originally sold the business? What about your two research assistants and the half-time secretary assigned to you? What about the production people who made your reports look so good? Take a closer look at that $750,000 of revenue. Was *all* of it attributable directly to your analysis, or was your analysis sometimes bundled with other products as a "freebie" to help win a sale? In other words, other people and other products may have contributed to your contribution.

You see how complicated this can get? It gets even more complicated when you are involved in multiple lines of products and services.

Sometimes, measuring your contribution is easier if you calculate your "replacement cost." This is the cost of getting what you do done for less—say, with someone younger or someone older, or someone off staff or someone on staff. You can benefit by calculating your replacement cost because your employer or client is busy calculating the same thing in search of the answer to one constant question:

"How can we get this person's job done for less?" If they can get your contribution while paying less for it, they can raise their value added. If that's the case, you'd better figure it out before they do.

On a brighter note, the value added formula can help you justify a raise or a fee increase. Suppose you are a product manager at a large commercial bank and you calculate your honest, actual, measurable, dollar contribution at $1.5 million in revenue. Suppose you're being paid $80,000 per year, plus a bonus of 10 percent of your salary. Even after you figure in benefits, overhead, and some support, your value added (or "net contribution") would be a *significant* multiple of your compensation, a factor of around ten. So you should march right into your boss's office and demand a raise, right?

It depends. It depends upon the extent to which that chunk of business depends upon your skills and relationships. Remember, a lot of people tripled their money on their houses and condos in the 1980s and got the idea that they were real estate geniuses. They somehow lost their touch in the 1990s when housing prices generally rose at a pace about one-fourth that of the early to mid-1980s. Similarly, many sales and account management people get the idea that they are major rainmakers and that the customers love them. You may be a major rainmaker because the company seeds the clouds every day. The customers may love the company or the service reps, not you. In other words, if you are the $80,000-per-year product manager at the bank in our example and you ask for a raise or a bigger piece of the action, you may soon find yourself replaced by someone ready to do the job for $60,000 and a 5 percent bonus. If, however, you found and grew those customers and they really do love you, you have a responsibility to yourself and, if you have one, to your family to get yourself a better deal. Try using the value added formula to justify it. It beats telling your boss how badly you want a summer house.

Often you and your employer know exactly where your value added stands without explicit calculations. If you've done a good job but have ridden the company's coattails, you both know it. If you've done a good job in spite of the company's massive screw-ups, you both know it. Of course, there are always human factors and emotions to muddy the waters, which is why I like the value added formula. Despite its imprecision, it at least attempts to measure what should be measured. And the underlying principle—add value constantly—represents the bedrock of multipreneuring.

To position yourself to add value constantly, and to feel confident of your ability to do so, you must answer two questions:

- What enables you to add value?
- Where can you add the most value?

You must answer these questions, not in some general, abstract way, but in specific, concrete terms. Answering them will help you maximize both your contribution and your pay. Why? Because both—and by extension your value added—are functions of what you do and where you do it. Value added hinges on the match between your core skills and the situations in which you apply them.

What Enables You to Add Value?

To add value, you must *know how to do something* that adds value to a product, service, or process. You must know how to do something that makes or saves money for your employer or client. That know-how and that activity represent your core skill or core skill set. A well-defined core skill enables you to add value. Ultimately that skill and your ability to use it to add value are what you are selling.

Define Your Core Skills

There are various ways of defining your core skills, and later you'll have a chance to define yours. There are also various ways of thinking about your skills. You may find it useful to start thinking about your skills from both the internal viewpoint and the external viewpoint.

From the *internal* viewpoint think in terms of

- the broad definition of your professional self
- the skills you enjoy using most
- the kinds of challenges you seek in your working life

In the previous chapter you came up with a *broad definition of your professional self*: communicator, teacher, advocate, whatever. This definition can either itself be a core skill or it can point to one or more core skills. For example, a teacher needs to motivate, communicate, demonstrate, correct, and persuade. That might be a skill set applicable to selling, facilitating workshops, or negotiating deals. A builder needs to envision structures, understand design, work with materials, draw upon the skills of others, plan on paper, and bring plans into reality. That might be a skill set applicable to operations research, information systems design, or product development. Incidentally, you do not necessarily have to think in terms of a set of skills. You might find it useful to single out the one skill that you identify with the most. But whether it is one skill or a skill set, the question is: What skill or skills does your broad definition of your professional self point to?

Think too of *the business skill you enjoy using most.* What skill or skills do you enjoy using so much that you lose track of time? Is there any skill that you would continue to use even if you weren't paid? While the unfortunate truth is that you cannot always make a good living using the skill you most love using, it is worth knowing what that skill is. Then you can seek ways of converting that skill into a financial contribution to a business.

Finally, *the activity that you have found most challenging* could well point to your core skill. When you find something challenging, you not only enjoy doing it, but also pursue greater proficiency at it. This means that you seek situations in which you can use that skill but find success somewhat hard to achieve. You seek challenge in that area so that you will develop in that area. What activity do you approach in this way? Where do you see the challenge in business? What do you care deeply about doing really well?

From the *external* viewpoint think in terms of

- the training, experience, and knowledge you have
- the areas in which you have been told you excel
- the areas in which you have succeeded financially

Your *training, education, experience, and knowledge* have given you skills. In what skills have you have been educated and trained? What thread or theme connects them? What kinds of activities do you always seem to wind up doing on the job? Think of the areas in which you worked or studied years ago. What has your experience given you? What did you get out of graduate school? What did you learn in law school, before you left it for the restaurant business? David Rye now runs a publishing company focused on outdoor sports books, but he sees as invaluable the skills he acquired years ago when he first worked with computers:

> The early skills that I developed in computer science and that whole area were very important in enabling me to do different things. Take, for example, the basic discipline of systems analysis and design. That one skill has been my vanguard, if you will, for a lot of things that I've done. I've applied it to writing, to management, to running a business. It has provided me with a logic and a methodical base with which to get into other areas, totally outside of computer systems design.

No matter how peripatetic a dilettante you have been, there may well be some connective tissue that defines a core skill. No matter how focused a specialist you have been, you may well have skills related to, but separate from, your primary area of focus.

Often others are better judges of our talents and skills than we are. *What have others told you you are good at?* Television producer Marge Heiser, with *Spenser: For Hire* among her credits, got into her line of work partly because when she was doing volunteer work on a telethon in Boston, a producer from New York saw her in action and told her she had what it takes. Not only did he happen to be right, but, equally important, his observation gave her confidence. What have you been told you are good at? While you're at it, consider what people have told you you are not good at. Also, what situations have you been chosen for by your employers? What task forces and special projects do you tend to wind up on? On performance appraisals, what have your bosses told you about your strengths and weaknesses? What compliments do you most enjoy hearing?

Finally, look at the bottom line. *Where have you succeeded financially?* You may hate market research, but if you have made a bundle at it, it would be hard for me to believe that you're not skilled at it. In a sense, applying the financial yardstick extends the exercise of considering the opinions of others. In business, money is the sincerest form of flattery.

The relationship between these internal and external considerations can be tricky. If you internally define yourself as a salesperson and you enjoy selling, but you've made no money at it and people say you couldn't sell ice cubes in hell, you have work to do. You may *think* you have the skills, but you may indeed lack them. If, on the other hand, the externals say that you're great at sales, but you don't think you are or you don't like it or you don't see it as challenging, you have a different problem. This problem may be psychological, but nonetheless real.

Most of us can define our core skill after giving it some thought. Many people come to see their core skills over time, through a combination of internal processes and external information. Note that multipreneurs make sure that they translate their core skills into concrete deliverables—that is, into a way of actually adding value. Take a look at the experience of two multipreneurs.

Sally Edwards defines herself broadly as a teacher. She has combined that skill with another skill set, that of the endurance athlete. Sally has converted her skills as a teacher and her experience as a triathlete into a business contribution. Thus her core skill might be defined as "teaching people about equipment for endurance sports and training."

Before she started Fleet Feet, Sally Edwards actually made money in triathlons. Then she applied her athletic expertise in the stores, testing shoes herself and relating to her customers' problems. She could teach customers about the shoes and other equipment. She wrote books on endurance sports, particularly on women in endurance sports, and her books have helped her launch a career as a speaker. In writing and speaking and in business, she sees her core skills as those of a teacher and athlete.

This skill set has been critical in her work in a new company called Trinity Fitness, which is applying heart-rate monitors to the task of calculating training zones for amateur athletes and their personal trainers. She sees this as a teaching task in that she teaches trainers and amateur athletes how to use heart-rate monitors in their workouts. Trinity is separate from Yuba Snowshoes, which Sally also runs. Here she sees her role as teaching people about the virtues and use of high-tech snowshoes. Sally's core skills enable her to add significant value in the sports equipment arena.

Courtney Nelthropp sees his core skill as the ability to deliver customer service, and he has brought this skill to bear in his quick-printing franchise. Courtney developed customer service as his core skill when he worked at IBM. He began his career in sales but found it was customer service that turned him on. Courtney told me, "I was always very high on customer service. I had quality programs (for my internal customers) long before it became popular." After leaving IBM and a U.S. software subsidiary of a British company that he was with for eighteen months after IBM, Courtney looked for a business in which he could add value by applying his core skills in customer service and quality assurance. He saw—correctly, as it turns out—that doing so in the quick-printing business would give him a real competitive advantage.

A lot of people start in sales. But not all of them develop a focus on customer service. A lot of people have internal customers. But not all of them develop quality programs to ensure their satisfaction. Courtney started in sales and developed an interest in customer service, took that with him to the staff side, then took it with him into the quick-printing business, where he gave it concrete expression. Find a similar thread in your own work experience, and you may well identify your core skill. Give it concrete expression, and you may have a business—and a competitive advantage.

Identify Your Competitive Advantage

Consider the concept of competitive advantage when assessing your core skill. Think of the competitive advantage Sally Edwards brings to Trinity Fitness or to Yuba Snowshoes. She can choose good equipment, test it herself, understand what works and why, relate to her customers, and choose employees who know what they're doing. As a bona fide expert in endurance sports, she knows where and how to promote her wares. She makes equipment for enthusiasts, and she is an enthusiast. So Sally not only adds significant value, but also has a competitive advantage in her chosen business arenas.

In defining your core skill, ask yourself: What is my competitive advantage? This helps you take your core skill farther into the real world, which is rabidly competitive. You must first define the core skill that enables you to add value, then compare yourself or your operation to others with a similar core skill. By comparison, you determine the excellence and marketability of your core skill.

If you have a clearly defined core skill and a clear competitive advantage, you are on the road to becoming a multipreneur. If you do not, begin now to define these terms for yourself.

Seeing yourself as having marketable skills is basic to multipreneuring. As interim-executive specialist Richard Plazza put it, "Those people who leave corporate life for the world of independent or interim employment do best if they believe they have a skill to sell. But many people either do not have such skills or do not see themselves as having such skills." For many people, this presents a serious problem. Some have functioned only as middle-management messengers in the feudal-corporate chain of command. Some only have what management consultant Emmett Murphy calls "second- or third-order skills" such as supervising and planning. If that is your situation, you must develop a primary core skill that enables you to add value directly to a process or product. When you have such a skill, you must find the product, service, or process that will enable you to maximize your contribution. That's the next step.

Where Can You Add the Most Value?

To maximize your value added, you must *apply your core skills* to the right situations. This means choosing your employers and assignments with care. Many people make long-term career mistakes by looking for work rather than looking for situations in which they can contribute the most or learn the most. One good rule of thumb for finding where you can add the most value is to apply your core skills where they are most needed.

Apply Your Core Skills Where They Are Most Needed

Where can you add the most value? There are two simple, but not necessarily easy, approaches to answering this question. I sum them up in two catchphrases:

- Find birds of a feather.
  or
- Be a lone eagle.

These are not strategies for finding work per se. They are strategies for finding situations that will maximize your contribution. Marketing and selling yourself is another matter, to be dealt with later.

Find birds of a feather means that if your core skill is in some area of accounting, work for an accounting firm. If it relates to high technology, work for a high-tech firm. If it has to do with marketing communications, work for a mar-com shop. This may not seem "new," but the reasoning here is that your value added will be high because your employer or client sells what you sell. They sell your skills and thus make money directly off those skills. They enable you to make a contribution by putting you in situations where you can make a contribution. If they know what they are doing, they know where the business is and have ways of exploiting these opportunities.

If you find birds of a feather—meaning birds of *your* feather—you'll be among people who work in your core skill area. The opportunities for learning can alone justify this approach. But be aware that many companies specializing in areas like accounting or high tech or marketing communications tend to be small or closely held or both. This means that they can be great places to learn and to gather experience, credentials, and contacts. However, often, unless you reach a certain level of management or account responsibility by about the age of forty, your actual contribution and your relative pay will diminish over time, and so will your career prospects. If you are motivated by money, staying around a partnership or small firm after you realize that you are not going to make partner or principal can be a poor long-term career strategy.

If you are an independent, one way to contribute to these companies is to offer them a very specific skill that they do not have but that complements what they have. For example, if you know accounting practices in South America or in the extractive industries, take this to an accounting firm that does not have it and show them how retaining you will add value. If you have core skills in multimedia programming, take them to a high-tech firm that lacks these skills. If your core skill is marketing communications for nonprofits, show a mar-com shop with no nonprofit accounts how you can make a dollar contribution.

You can also maximize your value added by joining a "boutique" or a specialty shop. Specialty shops abound in today's marketplace, especially given the boom in business services and consulting since 1980. There are outfits that only do product development, that research only the coal industry, that consult only about doing business in Vietnam. Whatever your core skill, no matter how narrowly you define it, you can find birds of a feather. If they sell what you sell, they know the value you can add, and they can expose you to clients who need your contribution.

Be a lone eagle does not, in this context, mean that you should work as a one-person shop. It means that you should maximize your contribution by working for an employer or client that lacks your core skill. Rather than be an expert in a flock of experts, position yourself as an expert among nonexperts. If the company is at point zero on the learning curve regarding your area, your value added will be significant in both perceptual and actual terms.

When you take your skill to a company that lacks that skill, be careful to make the right match. The employer or client has to somehow provide a platform on which you can add value with your core skill, even though they are not in the business of selling that skill. So in this strategy, you take, for example, your core skill in extractive industry accounting to an environmental consulting firm. You take your skill in multimedia to a newspaper or magazine publisher. You take your skill in nonprofit marketing communications to a company that wants to polish its image but has no corporate affairs office.

Since you are approaching people who lack your core skill, you must seek those in this group who can comprehend the value you can add. You must locate those who quickly understand that they face an opportunity or a problem that your core skill can enable them to address. Often these people will not put you on staff: if they thought they needed your skills that badly, they'd probably already have them in-house. But they will often be open enough to give a lone eagle a look and, if you structure the deal correctly, a chance.

In practice, the lone eagle approach often works best after you're already in the door as an employee or as a contractor on another project. Once inside, you are positioned to assess where the company needs your core skill. Make them aware of your skill. For example, after I left commercial banking and recruiting bankers, I worked in the product development group of Dun & Bradstreet Credit Services. There I came to be viewed as "the guy who should be involved in anything we're trying to develop for banks." Why? Because nobody else in the group knew banking, and I had not made a secret of the fact that I did.

Multipreneurs often succeed by working the front, the back, and the edges of the massive herd known as the business community. In contrast, most people just work where they happen to land, and sheer geography dictates that most people land toward the middle of the herd. So they wind up as accountants in accounting firms, where they stay too long after learning they can't make partner. They are high-tech people doing routine system maintenance at insurance companies. They are marketing communications people who don't get beyond writing plain-vanilla press releases and product literature. If you are in a similar situation, you may lack a clear concept of where you can best use your core skill to add value. Break away from the herd.

Adding Value: Process Plays

To generate significant value added, apply your core skill to a process that makes money or saves money—or both—for your employer or client. To add value, be involved with a process that adds value. Many companies now say, implicitly or explicitly, "You must either make something or sell something, or we can't hire you or keep you." Many companies have become quite insistent on this point.

Companies make money by bringing a product or service to market. They take inputs and add value. (In fact, the value added tax in Europe is calculated by applying a tax rate to the difference between what a company paid for the inputs and what it received for the outputs.) Value is added through various processes, including product or service development, purchasing and production, marketing and sales, distribution and delivery, and customer service. Each of these processes includes subtasks. For example, marketing includes market research, pricing decisions, promotional efforts, and public relations, among others. One of these subtasks could be your core skill.

An almost surefire way to maximize your value added is to (a) be involved in a process that is essential to your employer *and* (b) do all that you can to improve that process continually. Note the emphasis on *and*—you must do both (a) and (b). Involvement in a process without improving it makes you, at best, a caretaker. If the process is essential—like desktop publishing in a publishing company, for example—it must be as efficient and effective as possible or you will be replaced. If, on the other hand, the process is not essential, even if you improve it, you're not adding much value.

This means that when you go to work for a firm as an employee or an independent, you should quickly learn what the company "sees as essential processes. These will often be the company's "core capabilities." These may center on technological processes or marketing and sales or distribution or being the low-cost producer or whatever. Then you should gauge the extent to which your core skills will help you make those processes more efficient, more effective, or both.

This is, after all, what consulting firms often do. Marketing consultants help companies with positioning and pricing, both of which are essential. Operations consultants help companies improve production processes. Technology consultants help companies maximize the value of technology. You can, as an employee or independent contractor, add value by helping your employers or clients do the same. To add value to processes in a company, you must think not only about the type of company to approach, but also about the process you will impact and the way you will impact that process. (Right now we are not considering how you will sell the potential employer or client on this, but rather how you will sell yourself on it, by honestly finding where you can add the most value.)

Let's first consider the revenue side of the picture. What revenue-producing process can you help an employer or a client capitalize upon or improve? How do you know the employer or client sees this process as essential? How, exactly, does your core skill relate to this process? Can the company make money by reselling your skills to others? If so, how would your core skill help those others increase revenues?

Then, or alternatively, you must identify processes in which you can save money for your prospects. The most obvious way to save an employer or prospect money is to simply price yourself below market rates for the quality of work that you do. We discuss this tactic in the next section. Companies have become ruthless in their search for operational efficiencies, hence the outsourcing boom. Better still, if you can—without pricing yourself below market—perform a production process more effectively, more efficiently, or less expensively, you have a good chance of adding value.

Much of this analysis amounts to separating the essential from the extraneous. Examine the company. Ask yourself: How does this company earn its revenue? What processes are essential to this? How could this company improve these processes? How could I bring my skills to bear on these processes? How could I help this company make or save money by boosting the effectiveness or efficiency of one (or more) of these processes?

By some estimates, at least 80 percent of the people in this country are in the wrong jobs. This points to an abysmal mismatch between people's skills and their positions. But ultimately, we as individuals are responsible for this. To maximize your happiness as well as your value added, match your work to your skills—and when necessary, match your skills to the work available. Try thinking in terms of the diagrams below:

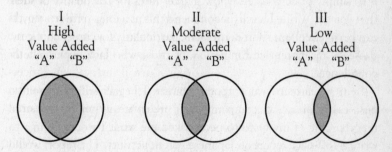

I	II	III
High	Moderate	Low
Value Added	Value Added	Value Added
"A" "B"	"A" "B"	"A" "B"

"A" = Employer's or Clients Needs and Primary Processes; "B" = Your Core Skills; ▓▓▓ = Value Added

Diagram I, the high value added situation, clearly represents the most desirable state of affairs both from your standpoint and that of your employer or client. If, instead, your position is best portrayed by Diagram III, the low value added situation, there are only three possible things you can do, given that you have to work for a living. You can change your work situation to fit your core skills, change your core skills to fit your work situation, or change both your core skills and your work situation. The latter move amounts to a complete career change.

Four Tactics for Increasing Your Value Added

Let's turn to four specific tactical moves you can make to increase your value added:

- Cut your price
- Increase your contribution
- Assume some of the employer's or client's risk
- Leverage yourself

Cut Your Price

Recall the formula: Value Added = Your $ Contribution − $ You Are Paid. As noted above, one obvious way to increase your value added is to simply price yourself below market rates for the quality of work that you do. While I hardly recommend this as a long-term strategy, it can be an excellent short-term tactic particularly for career changers, those in an apprenticeship period, or those who lack experience or confidence.

After a fifteen-year corporate career, I began selling myself to business information companies as a freelance writer of industrial reports. One of my first prospects asked me what I would charge to write a 180-page report on Japanese patent activity. The report would be based upon their data on patents filed in the United States by major Japanese companies. They would sell the report to their prospects through direct mail. I wrote a proposed table of contents and a work plan and offered to write the report for $6,000. Since, due to inexperience, I had underpriced myself by 40 percent to 60 percent yet seemed to have my head screwed on straight, I got the project.

However, after that initial project I had experience and a work sample, so I was able to charge my next client $12,000 for writing an industrial report.

It makes sense to underprice yourself when you know you can do the job up to quality expectations and you need the experience or the credential. Doing so almost ensures that you will make a dollar contribution beyond what you are paid and thus ensures relatively high value added. Even if you have experience and credentials, underpricing can be a useful sales tactic. In this tactic, known as "buying the business," you use low pricing to achieve a competitive advantage. But the long-term success of this tactic depends on your power to increase your rates after your client comes to depend on you—if he comes to depend on you.

Increase Your Contribution

As all of our "overpaid" athletes, actors, and entertainers (and their agents) have proven, if someone's dollar contribution is high enough, he or she can demand nearly any amount of money and stand a good chance of getting it. The television networks and other entertainment companies paying these folks are not (usually) crazy, although they sometimes turn out to be wrong. They are basing their decisions on an economic rationale, and the stars and their agents are basing their demands on the same rationale. The folks running CBS believed that David Letterman's initial five-year contract was worth $47 million because his expected dollar contribution in incremental advertising revenues was seen as greater than $47 million. This logic pervades the entertainment and professional sports worlds. It also works in much of the rest of the business world.

So how can you raise your contribution?

Beyond the techniques already discussed—which include having a core skill that can make or save money, applying your core skill to a company that needs it, and applying your core skill to a process that will benefit from it—you can raise your contribution by increasing your personal productivity and exploiting technology. (These will be discussed later.) But you can also increase your contribution by moving up or down the value or process chain. For example, if you do direct mail copywriting, you can get into graphic design, desktop publishing, or mailing services. If you are an executive recruiter, you can get involved with outplacement or executive skills development. If you make a product for retail sale, you can get into direct mail. Even if you work for an employer, moving up or down the value chain can increase your contribution. Unfortunately, in a corporate environment it can also lead to mindless (or mindful) empire building as an end in itself. We all know a vice president of sales who wanted to have marketing reporting to him, or a marketing veep who had to have sales reporting to him, and got what they wanted and then screwed it up. Like any tactic, moving up or down the value chain has to be properly executed.

This tactic of moving along the value chain resembles vertical integration, a growth strategy used all the time by companies that purchase or establish operations up or down the production and distribution chain. For example, a food packager will buy some farms (upstream in the process) in order to capture the farmer's value added (and profits) or buy fleets of trucks (downstream in the process) to capture the common carrier's value added (and profits). Like these companies, if you can move up or down the value chain *without* compromising quality, diffusing your efforts, or cutting your productivity, you can certainly increase your contribution and thus increase your pay.

Assume Some of the Employer's or Client's Risk

If your potential employers or clients are worried about the value you will add, you can often ease their minds by assuming some of their risk. What gives rise to this risk? The uncertainty of your future contribution ("Will this guy really make us a million?") versus the certainty of what they agree to pay you ("We're agreeing to pay this guy a hundred grand!").

Welcome to the wonderful world of pay-for-performance and fees based on results. These deals clearly make sense given the economic rationale. The fact that companies are reluctant to hire anyone who cannot make or save them hard dollars makes it relatively easy for you to structure these deals, provided you are focused on making or saving hard dollars for them.

This tactic may, technically, be misclassified as a way of raising your value added: under some deal structures and outcomes, your employer or client can *on the surface* wind up with less value added. (For example, say you actually do make them a million dollars, but you took a straight commission of 20 percent off the top, instead of $100,000.) I stress the term "on the surface," because part of your contribution, part of the value you add by entering a contingent-pay deal, is the reduction of the employer's or client's risk. After the fact, do they feel good if they bet the wrong way and you make out like a bandit? Rarely. But contingent pay is potentially one of the two most powerful ways to increase your pay.

Leverage Yourself

The other most powerful way to increase your pay is to leverage yourself. This tactic can be combined with that of moving up or down the value chain. It can be done either by outsourcing to other people or by replicating a product or service.

You can best leverage yourself through other people by using the producer-intermediary skills we'll examine in chapter 6. The idea is to add value by having more people make a contribution and to capture a portion of their pay in exchange for giving them the work. Basically, you hire freelancers and mark up their fees. This amounts to Capitalism 101. But you must handle it properly or you risk losing, rather than gaining, leverage.

When you leverage yourself through others, you face issues of contracts, pricing, and managerial and quality control and possibly legal and tax issues. Leveraging yourself through others can get out of hand and can wind up putting you in the position of running a company, which is far more complex and time-consuming than running a career, even a multipreneurial career. Worse, it does not necessarily pay better. But running a company—or a virtual company—is clearly an option for the multipreneur. You can get leverage through others without having to build an actual company.

The tactic of leveraging yourself by replicating a product or service is a valuable one and flows naturally from the nature of Information Age deliverables, which are generally focused upon, well . . . information. Information can be delivered through books and periodicals (including newsletters), broadcast and cable media (including databases), audio- and videocassettes, software and discs, consulting and speaking engagements, and seminars and workshops.

To gain high leverage from any product or service it should ideally be:

- proprietary and subject to copyright or trademark protection
- tangible and packagable
- salable through established channels
- convertible to other media
- applicable across other markets

If you have a product, a service, or an approach to adding value that is uniquely yours, it is considered *proprietary*. That means that you have an exclusive right to market and sell the product, service, or approach. You should take at least the basic steps to protect this right, meaning that you should copyright your materials and register trademarks or service marks. Note that an idea is not subject to copyright; only the expression of an idea is. That makes it easy for competitors to issue parity products ("knockoffs") to compete against your idea if it catches on. Their knockoff merely has to "express" the idea differently.

If, like Sally Edwards with her heart-rate monitors and high-tech snowshoes, you have a product, great. If, on the other hand, what you have is a service or an approach, you will gain more leverage if you translate it into a *tangible, packageable form*. By that I mean a book, manual, newsletter, workshop, seminar, audiotape, videotape, or software product. This not only reinforces your rights, but gives you something tangible to sell and, perhaps, for others to resell. The tangible form is really limited only by your imagination. For example, executive development consultant and author Paul Miller of the Miller Institute created *The Miller Report of Executive Development Potentials*, which is copyrighted and has an identity in the marketplace. Steve Levitt, president of Port Washington, New York–based Marketing Evaluations, did something similar with the Q Score, which rates the popularity of public figures among various audiences.

Once you have something to sell, you need to bring it to market. If you can do so yourself, you will be moving down the value chain and capturing revenue and profits from distribution. However, that can be a lot of work. If you just want added leverage, get someone else to sell it. Of course, they will get their cut, which may be even bigger than your share. If you want to develop ideas, get them to market, and move on to develop the next income stream, you should develop products, services, and approaches that you can not only render in tangible form, but that can be sold through *established distribution channels.* You've probably noticed that a lot of consultants, executives, and business owners have written books. Writing a book is not easy, but it does represent a proven way to package an approach and bring it to market through an established distribution channel of publishers and bookstores. Creating seminars that can be sold by a vendor such as the American Management Association is a similar strategy.

If what you are offering is *convertible to other media,* you gain yet more leverage. Craig Hickman introduced his packaging of his approach to management in *The Strategy Game,* released simultaneously as a book and software. Information is the most malleable of products. It can, with minimal investment, be packaged, repackaged, bundled, unbundled, and otherwise crafted to the needs of various users and markets. This is also true, albeit perhaps to a lesser degree, of many noninformation products and, of course, services.

To find new opportunities for adding value with what you offer, think about how your offering can be made *applicable to other markets.* If your core skill is credit risk management for commercial banks, can you apply your service and approach to large retailers? To the insurance business? To investment products? To mortgage-backed securities packagers? Also, in today's market it always pays to think internationally. Would someone in Canada, Mexico, or overseas deem your offering marketable on their turf? Are you afraid that the global market may be beyond you? Don't be. Foreign firms are just as hungry for new products, services, and approaches as those in the United States.

How to Analyze an Opportunity: The Value Added Perspective

Try using the formula, Value Added = Your $ Contribution − $ You Are Paid, and the underlying ideas, to analyze the opportunities that come your way. Because the economic rationale prevails in all business situations, the formula will help you assess everything from full-time jobs to project-based engagements. While your ultimate goal is to maximize your value added, you should pursue it by finding ways to maximize both your dollar contribution *and* the dollars you are paid. If you maximize both, you will truly maximize your value added in the long run.

To see if the opportunity you are considering will enable you to maximize your dollar contribution, ask yourself:

- How will the opportunity make use of my core skills?
- Will the opportunity give me access to processes that make or save money for the employer or client?
- Am I an expert among experts or a lone eagle in this situation? Or neither? How does that affect my ability to contribute?
- Do I know for certain that I can do this job? How do I know that?

To judge whether the opportunity will enable you to maximize your pay, ask yourself:

- What clear competitive advantage, if any, do I have here?
- How unique is the skill set I bring to the situation? Where else could they find what I offer?
- Could I increase my pay by assuming some of the client's risk through a pay-for-performance or a percentage-of-results deal?
- How might I be able to leverage this opportunity?

The above questions could have been phrased to elicit yes-or-no answers, but they are open-ended questions because you are better off analyzing your employment opportunities in depth rather than in checklist fashion. Careful analysis will help you keep your wits about you, tune your expectations, and draw up a game plan to put into effect after you decide how to add value constantly.

3

Manage Risk Aggressively

The security of long-term employment is gone. The security of lifetime employer-funded benefits is gone. The security of a mapped-out career path is gone. Even the security of a predictable work environment is gone. The opposite of security is uncertainty, and uncertainty equals risk. Clearly the current career climate presents increased risk.

As noted, individual capitalism is taking the place of corporate capitalism. The restructuring wave of the early to mid-1990s transferred large amounts of risk from companies to individuals, whether we liked it or not. In reengineering, the work of many staff positions came to be viewed as work that could be jobbed out. In effect, management said to many on-staff professionals, "We can't warehouse your talent until we need it, because that puts the inventory risk and the associated costs on us. From now on, you can bear that risk. Take your talent yourself and sell it on the open market."

In a sense, we are moving closer to true capitalism, which has always been about individual risk. People own private property, including money, and other resources such as time, talent, and energy, which they put at risk in enterprises in exchange for a hoped-for, yet uncertain, return. The individual component of risk was masked by the corporate-feudal economy. Thus our individual careers now appear—and in fact are—more risky than those of business managers and professionals throughout most of this century. How should you deal with this increased risk? Recognize it, then manage it.

Recognizing Risk

Risk comes in various forms. The financial world recognizes this, because in finance risk management represents a fine art and an advanced science. People in finance think in terms of the following types of financial risk, among others:

- inflation risk: the possibility that inflation will erode the value of investment income or financial assets
- interest rate risk: the possibility that a bond will lose value if interest rates rise
- credit risk: the possibility that a borrower will be unable to repay a debt
- foreign-exchange risk: the possibility that foreign-exchange fluctuations will erode the value of overseas income or assets
- political risk: the possibility that civil turmoil or nationalization will undermine an investment's value

Isn't this like the Eskimos having many different words for snow? Managing your career has become as risky as finance, so I've identified six kinds of career risk we all now face:

- financial risk: the possibility that some or all of your income will be lost, interrupted, or voluntarily forgone
- benefits risk: the possibility that some or all of your benefits will be lost, interrupted, or forgone
- professional risk: the possibility that your career will be ended or undermined
- interpersonal risk: the possibility that you will jeopardize others who depend upon your earning power and emotional stability

- emotional risk: the possibility that you will feel fear, anger, regret, or powerlessness
- creative risk: the possibility that you will waste time, energy, and goodwill on a fruitless endeavor

Risk is the bête noire for many of us. If most of us lead lives of quiet desperation, it may well be for lack of risk-taking behavior. Understanding risk will help you think about it more productively. If you understand the various risks you face, you can better decide which ones to assume. Risk management involves considering downside possibilities, such as the potential for lost income or the chances of careerus interruptus. However, risk management is also about upside potential, because risks are assumed in anticipation of rewards. Finance recognizes a risk-return trade-off. Investors do not assume risks for kicks. They assume risks because of the upside financial potential. Similarly, career risks hold upside potential. For example, the upside potential, the possible reward

- of financial risk is increased or more certain earnings
- of benefits risk is a benefits package that you control
- of professional risk is a more flexible and, ultimately, more secure career
- of interpersonal risk is improved relationships and freedom from confining roles
- of emotional risk is personal growth and greater happiness
- of creative risk is higher levels of function and fulfillment

Multipreneurs have risk management tools at their disposal. Any of these tools can be applied to any, or all, of the career risks just identified. These risk management tools include

- planning and preparation
- managing expectations
- diversification and portfolio approaches
- insurance policies

- sharing and swapping
- escape routes and fallback positions

Before addressing these individually, listen to what market researcher Ray Shu has to say about risk, then examine more closely the dimensions of risk in the career management game today:

You have got to take risks. If you don't take risks, you have no idea what you can do. I failed on my last risk in the company and that had to do with my leaving, but I had a good time and I learned a lot. If things don't work out with what I am doing now, I can go do whatever else I want. I can open up a shoe store if I want to. Some people think that's crazy for a Ph.D., but I can do what I want with my life. If you have that attitude, you can do anything.

Place Your Bets: The Dimensions of Risk

Until now you have probably thought of career risk as an ugly, amorphous blob of financial loss and slipping social status. Since most of us are working mainly for the money, financial losses tend to loom largest. Yet since our professional identities are basic to our overall identities, we are also touched by the interpersonal dimensions of career risk ("What will my in-laws think?") and by its emotional dimensions ("Why the hell am I doing this at my age?").

In today's world of financial management, just about any type of risk can be isolated and hedged. The same is true in today's world of career management. But in either world, you have to understand your own risk profile. For example, some investors buy only U.S. government paper, because they know they can't sleep at night if even a penny of principal is at risk. They have no tolerance for credit risk, so they purchase only investments backed by the full faith and credit of the U.S. government. Of course a stockbroker would call them crazy, but they aren't crazy. They are simply extremely risk averse. I believe we should assume, and manage, sensible career risks. If, however, you are intensely risk averse in this area, you should at least know that about yourself and know what you can do in light of that.

Let's examine career risks in greater depth and then compile your risk profile.

Financial Risk

This is the biggie, because a business career is essentially a financial transaction. We work for the money. If we lose our job and cannot replace it, if we lose a client that represented 50 percent of our billings, we lose money. Financial risk must be measured in light of three elements (excluding benefits): income, obligations, and wealth.

Income is the regular, short-term return for working. The degree of financial risk you face depends not just on the size of your income, but on the size of your obligations. These include regular, short-term obligations like food and utility bills, mortgage or rental payments, car payments, and credit card debt, as well as long-term obligations such as your children's college tuition. (Upon arrival, long-term obligations become short-term.)

Over time, as you balance income and obligations, you accumulate wealth (through positive cash flow), accumulate debt (through negative cash flow), or break even. Wealth, net worth—that is, the value of assets minus the value of liabilities—mitigates financial risk. Enough wealth—enough to throw off interest and dividend income sufficient to cover your obligations—can eliminate the financial risk inherent in working for a living. In fact, enough wealth can eliminate your financial need for work. It can also eliminate the risk of retiring broke or of not being able to retire or slow down at all.

Many people do not think rationally about money, which is understandable since money is a loaded concept, symbolizing success, failure, effort, laziness, power, powerlessness, and status. Many people even associate money with intelligence or character. One way or another, money drives many people crazy. The pursuit of money or of a certain lifestyle can itself sharply limit your ability to take risks. Charles Cates sees it like this from his position as an outplacement professional:

> I don't think that many people who work for a large organization and have the corporate perks and a pension plan

and the feeling that they are going to have that job as long as they don't screw up want to cash all that in for a freelance lifestyle or for constantly going from one company to another. It's emotionally tough.

Longtime multipreneur Sally Edwards looks at it this way:

> The risks [of pursuing an independent living] are perceived as very high for most people, but a lot of that perception flows from the entire American system of debt and responsibility and peer pressure. Really, you just have to decide what is important to you. I think that people should be who they are and not try to be what they are told they should be. But our entire system constantly tells people what they should be, and it takes a lot of strength to fight that.

In general, the more rationally and analytically you deal with money, and with financial risk, the better off you'll be. Realize that part of that rationality is keeping money in perspective and not allowing financial risk to dominate every career decision. Few of us are level-headed enough in our dealings with money, preferring drifting, dreaming, denial, or all three. There is a real difference between managing financial risk and either ignoring it or letting it dominate your career.

Benefits Risk

If you work as an on-staff employee, your benefits are subject to the same risk as your salary, except that two added elements have recently increased benefits risk: employers are reducing benefits, and they are transferring more of the cost of benefits to employees. In addition, there are uncertainties surrounding unfunded pension liabilities. Many observers view the billions of dollars of retirement benefits for which companies will become liable, but are not funding, as a time bomb. If it explodes, it will doubtless be in the faces of retirees.

To measure benefits risk, think in terms of your ability to finance your own "disaster relief program." If you or your spouse became disabled, if one of you became ill and required expensive medical care, if the main breadwinner died, could you handle it financially? This is the way to measure benefits risk: What would be the financial impact of these events, and how would you adjust financially? Most people believe that accident, illness, or premature death will not befall them, and most of them are right. Yet if you're in the minority that is wrong, it could quite possibly ruin your life and the lives of your dependents. Benefits—life, health, and disability insurance and a retirement plan—are necessities.

If you are self-employed and funding your own benefits, your benefits risk may be lower than if you were a full-time employee. If you assume the risk, it more explicitly becomes yours to manage. However, going without benefits, particularly without health, life, and disability insurance, especially if you have a family, is assuming too much risk. Get covered, no matter what it takes.

Professional Risk

Aerospace engineers couldn't find work in the early 1990s thanks to defense spending cutbacks. Thousands of financial services professionals hit the bricks after the 1987 stock market crash. Mainframe computer designers must scramble for fewer slots, given the rise of the PC and the decline of IBM's traditional business. As health care restructures, even physicians, once proudly independent professionals, are being corralled into managed care programs and seeing the nature of their profession change.

The emergence of the new economy has heightened the professional risk for middle managers in all industries. Charles Cates of the outplacement firm EnterChange notes, "If you can't put your hands on a computer or on a machine and do some actual work, or if, on the other side of it, you haven't been at the real strategic decision-making level of management, you are pretty vulnerable."

Professional risk is real. It affects us as individuals. It is not dictated solely by the fortunes of your company. It can stem from economic cycles, public policy initiatives, technological developments, or foreign competition, as well as from managerial malfeasance, misfeasance, or stupidity.

Every profession holds risks, and they can be tough to measure.

Often by the time risks are apparent, it's too late to protect yourself. There are, however, two straws in the wind to watch for: changes in technology and changes in the economics of your industry or in your suppliers' or customers' industries. When personal computers are in more than one-third of U.S. homes, which they now are according to New York City–based Jupiter Communications Company, you have technological change. When health care costs are projected to grow from 12 percent to 16 percent of gross domestic product between 1990 and 2000, you have changes in the economics of an industry.

Of course, multipreneuring is itself the best overall tool for managing professional risk. The true multipreneur has a diversified portfolio of skills that can add value to a variety of processes in a variety of settings. That diversification represents the best defense against professional risk.

Interpersonal Risk

Interpersonal risk can be the toughest form of career risk to assume, because it involves others, generally others who are close to you. If you have a spouse and children (or just children) or an aging relative depending on you for financial support, you clearly have more at risk than if you did not. You therefore cannot make career plans in a vacuum.

Interpersonal risk entails more than the familial aspects of financial risk. Depending upon your values, personality, and philosophy, you may see high interpersonal risk where someone else would not, or vice versa. For example, for some people, losing or leaving a high-paying job without a "socially acceptable" alternative entails a loss of face. Friends and neighbors may want an explanation. Social pressures and awkward situations may arise. Such interpersonal risk stems from the issue of professional identity discussed earlier.

Another source of interpersonal risk involves the relationships you form on the job. If you leave an employer, for whatever reason, you leave a social structure, friends, colleagues, and clients. Many independent operators, corporate nomads, and sole practitioners find such losses among the toughest to resolve. Atlanta-based market research consultant Ray Shu was among those who missed the social aspects of having an employer:

> I actually left a pleasant home-based office and took on the expense of a turnkey office at Executive Suites in Atlanta in order to have a place to see other independent operators every day. You know, we talk about how our business is going, business conditions, national politics, and just about the place where we work. Some of us go out for a few beers on Friday. It's more like being at a company with co-workers.

Measuring—and addressing—interpersonal risk is a highly individual matter. For example, if you are involved in a family-owned business, the interpersonal dimension is amplified. Interpersonal risk revolves around your unique set of relationships.

Emotional Risk

This is another biggie among the risks, because a lot of emotion surrounds our concepts of work, success, and failure. Feeling fear or insecurity can itself cloud your thinking. To analyze your career situation and to objectively measure the risks you face, you must separate your fears and feelings from the other, more external risks. But make no mistake: dealing with career issues strikes at the very root of your personality, involving your level of maturity and your ability to face up to your strengths, weaknesses, and limitations and, for that matter, your mortality. At times you must expect to feel confused, vulnerable, and off kilter, but if you maintain perspective, facing emotional risks can result in big payoffs. Management consultant Emmett Murphy has thought deeply on this matter and has concluded:

> The fundamental question to ask is this: "Is what I am doing with my life—the time I spend at work and, for that matter, outside work—in sync with the real challenges that the world faces today and with what I can bring to those challenges?" The sooner this issue is put on the table, the sooner adaptation occurs. This requires a stark analysis of whether

our life's time is being spent properly. The answer to that question and the ensuing realizations often involve a grieving process in which you say, "Holy smoke, I've been out in left field." But that confrontation and that realization leads to new knowledge about oneself, and that knowledge in turn becomes a mandate for action and a motivator.

In other words, you must confront the fact that you have one certain life on this planet and that you spend most of it working. I have often thought that business is not about money, but about character. To manage the emotional risks involved in having a career, you must confront yourself and find that you either have, or can develop, the character needed to deal constructively with the fears or insecurities that hold you back.

Creative Risk

Does a business career involve assuming creative risks? When we talk about creative risks, we are usually discussing filmmakers, playwrights, novelists, musicians, choreographers, painters, and other artists. We talk in terms of the creative risks they take when they depart from the tried and true in their field or in their methods. They risk their time, efforts, and energies when success is not assured, even success in terms of the desired effect, let alone critical or commercial acceptance. The willingness to assume creative risks often stems from the self-knowledge gained by coming to terms with emotional risks.

In business, in order to move ahead in your career or to forge a new career, you will at times have to take creative risks. You may have to take creative risks to make your work stand out, to establish a new organizational structure, or to move into new territory. In such situations you risk wasting time, energy, and resources. You may find yourself up against the organization. You may expose yourself to criticism or ridicule. However, to stick with the tried and true when you know the situation calls for more does not mark the path to success.

Measuring creative risk entails judging the extent to which a course of action represents a departure from the "safe" route and measuring the time, effort, energy, and resources involved in pursuing the risky route. As with any risk, you must also consider the potential return. Please know, *big* payoffs, emotional as well as financial, often accrue to those who gamble on their talent and win. Why? Because creative risk often brings out the very best in us.

Your Risk Profile

Now it's time to assess your career risk profile. This profile gauges your relative willingness to assume various career risks. Do not worry about constructing the profile in the absence of data on the potential returns. As in investing, higher risks generally promise higher returns in career management, but an individual's ability to deal with risk tends to be independent of that. In other words, risk-averse people tend to avoid high risk even in the face of potentially high returns.

Please check the appropriate columns, but remember: *you must wind up with two check marks in each column.* This forces you to make choices, just like real life. If there happen to be three types of risk you would like to place in the "will assume" column, bump the one you like least into the "would assume" column. If you see four types of risk you feel you "must avoid," you will have to bump two into the "would assume" column. If you then have four in "would assume," you'll have to bump two into "will assume."

	Will Assume	Would Assume	Must Avoid
Financial Risk			
Benefits Risk			
Professional Risk			
Interpersonal Risk			
Emotional Risk			
Creative Risk			

You might find it useful to think of these risks as being on a continuum, with financial risk at one end and creative risk at the other. Financial risk and benefits risk tend to be more easily measured and more subject to numerical analysis than emotional risk and creative risk, which are difficult to measure and less subject to rational analysis. Professional risk and interpersonal risk tend to fall in between, having both a measurable/rational dimension and a nonquantifiable/intuitive dimension.

Now consider the choices you made. Think in particular about the types of risk you feel comfortable assuming and those you must avoid. Did your profile point to a greater willingness to assume emotional and creative risks? If so, think about the process by which you prepared that profile: Is it that you are truly willing to take on emotional and creative risks? Or are you simply committed to avoiding financial and benefits risk? Are you willing (and able) to assume financial risk because you have a large nest egg? Or do you find it difficult to take financial risks because you have financially needy dependents? If that is the case, aren't there some interpersonal risks you must assume?

There is nothing right or wrong about any given risk profile; it merely offers a way for you to think about career risk. It is information for you to consider. And now that you've assessed your personal reactions to the different kinds of risk, look for external evidence that supports or contradicts your profile. Are the choices you made here reflected in the way you live your life? If avoiding financial risk is important, do you have a healthy savings account? Is your lifestyle in keeping with your income and wealth? If you're open to assuming financial risks, have you ever done so? If you want to be able to assume greater risk, or at least be able to handle the increased career risk posed by today's marketplace, you need the right tools, and you need to know how to use them.

Power Tools for Managing Career Risk

While these risk management tools can be applied across the spectrum of career risk, you may find some more effective than others for managing a given risk. For example, managing expectations is ideally

Risky Business

Before examining risk management tools, it is important to study the risk-return matrix below. You can use it as one more tool to characterize work situations as well as your relation to career risk. A situation can offer high risk and a high return, high risk and a low return, low risk and a high return, or low risk and a low return. I've broadly classified the individuals whom we would likely find working in each situation.

		Return	
		High	Low
Risk	High	High Roller	Short Timer
	Low	Lucky Duck	Rut Walker

- The High Roller seeks high returns and is willing to assume high risks in pursuit of these returns.
- The Short Timer gets into a high-risk/low-return situation and, absent extremely high motivation, will not be around for long because high risk will wipe you out if the returns can't sustain you. One exception: dedicated artists.
- The Lucky Duck gains high returns in a low-risk situation. Few situations offer such a sweet deal, especially at the outset. In fact, it takes years, even decades, to develop setups like this. When you do, you're golden.
- The Rut Walker is content (or, at least, quietly desperate) with low risk and low returns. This quadrant is where you will find the majority of people in the workforce. There is security in a rut, but there are also low returns.

Where do you want to be?

suited to interpersonal risk, while diversification is geared more toward financial and professional risks. But again, choosing the tool to use, like choosing the risks you'll assume, is a highly individual matter. I urge you to choose as many of these tools as possible. Use all of them, to the extent that you can, on the career risks you face. Why not hedge your bets? Why not give yourself every possible chance to succeed?

Planning and Preparation

You cannot manage a risk that has already materialized as an outcome. You cannot write a prenuptial agreement after you are married or buy fire insurance on a house in cinders. Planning and preparation represent the essential risk management tool and the framework for the use of all the tools that follow. Risk management *is* planning and preparation.

Serial executive Hall McKinley has adopted planning and preparation as a bedrock philosophy:

> You cannot get prepared for sudden job loss, and everything that that entails, after you have lost your job. You have to be ready for it. You have to be prepared and have a plan before it's time to execute it rather than have to make it all up under pressure.

The opposite of planning and preparation is denial and rationalization. I have seen people deny that they were at risk of losing their jobs while all those around them were being laid off. I saw a fellow continue to show up for work even after his firm stopped paying him. They obviously wanted him to leave, yet they lacked the maturity and ego strength to tell him so, so they just stopped paying him. He rationalized it by saying, "Times are tough. A lot of firms in my business have had to cut people's pay." After several weeks they fired him on a pretext.

Again, to manage risk you have to recognize it, then plan and prepare for it.

Planning should be undertaken on short- and long-range bases. Of course, your risk profile and your needs will change as your life progresses. You will face different risks at different times. Professional risk generally increases with age since your earnings tend to grow and your skills tend to become dated. Thus a lot of people are forced into early retirement. Interpersonal risks tend to be easier to take when you are young and less encumbered with family responsibilities. The long-term perspective can help you better understand and manage career risk.

Managing Expectations

As noted, managing expectations can help you manage interpersonal risk, which often involves those close to you. If your family depends on your earnings, it is unfair to put their livelihoods at risk without their knowledge and, in most cases, their advice and consent. The burden of doing work you despise in order to support others can be intolerable. But if you have responsibilities to others, you must help them adjust as you deal with your career challenges.

You have to talk these matters over with your spouse or aged parent and, when appropriate to their ages and maturity, your children. If your job is at risk, you must share that information with your spouse. If you are undertaking a risky venture, if you are putting joint money or a shared lifestyle at risk, if you may lose your company-funded benefits, you must have a series of calm, clear-headed discussions about it.

This is not always easy. Marriages and families are freighted with roles and expectations, and when these roles and expectations stand in the way of our dreams, things can get overheated, even ugly. Try to avoid that, but not at all costs. It is better to be straight-forward and honest and risk it becoming ugly than pretend to go to work at the accounting firm while trying to become a performance artist and cashing in the family's investments so you can "deposit paychecks." Your loved ones can be a tremendous resource to you and can help you deal with the emotional risk involved in career advancements and setbacks. Give them the opportunity to empathize and to prepare their own plan of action, whether that involves a part-time job or a temporary lifestyle adjustment. As Hall McKinley states:

> One of the most important things in terms of handling career setbacks as a fact of life, as opposed to a complete loss of identity and self-esteem, is to deal properly with your spouse. There may be terrible things happening in your career, and they are hard on you and on your spouse. But if you have prepared him or her realistically for the possibility that you could be laid off or fired, you are in a completely

different world than if you have not. If they are mentally and emotionally prepared, they are in a much better position to deal with it themselves if and when it does happen and to help you deal with it.

You also have to manage risk by managing the expectations of your employers and clients. Here you may have to manage expectations in the more traditional sense of the term, by underselling or overselling yourself. Just be aware of what you are doing, and avoid increasing your risk by setting people up to expect too much or too little. Managing your employers' and clients' expectations becomes especially important when you involve them in something inherently risky, for example, when you take creative risks with their time, money, and resources.

We all have dreams. Multipreneurs act on their dreams. But when they do, the smart ones do so by sharing the truth as fully as possible with all concerned parties.

Diversification and Portfolio Approaches

Diversified skills and diversified income streams lie at the heart of multipreneuring. Ideally you need a portfolio of skills useful in adding value in various situations and a portfolio of income streams from various sources. Never has the old saw "Don't put all your eggs in one basket" been truer.

Diversification means spreading risk across various areas. In investing, a diversified portfolio enables you to manage risk by mixing securities of different types, from various industries and regions. Investment professionals avoid concentration in a single company or industry. There is also the concept of countercyclicality: some investments do well in boom times; other (so-called defensive) investments do well in recessions. The goal is to construct a portfolio that maximizes the return for a given level of risk.

Consider a similar approach. Many people have gotten sandbagged because their careers, their earnings, and their skills were concentrated in a single area. As a multipreneur you must learn to add value in a variety of settings and industries. That's diversification. As a multipreneur you must develop multiple sources of income. If, as an independent contractor, you have earnings coming from several divisions of one large company, you are more diversified than if you were in only one division—but you are still concentrated in one company.

How can you become diversified? Frankly, diversification may be difficult to seek as an end in itself. Most multipreneurs did not wake up one morning and say, "You know? My skills are just too concentrated in one area. And look, my sources of income aren't diversified enough." (Although Florida-based teacher-publisher and former pharmacist Arnold Goldstein revealed, "I've never liked having only one source of income because then I'm just too dependent on one boss or one job or one business.")

Most multipreneurs have developed multiple skills and incomes by developing their interests. And most are interested in a lot of things. They read everything. They listen to everyone. They keep up with industries other than their own. They see the value of cross-pollination. To some observers, a multipreneur may appear to be an unfocused dilettante. But unlike an unfocused dilettante, a multipreneur converts his or her multiplicity of interests into skills and earning situations. Probably the best way of doing this is by developing business opportunities across related, but separate, areas.

Craig Hickman, who among other things is the half-time editor of *Utah Business* magazine, has set it up like this:

> I don't devote all of my time to any one thing. I spend time now as a magazine editor, but that also serves at the base for expanding the magazine into other businesses, like a business resource center providing books, audiotape programs, video programs, and motivational and training materials. I am also doing product development for Franklin Quest, a publicly held company that sells business and personal productivity tools. I've written eight nonfiction books, and now I'm working on a novel. My career right now involves a spectrum of things, and it is important for me to keep that spectrum broad.

Staying broad allows me to stay in touch with what's going on, with what makes people tick.

Craig is an excellent example of someone who has taken his core skill, which you may recall he describes as "conceptual thinking," and uses it to develop a true portfolio of activities and income streams.

Insurance Policies

When it comes to managing certain risks, you can't beat insurance. I mean real insurance, insurance policies. For managing financial, benefits, and some aspects of interpersonal risk, there is almost no substitute. I believe that you should have health and disability insurance at all times even if you are single, and if you have a family, you should have life insurance. Insurance exists to manage these financial risks. Unless you have massive amounts of money saved, there really is no other way.

Insurance helps you manage benefits risk by enabling you to create your own portfolio of benefits—self-funded when necessary. Chapter 9 will cover how to be your own benefits manager, but know now that there is no way around it. Hoping you don't become ill and hoping you don't have a disabling accident are not risk management tools. Insurance policies are.

There are other "insurance polices" that help you manage the risks of the multipreneurial life, including employment contracts, letter agreements, kill fees, and agreements on billable expenses. These tools enable you to have that most fundamental of risk management tools, a clear understanding of the transaction and of the responsibilities of each party.

You can, with the right agreement up front as "insurance," do much to reduce the financial risk and the professional risk in a given situation. Despite our reputation for litigiousness, Americans still like to do business on a handshake. No one welcomes a barrier on the road to a deal. But if someone does not want to sign or acknowledge a simple letter agreement documenting each party's responsibilities, you are entering a dicey situation. If the client balks, citing the excuse that it is all too straightforward to require anything on paper, point out that because it is so straightforward it will take you only a few minutes to get it on paper and in the mail to him or her.

Sharing and Swapping

Chapter 2 mentioned ways of sharing risk though contingent-pay arrangements. Use them. The percentage of your salary or fee that you can afford to have paid to you on contingency depends on the situation, its risks, the required skills, your abilities, the time horizon, and the measurability of the results. You can often maximize your upside potential in a deal as an employee or independent contractor by taking contingent pay. (One of the beauties of having multiple income streams is that you can afford to get into some high-risk/high-return situations if you have a baseline income from lower-risk/lower-return activities. This is a common multipreneurial strategy and one I use a lot. My baseline income as a corporate trainer let me get into the riskier business of freelance business writing, and both of these allowed me to try the still riskier business of screenwriting.)

If you are married, you can share or swap risk with your spouse. Many a two-income household temporarily forgoes one income, and a portion of its lifestyle, to send one of the parties to graduate school or both parties in succession. (My wife and I did the latter.) This also works for career changers and entrepreneurs. You can assume the financial risk and benefits risk because your spouse can hold up the financial and benefits end while you prepare for a new career or underprice yourself to build a new practice.

You can also swap risk across time, if you have the know-how and discipline to plan. If you know—with complete certainty—that you have a secure position that you can return to, you can perhaps take a flier on a venture now. In fact, it is always good risk management to have a fallback position.

Escape Routes and Fallback Positions

You've heard the phrase "I can always go back to waiting tables"? Whether said in earnest or in jest, it clearly translates to one, or both, of the following: "I don't have to take this guff forever" or "If this doesn't work out, I'm not going to starve." One way it is a declaration of independence; the other way it is a plan "B" formulated in recognition of the risk of plan "A." As serial executive Hall McKinley put it:

> You have to understand the difference between retreat and defeat. A retreat is when you have a strategy in which you fall back to a previously prepared position, regroup, and launch another attack. It is an organized withdrawal. It is not a defeat, in which you are driven back on someone else's terms. You understand, up front, that with every opportunity to advance, there is the possibility that you are going to have to retreat. So you prepare for that possibility. A retreat differs from a rout.

Escape routes and fallback positions can consist of taking stopgap employment (that is, a job you'd normally not consider taking), returning to "corporate life" (which I have done twice, once after a year and a half as a headhunter and once after five years as an independent writer, consultant, and trainer), undertaking additional training or education (which you sometimes see as necessary only after failing without it), cranking down your lifestyle and taking a rest, or, if you can handle it, moving in with, or not moving out on, Mom and Dad (or Mom *or* Dad, as the case may be). Provided you have prepared yourself and others emotionally and otherwise for these contingencies, they represent prearranged positions to which you may retreat.

Escape routes and fallback positions differ from diversification strategies. They are not simultaneous in time, and they are second choices rather than dual first choices. There is nothing wrong with this. No bank wants to call a loan or seize collateral. But whenever possible, banks have provisions that enable them to call loans (for nonpayment or even on evidence of eroding borrower finances), and most try to get collateral of some kind.

This brings up two points. The first is a practical issue. You should not only have an escape route or fallback position, you should also have flags that will trigger your movement in that direction. The most common flag is something like "If I don't achieve such and such a result by such and such a date, then I will . . ."; but the kind and number of flags are limited only by your imagination. Note, too, that flags are excellent for managing interpersonal risk. If you are leaving a senior-level position with American Express in order to become a famous fashion photographer, your spouse might ask about plan "B." In most healthy households a spouse would have a right to do so. And you can say, "If I haven't shot a cover for *Vogue* within three years, I'll hang up the camera and go back to financial services."

The second point is more psychological. The question "What will I do if this doesn't work out?" poses a problem for some people because they see acknowledging the risk of failure as courting failure. I understand their point, but it smacks of superstition. Fire insurance does not cause fires. Spare tires do not cause flats. Think of escape routes as risk management tools rather than as admissions of the possibility of failure. The escape route, the fallback position, plan "B" should free you up. If you find it hobbles you, then by all means forget about it. Put it completely out of your mind—but only after you've figured out what it is.

How to Analyze an Opportunity: The Risk Management Perspective

To analyze an employment opportunity—whether full-time, project based, or something in between—or to assess a contemplated career move, try the following:

Risk/Reward Assessment

In the "Risk Assessment" column on p. 86, rate the opportunity on a scale of one to ten for each type of career risk:

	Risk Assessment	Reward Assessment
Financial Risk	_____	_____
Benefits Risk	_____	_____
Professional Risk	_____	_____
Interpersonal Risk	_____	_____
Emotional Risk	_____	_____
Creative Risk	_____	_____

Then, in the "Reward Assessment" column, rate the opportunity's potential rewards in each of these areas on a scale of one to ten. Be careful. It is easy to see potential rewards as certain rewards or to believe that long-term rewards can enable you (or your loved ones) to bear unbearable burdens in the short term. It is also easy to "assume away" risks. Specifically, you might think that the financial rewards will be so high that the lack of benefits doesn't matter. In fact, until the financial rewards materialize, any lack of benefits is very real and leaves you exposed. It is also tempting to believe that emotional and creative rewards will carry the day on all counts, outweighing the potential lack of all other rewards, plus the presence of all risks.

Here is where self-knowledge and knowledge of those around you are so important. If you are a man who wants to stop selling mutual funds and start building wooden boats, you have to realize that it is *your* dream career, not necessarily your wife's concept of her husband's dream career. Your wife loves the mutual funds salesman (presumably), and she might find the going more than a bit rough as you learn woodcraft and then set up shop. Are you sure she can handle it, as she claims she can? Or is she just trying to be a trouper and support you, come what may? While you're at it, ask yourself, are you really built for boat building? Your love for wooden boats had better be true, mad, and deep to carry you through the long hours, low pay, rough conditions, and social dislocation such a career move can hold. Yes, it's okay to dream, but it's also okay hedge your bets. Which is the final part of this analysis.

Risk Management Tools Inventory

Now that you have rated the risks and rewards of the opportunity, examine the risk management tools at your disposal. Regardless of the rewards, how are you going to hedge the risks you identified above? You need a tool or strategy for each risk.

Risk Management Tools and Hedge Strategies

Financial Risk   _____

Benefits Risk   _____

Professional Risk   _____

Interpersonal Risk   _____

Emotional Risk   _____

Creative Risk   _____

Here are some examples of specific tools and strategies:

Financial Risk: Use savings or spouse's income, crank back the lifestyle, incur debt

Benefits Risk: Use spouse's benefits/have spouse get benefits, fund own benefits, reduce benefits (but maintain a minimal package), leave job and fund own benefits under COBRA (discussed in chapter 9)

Professional Risk: Continue part-time, continue as project-based independent contractor, make other arrangement with current employer, explore similar opportunities elsewhere if current employer is not amenable, take leave of absence, develop the new opportunity by moonlighting or through part-time or project work

Interpersonal Risk: Discuss the opportunity, risks, rewards, and your risk management strategies with those who depend upon you financially and with trusted friends and advisers and, if possible, with your employer or potential employer—and develop mutually agreeable positions

Emotional Risk: View the opportunity in the context of your long-term goals and needs and, to the extent possible, honestly accommodate these goals and needs and face your fears and hopes

Creative Risk: Honestly assess your skills and talent and motivation, interview others who work in the area, plan exactly how you are going to learn what you need to learn and how you are going to learn it (see chapter 5), get additional education or technical training if necessary, work to deepen your belief in your mission.

After you identify risk management tools to apply to the situation, look back at how you rated the risks and the rewards. Can you reconcile any positions in which the risks are high and the rewards are low? Do you have risk management tools for each high-risk area? When you have fully analyzed the opportunity, alternately reflect upon it and then let it alone. This way a clearer picture and more fully developed answer will emerge. Avoid analysis paralysis. Do your homework, then let it alone and see what the answer is.

Much of what's in this chapter may strike you as codified common sense. Yet if it is so common, how do so many people get into such horribly screwed-up career situations? Here's how: through denial, rationalization, magical thinking, hoping against hope, and similar mental gymnastics. After a downside risk materializes, after the dust of a career crisis settles, the postmortem usually goes like this: "The signs were there. I just didn't want to see them. People tried to tell me, but I didn't listen. A lot of this mess could have been avoided."

How could it have been avoided? By recognizing and managing the risks inherent in virtually every work situation. When it comes to dealing with career risk, make "realism" your watchword. Remember, risk is not to be avoided, but recognized and managed.

4

Work Productively and Flexibly

Whether you work on staff, as an independent operator, or anywhere in between, you now have more to do and you have more varied things to do. Multipreneuring begins with the assumption that you not only have to perform multiple tasks, but that you will actually seek them out in order to broaden your skills and opportunities. Part of a multipreneur's job description, if there were such a thing, would read "Must be able to handle multiple tasks simultaneously and perform each of them well." Thus, working productively and flexibly is a necessity for the multipreneur.

How you go about working productively and flexibly will differ depending upon whether you work on staff, as an independent, or as some combination of the two. When you work on staff, you have two tremendous assists to productivity: structure and infrastructure. Structure arises from something as simple as an in-box or a job description. An in-box gives you things to do. A job description gives you a defined set of tasks to perform. In fact, the entire purpose of the organization is to give you things to do. Infrastructure also arises from the organization, in that the company gives you co-workers as well as systems, from the information system to the mail distribution system to the reward system, that (usually) support you in getting things done.

Those who leave corporate life to pursue an independent living often feel lost, at first, without the external structure provided by an organization. That feeling is completely natural, because the organization motivates and directs its employees, and it often takes time for former employees to develop internal motivation and direction.

The lack of infrastructure also frustrates many a fledgling independent operator. The standard complaint is, "I have to lick every stamp." For the independent there is typically no secretary, no research assistant, no copy department (and usually no copy machine), no sales force, no treasurer, and no stamp licker. Since life outside an organization provides no infrastructure for getting things done, it is often filled with tasks representing an unproductive use of a highly trained individual's time and energy.

Organizations boost productivity by providing structure and infrastructure to those doing the work of the organization. Yet while an organization usually boosts group productivity, it does not necessarily teach us how to boost individual productivity. Working in an unstructured environment can be tougher than it looks. When independents have trouble working alone, it is not just that they miss their friends and their routine—it is often because they literally don't know what to do. Having grown used to having their time and tasks structured for them, they often panic when called upon to manage their own time. Instead of productivity and flexibility, the result is often repetition of a routine that helps keep the panic at bay but does little to blaze new trails or create momentum.

The principles of productivity and flexibility center upon creating the structure and infrastructure you need in order to be productive and to develop a truly flexible mind-set.

Working Productively: A Matter of Focus

When we think of working productively we typically think about getting lots of things done and getting them done quickly. However, the way to be truly productive is not to get lots of things done, but to get the *right* things done. To be productive you need to create a structure and an infrastructure to support you in getting the right things done. What are the right things? The things that add the most value, of course. Consider the advice of Holliston, Massachusetts–based political and media consultant Todd Domke:

> The issue of productivity starts with wanting to do the work you're involved in. The work itself has to motivate you because you enjoy it immensely or you feel it is important or fulfilling. You have to be honest with yourself about this. If you are trying to do work that you basically dislike, productivity becomes this big issue because everything is forced. If you really enjoy the work and find it fulfilling, all you really require to be productive is a need for the money and a deadline.

If you don't enjoy the work itself, you must constantly try to motivate yourself to do things you really don't want to do. Think about situations in which people have to do work they dislike—for example, when managers who hate to write have to write reports or when salespeople have to make cold calls. What happens? Procrastination. Skylarking. Trips to the water cooler. A sudden interest in organizing files. Don't set yourself up by getting into, or staying with, work you dislike.

If you develop a broad enough definition of your professional identity and define your core skills properly, you stand a good chance of having work you enjoy. But if you find yourself terminally unproductive, look first to your basic motivation. If that is missing, try to find work you enjoy. Listen to what consultant Joanne Pratt has found:

> What keeps many of us going is the high of being your own boss. It is exciting to be determining your own destiny, to be testing your own ideas even though you know some of them are going to flop. Many people in corporate offices count the minutes until the next break or until lunch or until the day's end. But those of us who are determining our own destinies get totally caught up in our work and don't even think about the time.

Once you are doing work that you find enjoyable and fulfilling, increasing your productivity begins with an analysis of activities you are—and should be—doing, followed by the need to structure your work and put the proper infrastructure in place. Finally, you should monitor the way you work and use specific tactics to improve your productivity.

Productivity Analysis: High-Return versus Low-Return Activities

In our complex, demanding world, we need simple rules to guide our behavior. One of the most valuable things I ever heard was that the major reason people fail in major endeavors is that they don't relate their day-to-day activities to their long-term goals. It is easy to get caught up in performing tasks that can be described as maintenance or "housekeeping" or that meet short-term goals. But these tasks will not necessarily bring you closer to your long-term goals.

Presumably you're reading this book because your long-term goal is to reach high levels of function, income, and independence. To reach that goal as a multipreneur, you must spend your time, every day, on activities that lead to higher levels of function, income, and independence. I call these activities high-return activities, and they usually also add increasingly greater value for your employers and clients. Activities that don't either contribute to your long-term goals or add high value for your employers and clients are low-return activities.

To be truly productive, you must have a clear idea of your professional goals and a clear idea of what it is you do that adds value. When these ideas are clearly established in your mind, you must then identify which activities support these goals and add value and which do not.

For multipreneurs, the high-return activities of marketing and selling themselves, organizing and executing projects, and learning new skills typically produce high value—and revenue. Everything else can be categorized as low-return activities, including administrative tasks (maintaining files), work-related errands (going to the copy shop), and professional courtesies (listening to sales pitches from salespeople referred to you by friends). New York City–based book producer Roseann Hirsch has found:

The key is to spend time on the thing that is going to bring in the money. Very often I will actually ask myself, "Is this going to bring me money?" When you work for someone else, you develop sloppy habits in this regard. When you work for yourself, you have to adjust your focus. You have to learn that sometimes you have to let your files stay messy while you write that proposal that is going to bring you big bucks. You really have to prioritize. It is so easy to get sidetracked. You have to stay on the money track if you want to be successful.

Note that low-return activities are not no-return activities. Having orderly files, copies of correspondence, and necessary supplies is important, but you have to get these things done with a minimal investment of time and energy. It's also important to realize that the returns among high-return activities can vary depending upon your business and what you do best. For example, in sales some people see cold calling as a low-return activity, while others see it as the only way to get business (and therefore as a high-return activity). This is in spite of the fact that the average percentage of calls that result in an appointment is around 5 percent. Their value depends upon you and your business.

It takes time to identify the returns on various activities, but it is time well spent because the resulting knowledge can help you boost your productivity tremendously.

Think Binary

Simple rules help you be productive, and a simple way to decide what to do is to "think binary." Here is how I once developed a binary thinking system when I needed one:

After I decided to become a writer, I made slow progress for several years because I wasn't spending enough time learning the craft, pitching proposals, selling projects, and writing. I had a managerial job. I was too busy. I had to meet short-term financial obligations. I had to get promoted again. But my writing career got moving when I developed the following attitude: "There are two types, and only two types, of activities: those that move me toward becoming a writer and those that move me away from becoming a writer." This mantra gave me a sense of direction. When I engaged in the activities that supported my goal, I could feel myself being pulled toward the goal of becoming a writer, and I enjoyed the sensation. When I did things that did not support my goal (as necessary as some of them were), I felt myself being sidetracked, and I disliked that feeling. I quickly found myself doing more of the right activities and avoiding the wrong ones.

Whatever device you choose, you must relate your daily activities to your professional goals and to the goal of adding value. This means spending the bulk of your time and energy on high-return activities.

Structuring Your Time and Tasks for Productivity

Once you've identified high-return and low-return activities, you have to invest the right proportion of time in these activities. An organization manages your time for you. The boss, the in-box, the telephone, the fax machine, the production schedule, the sales quota, and the monthly activity report all tell you what to do and when to do it. But without them, the choice is yours. How are you going to structure your time? Without these motivators, how will you be productive?

To structure your time and work productively, you must

- motivate yourself
- allocate your time proportionally to the return
- schedule tasks around your peaks and valleys

Motivating yourself calls for big goals. To locate big goals, look not just to the work you want to do, but to your dreams. None of the corporate objectives I've had set before me, none of the entreaties I've heard from platform or pulpit, have motivated me as much as my own dreams. We all have dreams. Sadly, most of us don't act on them.

This echoes, and is meant to echo, the comments about risk taking in the previous chapter. Many of us refuse to take the risks necessary to realize our dreams. Many of us believe—falsely, in my view—that our dreams are either unworthy or unreachable. Don't deny yourself. Translate your dreams into motivating goals and then identify the activities that will move you toward your goals.

Allocating your time proportionally to the return means that you don't set aside an hour a day to lick stamps. (If you send out that much mail, get a postage meter.) Reasonable allocations of time among the major activities of selling, executing, and administrating business run, respectively, about 40-50-10 percent or 25-70-5 percent or thereabouts. The balance between selling and executing business will vary with the length of time you've been in business and the annual or monthly phase of your business cycle. However, the time spent on administrative tasks should be very low relative to that spent on selling and executing business.

There is also the issue of allocating time within a given high-return activity. For example, in sales, as noted, there are higher-return and lower-return activities, depending on the kinds of activities (prospecting by mail versus telephone, or selling by proposal versus face-to-face) and the kinds of prospects (banks versus high-tech firms) you face. It is up to you to figure out where the greatest returns lie. In executing business, you'll find (if you haven't already) that certain types of projects and clients suck up your time, teach you little, and pay you poorly, while others actually yield a higher return for less time and hassle. You must monitor all activities with an eye toward the return.

What about part-time work or stopgap employment? You may spend half your work time on a "bread-and-butter job" while you work toward bigger goals. Yes, such an arrangement can blow a real hole in your week, every week. (So can a full-time job, for that matter.) If you can't find part-time work that is synergistic with your larger goals, you must keep those goals in front of you, remember that the job is a means to an end, and keep it in its place, which might be down in a valley rather than up on a peak.

Scheduling around peaks and valleys means considering your energy levels and your short-term and long-term rhythms when you structure your time and tasks. During peaks, your energy and mental acuity are relatively high, while during valleys they are low. Of course, circumstances, such as a deadline or an opportunity, as well as your ability to motivate yourself at will can affect these peaks and valleys, but in general peaks and valleys refer to your natural rhythms. Scheduling cold calling during a valley is self-defeating. So is using peak time to organize your files. You can increase your overall productivity with no extension of your working hours by simply watching yourself—your energy level, attention span, mental acuity, and efficiency at certain tasks at certain times—and scheduling accordingly. Use the peaks for high-return activities and the valleys for low-return or routine activities. Look forward to the valleys as down time. There are time management experts who will tell you to view all time as time when you are "up" or "on." That's hooey. Everyone needs down time.

Each of us is ultimately responsible for structuring our time and tasks, but this fact simply becomes more obvious for the multipreneur who doesn't have a full-time employer.

Three Structural Questions

In structuring your time and tasks for productivity, you face three simple questions:

Informational:	What should I do?
Motivational:	Why should I do it?
Practical:	When should I do it?

In answering these questions, you will begin to create a structure to replace the one that the organization used to provide. That structure will tell you what to do as surely as the organizational structure did, probably more surely.

Building an Infrastructure to Support Your Productivity

Too many independent operators operate too independently. Some are loners by nature, while others simply don't know how to get the right support. Many are underresourced. Some hate to spend money even to make money. Others don't know what they need, much less where to get it.

To be productive, any worker, whether a laborer, knowledge worker, or salesperson, needs some degree of infrastructure. You need support from other professionals, such as accountants or technicians, who can perform certain tasks that you cannot or who can perform them better than you can. You need a workspace, equipment, supplies, and systems. You will dramatically undercut your productivity if you believe that you lack the time, the money, or the need for such things.

Infrastructure should be broken into two categories: human infrastructure and physical/systems infrastructure.

Human infrastructure is typically what people who leave full-time employment miss the most—and not just because it helps them get things done. Ray Shu, the former Coca-Cola market research manager and current independent market researcher, observes:

> When you leave the corporate environment, all of a sudden you are alone. I used to have fifteen to twenty employees and I used to get into political fights day in, day out. You know? You hate that while it's going on, but the thing is that once you are removed from it, that is what you miss the most. That's half the fun. People bitch and moan about it, but it really is half the fun.

While Ray's phraseology was unique among the multipreneurs interviewed, anyone who's ever worked in a large organization knows what he means. From the standpoint of productivity, co-workers generally help us get things done and serve as sounding boards, advisers, and sources of information and ideas. Book producer Rose-ann Hirsch sees both sides:

> I can pursue any idea I think might fly as a book. That's not necessarily the way it works at a publishing house, where you can go to an editorial meeting and twenty-nine other people have to give the imprimatur before you can go ahead with it. But I also miss [being on staff and] benefiting from the give-and-take of editorial meetings.

To be productive, you need at least two or three trusted colleagues with whom you can test ideas and talk over situations. A smart, objective adviser who has your best interests at heart will help you steer clear of bad deals, catch errors early on, and weed out poor ideas before you waste time and energy on them. I have about five such people in my life whom I call upon in various situations, in addition to my agent. I in turn act as an adviser to a similar number of people (however, not necessarily the same ones).

Don't be afraid to reach out for this kind of help—it's not as though you should face things alone. You can even benefit from a formal mentor program, such as SCORE (Service Core of Retired Executives) or the Small Business Association's WNET (Women's Network for Entrepreneurial Training), both of which helped multipreneur Michèle Van Buren:

> WNET is a mentor-protégé program the SBA established about four years ago. I've been working with my mentor in the program in Boston for the past three years. She worked closely with me at the start, helping me get my business up and running. For example, she had been very involved in getting press for her company, and through her guidance and encouragement I started doing the same for myself. Earlier the people from SCORE were similarly helpful and encouraging about the mechanics of getting a business formed.

Certain situations can make it tough to get help. If you've relocated to follow your spouse, it makes good business sense to stay in touch with your friends and associates back home, at least until you're settled. Try plugging into formal sources as well as into networking groups, professional associations, and local chapters of your alumni association for sources of advisers and friends. If necessary, start your own networking group.

To maximize your productivity, offload every low-return task you can. This means getting and paying for help with tasks you dislike, put off, don't do very well, or don't do at all, but that must be done. There is lots of good help out there. Ask yourself: What's my time worth? That question can be answered mathematically and objectively. Look at your salary or fees. You might find the answer depressing. However, your time might be worth more if your low-return activities were taken care of by someone else, so that you could spend more time on what counts. Be sure to get the help you need.

In terms of physical infrastructure, if you are on your own even part-time or intend to be, you *must* have office space. Forget the kitchen table. Forget a corner of the living room, especially if you have kids. The matter of the home office versus outside office space will be examined in chapter 9, as issues like office space fall into the "take care of business" category. Know that you have a wide range of options for establishing a physical infrastructure. Commit yourself to getting what you need.

The final element of infrastructure has to do with systems, which you need to maximize your productivity. "System" means an information system that tells you who got what sales letter on what date, who owes you money, whom you owe money to, and so on. Although it would be best to do it yourself, at least for some period of time, such a system can be maintained by a freelance office manager who comes in once a week. However it gets done, you must effectively track your money, projects, invoices, proposals, and subcontractors.

You also need a system of rewards. In any company there are perks, freebies, social functions, and so on, as well as more formal, albeit nonmonetary, rewards. Will you be more productive or better connected if you have lunch with a friend or contact every Wednesday? Will a monthly dinner with your spouse, just to keep him or her up-to-date on your business, be useful? Should you get a massage once a week? Or use Friday afternoons in the summer to play golf with a like-minded independent operator or client?

To some readers, such ideas may seem indulgent or unproductive. (Others, of course, are yelling, "Hot damn!") But many independent operators, not to mention full-time staffers, fritter away hour upon hour, then say they don't have time for those things that would really lift them up. With the right infrastructure in place, you'll be better positioned to be productive and to enjoy its rewards, perhaps by combining business and pleasure or by occasionally saying, "The hell with business this afternoon."

Ten Tactics to Improve Your Productivity

Once you've identified your high- and low-return activities and created some supporting structure and infrastructure, achieving productivity calls for tactics to combat the forces working against you. Here are ten:

1. *Compartmentalize and bundle low-return tasks.* Don't get into reactive mode with low-return activities. Stay in control by placing them in pigeonholes, then doing a group of them at once—during a valley. Such tasks include routine product literature mailings, going to the copy shop, paying bills, and buying supplies.

2. *Schedule smartly and realistically.* When you draw up your schedule, be sure to include down time, "fudge factors," and buffer time. The latter is especially important. Anticipate, and allow for, delays, late deliveries, broken commitments, and people being out of town.

3. *Call people you need as soon as possible.* Millions of people walk around every day saying, "I've got to call this guy." What's stopping them? If you put off calling someone you are going to need in the future, you risk their having a full schedule or being out of town. Also, always phone ahead for reservations, items in stock, and directions.

4. *Get feedback—and cut your losses—early.* You can waste months chasing a bad idea, a worthless deal, or someone with nothing to offer. After you shape an idea, get fast feedback on it from a friend or the marketplace. If you have doubts about a deal, run it by someone sooner rather than later. Don't dance for weeks with people who aren't serious.

5. *Master the five-minute phone call.* The reason we don't keep in touch with people is that we make it too time-consuming. Call and say, "I really only have a few minutes before my ten o'clock, but I wanted to stay in touch." Call more often, but make calls shorter. If you get the incoming call, tell them you're jammed, then spend just a few minutes. If they need to unload, schedule a time in the next twelve to twenty-four hours.

6. *Insist that all meetings have a closing time.* This is an old one, but it really works. The attendees can schedule their day better, and the closing time helps people push forward at the meeting when things go astray. ("We only have three hours left, and we have to reach a decision.")

7. *Manage your family during work hours.* When you work on staff, your family easily understands when you are at work. This understanding can vanish if you work at home full- or part-time or even if you become self-employed outside the home ("Gee, you can take a day off, can't you? You're the boss!"). Also, if you have seen your earnings tumble after a job loss or a move into a new business, your spouse may see your work as less important than it had been, which can create tension over the division of labor on homemaking activities. Such situations call for open communication and explicit scheduling of activities.

8. *Stop throwing time away.* If you don't know how you waste time, watch yourself for a week or two. Main offenders: browsing in the library or stationery store; taking long breakfasts, lunches, or breaks; smoking during work hours; rifling through junk mail; standing on lines and sitting in traffic. If you've factored these activities in as down time, fine. However, too often they are simply low- and no-return activities.

9. *Demand immediate action when a service provider stalls you.* Your computer is broken. You need a physician referral. A delivery is late or lost, or they sent the wrong item. You phone the company and find yourself stunned yet again by the remarkable insouciance of their "service" people. Their attitude: "I'm underpaid, and your problem is not my problem." Make your problem their problem at the first sign of this attitude. Come on strong early in the game. Make it clear that they screwed up, and it is hurting you. Get names, direct dial numbers, and supervisors' names. Tell them—don't ask—what they have to do to

fix the situation, then demand a deadline. If they can't agree, keep saying, "I'm very sorry, but I just can't accept that," and keep going higher.

Tip: Many "service" people are actually cost-controlling gatekeepers instructed *not* to send out a service rep unless your computer exploded and *not* to refer you to a medical specialist unless you're having a near death experience. Cut these people off at the knees. You have the right to the service call and the right to see a specialist.

10. *Use time management systems and tools*. If you have not read *How to Get Control of Your Time and Life* by Alan Lakien, do so. It is the classic of the genre, and it got an entire generation to use prioritized "to do" lists. Tools such as computer-based calendars and ticklers, as well as paper-based planners and schedulers like those by Day-timer and Franklin Quest, can boost productivity as long as you don't spend more time with them than on the tasks. I write everything down on pieces of paper that I keep in a money clip in my pocket, from my major goals to the loaf of bread I have to pick up that evening. Whatever works.

It takes time to find a productive way of working independently and of maintaining your productivity as you put together a living from various sources. It will not happen by itself. It definitely takes planning and it is a necessity. David Rye tells his students in his how-to-run-a-business class:

They have to methodically plan what they want to do, where they are going, and what tasks are required to get there. They have to work very smart. I tell them that if they are going to be working on their own, they should look to achieve a productivity level at least twice that of their counterparts in the corporate world. Almost any independent is competing against established businesses at some level, so striving for double productivity is a kind of insurance policy to promote success.

Flexibility: The Ability to Handle Change

Flexibility is the ability to deal effectively with change, whether that change is generated within you or from outside. Flexibility has become as important as productivity, because the business environment is demanding flexibility just as insistently. To be a multipreneur *is* to take a flexible approach to using your skills, making a living, and managing your career. If we are flexible, we can move from activity to activity, from task to task, from situation to situation, with little loss in productivity.

As with so many aspects of multipreneuring, the need for flexibility applies to us whether we work on staff, as independents, or anywhere in between. During the downsizing wave of the early 1990s, one buzz phrase that made the rounds was "fungibility of resources." This was management's way of saying that anyone could be asked to do anything. Many companies have long used rotational programs to round people out and expose them to all areas of the business. But real cross-functionality has become highly valued. Given the realities of flat org-charts and fewer opportunities for promotion, companies are using lateral moves to "reward" people and teach them new skills to be used either at the company or at a future employer. So flexibility is the order of the day, even for those on staff. For those off staff, it is essential to survival.

Beverly Kaye, career development and in-placement consultant in Sherman Oaks, California, sees flexibility as a set of attitudes:

> It is a mind-set or set of mental models, for the way people approach the world. It is now the attitude you carry with you that will make or break you in the new organization. It's our ability to adapt. It's our ability to deal with ambiguity. It is these things that count, rather than being technically brilliant or the best delegator. It's flexibility that is so important.

In the research I've done among multipreneurs and career management professionals like Bev Kaye, the following abilities emerged as constituting flexibility:

- the ability to work well with a broad range of people
- the ability to work well in a broad range of situations
- the ability to change your mental focus rapidly
- the ability to function well as a member of a team, but without traditional "corporate" motivations and structures
- the ability to live with ambiguity

We often think of flexibility as a personality trait. Clearly some of us have more flexible or more rigid personalities than others. However, it will be more useful to think of flexibility not as a personality trait, but as a set of abilities, the five abilities noted above.

How to Increase Your Flexibility

To expand your ability to work with a range of people and situations, think in terms of bandwidth: broaden your bandwidth by seeing people clearly and by grasping the fundamentals in situations. To focus flexibly, try developing rapid response capabilities. To work as a team member in the absence of traditional structures and motivations and to live with ambiguity, you must develop your own set of external and internal supports.

Bandwidth: How to Tune In

In conversation we talk about "being tuned in to what someone is saying" or "being on the same wavelength." Bandwidth refers to the fact that we all must operate on a broad range of frequencies, given the number of people and situations we must deal with today. However, within that bandwidth we must still be able to focus on the important things. Multipreneur and *Utah Business* editor Craig Hickman feels this way about it:

> We are all going to have to learn to deal with that feeling of being spread too thin. I don't think that the way to deal with it anymore is to narrow the bandwidth. But there are two contradictory things at work in what Bill Gates has called the Age of Bandwidth. On the one hand, you can't narrow the bandwidth because, even if you are in just one business, the scope of competition and substitute products and

opportunities is much broader than it used to be. We don't
have the luxury of being able to zero in too narrowly. Yet on
the other hand, a big part of reengineering is about redesign-
ing work so that you eliminate stuff that is ineffective, unproductive, or unimportant. Put these two things together
and what have you got? The amount of work where you can
really add value is broadening, but at the same time you have
to be constantly reevaluating your priorities.

Pulling this off demands almost double-jointed flexibility. Think
of it as having the ability to tune in to a lot of channels sharply, then
having the freedom to decide which ones to stay tuned in to. To be
able to deal with a wide range of people and situations, you have to be
able to relate to them, to tune them in. With some people, you must
be willing to come to grips with your prejudices and preconceived
notions in order to see others clearly. With some situations, you can
use frameworks to help you connect by quickly grasping the fundamentals and the issues involved.

As Newton, Massachusetts–based executive development consultant Paul Miller has pointed out, by understanding your prejudices
and preconceptions about others, you are better able to tune them in
because you'll tune out the static produced by those attitudes. If you
have notions about others based upon their color, sex, appearance,
accent, class, marital status, political affiliation, place in the organization, technical specialty, and so on, you see them less clearly as
individuals. The extent to which this occurs is proportionate to the
intensity of these beliefs. To the extent that you believe your preconceptions about others, your approach to them will be rigid and your
flexibility limited.

The damage done by racial and gender prejudice is well documented. But on the job plenty of damage can be done because "a
creative" can't understand "the suit" or because the suit doesn't trust
the creative with money, or because management thinks that the
MIS (management information systems) people don't care about
business or the MIS people think management doesn't care about
technology, or because the boss thinks the subordinate is always
wrong or the subordinate thinks the boss is always right.

Probably the biggest mistake anyone can make would be to

believe that we are free of prejudice toward others. A better starting point might be to acknowledge your prejudices and then mentally allow for them in your interactions. Unless your multipreneurial career is going to include a stint in sainthood, this may work better than trying to rid yourself of any preconceptions or, worse, believing you don't have any.

To tune in to a broader range of situations (as opposed to people), you have to know at least something about a lot of different things. You have to be well informed, of course, but equally important is an understanding of how various classes of situations work. This will be covered in greater depth in the next chapter, on learning, but consider this: If you understand the fundamentals of how, for example, financial instruments work, then you will be able to understand a new financial instrument when one comes along. Similarly, if you know the broad fundamentals of a business process, such as inventory management, or of an industry, such as telecommunications, then you have a basis for understanding a broad range of similar situations.

When we feel left out of a conversation, when we don't know what someone is talking about, it is often because we don't know the fundamentals and because we have no frame of reference for organizing or evaluating the material coming at us. As a multipreneur, your goal should not be to know everything about everything, which is impossible, but to know enough to ask good questions. Questions enable you to get at the main points and understand the goals, roles, and problems in a situation.

If you understand your preconceptions about others and you grasp the fundamentals of numerous situations, you will broaden your bandwidth. But will you be able to stay tuned to a single channel?

The Ability to Respond Rapidly
We need to be able to tune in a single channel—and then act quickly. The ability to respond rapidly provides an advantage in the marketplace, because of the pace of change in today's economy. Management consultant Emmett Murphy looks at it this way:

> The new environment demands rapid response capability in terms of creating and using information. This is very different from the old paradigm. A lot of very bright people have

up to now been taught how to be corporate bodyguards, but not how to create, acquire, and use new knowledge in reponse to the quickly emerging demands of the marketplace.

The ability to respond rapidly differs from habitual responsiveness, which can erode your flexibility in that you have fewer choices and, worse, they are determined by outside events. Broad bandwidth makes an enhanced range of opportunities available to you, but the

A Word on Business Literacy

The value of an MBA is not that it makes you a master of business administration, which of course it does not, but that it gives you "business literacy." So does an undergraduate business degree. So does enough varied business experience. Wherever you get it, this broad understanding of business is invaluable. For example, many businesspeople are alarmed by the fact that many educated, intelligent American adults believe that the average large corporation earns profits of up to 25 percent or more on its sales annually. (The actual number is in the 5 percent range.) No multipreneur can afford this degree of naiveté.

People with true business literacy understand the basics of finance, accounting, production, inventory management, distribution, sales, and marketing. They can apply this knowledge to industries and companies and place things in the context of the local, national, and global economies. They understand the relationships among management, employees, shareholders, customers, and suppliers and the role of profits, competition, trade, and regulation. Lack of this basic knowledge, which is readily available in books, magazines, and courses, will hobble you. The greater your level of business literacy, the broader the number of situations you will be able to grasp, not necessarily because you instantly understand that particular situation, but because you can ask useful questions and understand the answers.

flexibility of your response is often determined by your ability to respond rapidly or to choose not to respond rapidly—or at all, for that matter.

You need to decide explicitly when rapid response is, and is not, necessary. Is your client willing to pay for rapid response? Will rapid response enable you to gain a competitive edge? When is it a requirement? When is it a case of "hurry up and wait"? The volume of information and work we deal with has created a crisis environment. Don't reflexively buy into it. It is up to you to distinguish between the things that require rapid response and the things that do not, when it is worth it and when it is not. You cannot rely on others to do this for you, nor can you react immediately to everything that purports to require rapid response.

Rapid response capability must be grounded in your knowledge and skills, business relationships, technological capabilities, and time management ability. If your skill set is narrow or outdated, you will be able to respond rapidly in only a few situations. To develop rapid response capability as a competitive advantage, you have to see flexibility and speed of turnaround as virtues and put together the skills and relationships accordingly. This means continually updating your skills and cultivating new relationships. It may mean having a network of freelancers whom you know and trust. It might mean leasing rather than buying equipment, or it may mean overbuying so that you can accommodate future applications.

Most people think of rapid response as an intense customer-service orientation or the ability to move fast, and indeed it does include these things. However, the ability resides in the breadth, depth, and applicability of your resources. The corporate move to looser organizational forms such as virtual corporations and self-managed teams reflects this need, and in the chapters that follow you'll see ways of developing the ability to respond rapidly.

External and Internal Supports

To function as a team member and to live with ambiguity, you need to develop external and internal supports that enhance your flexibility.

External supports ensure that your skills, work arrangements, and finances support you. How much flexibility do you have if you have only one skill and can apply it in only one industry? How much flexibility do you have if you have presold 90 percent of your time for the next year? (That might be a good thing, of course, but you have to consider the effect on your flexibility.) How much flexibility do you have in negotiations if your rent or mortgage payment hangs on the outcome of every deal? Flexibility is a set of mental attitudes, but you are either going to help yourself or hurt yourself with your external setup.

Internally you need personal qualities that support you. Flexibility requires humor and perspective. If you regard everything in life-or-death terms, there'll be no room for flexibility and you'll be miserable. As someone who has generally managed to keep business in perspective, I often feel sorry for those who don't. How can they be so serious about something as gamelike as business? Haven't they heard that life is too short?

Incidentally, game psychology has helped millions of people keep business in perspective. You train hard and do your best. You play your position and let others play theirs. You win some. You lose some. Some get rained out. Money buys equipment and pays the bills. Argue with the owners or the umpire only when it's important. Listen to the coach, but find what works for you. Get a good night's sleep. Plan for the day when you can't play anymore. And remember, it's only a game.

You also might just consider what increased flexibility could do for you and your relationships with others. In an environment as unpredictable as our economy, rigidity can kill you, literally, and it can be hell on the people around you. You want to be flexible? Lighten up. This is business, not Greek tragedy. Your spouse and kids will thank you, and so will the rest of us. You'll thank yourself, too.

Productivity and Flexibility: Two Aspects of Control

In a very real sense, the principle of working productively and flexibly centers on the issue of control. Productivity requires you to exercise control. Flexibility requires you to let go.

To be productive you have to control your job content, your time, and your working conditions. The content must comprise tasks that suit your tastes and talents and add value. The time you spend on a task must be appropriate to the return. The working conditions must be fair and favor your getting things done efficiently: you require the right structure and infrastructure.

To be flexible you must understand on a deep level that you control very few of the factors that affect your success. The national and international economy, the global marketplace, the regulatory and tax environment, and the behavior of other people all lie beyond your control. Lack of flexibility often stems from a failure to understand this, which is why game psychology can be so useful. Aside from adopting the right attitude, you can enhance your flexibility by developing a broad bandwidth, business literacy, and the ability to respond rapidly as well as multiple skills, multiple income streams, and multiple career options—in other words, by becoming a true multipreneur.

5

Learn Continually

Continual learning is the only way to adapt to continual change. What's more, the rapid rate of change in today's marketplace demands that we learn rapidly. It has never been a good career strategy to stay in a job after you have stopped learning from it, nor has it been good to job-hop habitually, always leaving before you learn all the useful things you can about a business. But today the stakes are higher, so two key questions have become even more important:

1. What do you need to learn?
2. How can you best learn it?

Only you can answer these questions for yourself, because only you know your individual career situation, and you must consider these questions in that context. However, there are strategies and techniques for learning continually and for becoming what I call an instant expert in a given skill or area of business.

Serial executive Hall McKinley notes the impact continual learning has on career management:

> You must look at opportunities with "What can I learn?" at the top of the list, rather than how it will make me look or how it will aggrandize my position. Because how you "look"

is irrelevant if the company doesn't need you. You must look at things in terms of what you can learn, how a job enhances your set of skills, and how it makes you unique. It is not that as a multipreneur you are always worrying about getting a job. It is that you are always concerned with enhancing your skills.

How Multipreneurs Learn

Continual learning is so prevalent among multipreneurs that it's not clear whether they are learning continually because they are multipreneurs or they are multipreneurs because they need to be learning continually. In any event, multipreneurs typically learn by plunging into an area, immersing themselves in information, and going directly to practitioners in that field. As management consultant Emmett Murphy put it:

> That is the singular skill—the willingness to engage in the active search for knowledge on a day-to-day basis. If people acquire that skill, they will succeed, period. These are people who are willing to get off their fannies and get out on the front lines. They are information seekers. They are natural learners, and that's the single most important skill. It has nothing to do with whether they are introverts or extroverts. They are just learners. Some people are learners by nature, but you *can* cultivate the habit, by getting up and getting involved in the areas you want to learn about. Eventually, a light bulb goes on. But it goes on only after a process of reflection on how the pattern of your life is productive and how learning what you need to learn can make you more productive.

In our society, the necessary information is readily available in all its various forms. Multipreneurs use them all, but they are distinguished most by their willingness to plunge into learning. Here are some examples.

Market researcher Ray Shu notes:

I read a lot and talk to others a lot. I just call whoever comes to mind. The learning process is a lot of Q&A sessions. If you are afraid of asking questions, you will never learn anything. Also, most people will help you if they know something and you don't.

Publisher-teacher David Rye uses a mixed bag of tools:

Depending upon what I have to learn, the process might entail anything from a trip to the library where they have an easy-access database to the scanning of the local university course catalog to find classes that would be of help. I also use consultants and conferences. Since Boulder is a university town, it is easy and inexpensive to get an education in a topic.

High-tech sporting goods multipreneur Sally Edwards will just jump into something new:

I ask lots of questions. I read a lot. I take classes. I talk to people. To learn buying and inventory management, I talked to a lot of people. I also got an MBA, but mostly because I got tired of people asking me what credentials qualified me to run a business.

Mike Pickowicz, pet-product developer turned video chain-store owner, uses total immersion:

I inhale information. Right now I am getting into CD-ROM as an extension of my video business. In two weeks I'm going to a conference on the subject. I'm talking and listening to everyone I can. I'm constantly thinking about CD-ROM.

Communications and multi-image producer Michèle Van Buren reads, but with a conscious process of assimilation and synthesis in mind:

I read everything I can, everything I can get my hands on. I surround myself with information. I read things over and over it until it sounds like something very natural to me, very common. That's what I did when I started my business. I read everything I could find about how to be in business and how to be a consultant. I read every day. When it started sounding repetitive, I felt that I was getting the gist of it. I've encouraged others to do this, too. I tell them to buy lots of books, read them until they're very familiar with them, and then see how they can use what they've learned.

Of course, multipreneurs also learn on the job, by working on various projects and in various businesses. Most of what we learn we learn by doing, but whether you need to use a formal source of information or an on-the-job strategy, you'll benefit by staying on top of all the techniques you can use to learn something new.

Techniques for Learning

The learning technique you'll use will depend upon what you must learn, how much you must learn, how you tend to learn best, and the time and money available. The more techniques you have at your disposal, the better positioned you are to learn new skills and explore new opportunities. We'll examine first five "formal" techniques, then five "on-the-job" techniques.

Formal Techniques for Learning

Research and Writing
If you research and write about a topic, you will inevitably learn about that topic. A desire to propose the idea of a captive venture capital fund to Dun & Bradstreet led me to research that topic so I could write about it knowledgeably and present a credible proposal to management. If you research a topic for any purpose, be it an article for a magazine or newsletter, a presentation to your professional association, a business plan, or a proposal to a potential client or employer, you have a vehicle for learning about that topic. This, of course, is why you are made to write papers in school. To write about something, you must find material, then structure and synthesize it. In the process, you learn.

Interviewing Experts

Whether or not you're doing formal research, experts can be very generous with their time. They are easy to find since they're always either giving interviews or writing. When you see them in the media, clip the article or write down their names and affiliations. Do enough homework so you can ask good questions and display genuine interest. Call them and tell them that you'd like to talk with them about their work sometime at their convenience for about twenty or thirty minutes. When they ask why, tell them, or say you're planning a career change. Write down your questions beforehand, call when you say you will, and use the questions as a jumping-off point. Stay loose. Take notes. You may get in over your head, but dealing with that can in itself be useful.

Continuing Education and Training

If you work for a company with a tuition reimbursement plan and you want to pursue courses or a degree related to your work, you'd be foolish to pass up the chance. A fair portion of my MBA, and those of countless others, was funded by employers. It is part of the benefits package, which is part of your total compensation.

Many companies lavish training in practical business skills on their employees. It pays to be selective, but free training in a business skill is worth pursuing. The most common types offered are software usage; selling, telemarketing, and direct mail; customer service; writing and public speaking; project management; time management; negotiation and conflict resolution; supervisory and management skills (including specific skills such as conducting performance appraisals, hiring and terminating properly, delegating, and so on). Many people spurn such training, thinking that they lack the time, don't need it, or wouldn't learn much. While the quality of such training varies, you benefit from focusing on a skill for a day or so and usually get at least a few ideas you can use. It's worth the time invested.

Using Books, Magazines, Tapes, Databases

Multipreneurs are voracious readers, and magazines give you a real feel for an area and the current hot topics. Tapes certainly have their place (in your car's tape deck if you drive to work or in your Walkman if you don't). Databases are an incredible source of information. Use a decent one, with several hundred or more publications on file. Search on just about any subject and you'll be awash in articles—which can be a problem. Take care to begin your search with a narrow focus and then broaden it or you can waste time and money on lots of files and articles you don't want or need.

Books, magazines, audiotapes, and videotapes are free at the library, or you can buy them. Databases, whether CD-ROM or electronic, usually cost money, often a lot. An information-on-demand firm or information broker can be useful, but be sure to get agreement up front on the charges you'll face. If you hook up directly to a database, be sure you understand and can afford the charges, which can mount rapidly if you are not proficient with the search protocols or if you browse for too long.

Joining an Association

Join an association and you will be inundated with information. I joined the Bethesda, Maryland–based World Future Society, and they sent me so much material that I started longing for the past. Most associations have open memberships, and even those oriented to the trade offer literature to nonmembers (at nonmember rates). Not only does an association send you the material that it produces itself, but, through the magic of mailing lists, related outfits soon learn of your whereabouts. Until you join an association in your area of interest (and there probably is one), you haven't scratched the surface, nor will you know about the conventions, seminars, workshops, forums, field trips, cruises, and other gatherings of like-minded individuals. Associations expose you to scores of experts and at times to actual employment and project opportunities.

On-the-Job Techniques for Learning

Expanding Your on-the-Job Responsibilities

If you are currently working full- or even part-time, often the easiest, least expensive way for you to learn something is right there on the job. This is especially so if you want to learn a business skill such as sales, marketing, budgeting, finance, management, or technology. You can work on the sales, marketing, budgeting, financial, management, or technological aspects of the work of your current department, or you may be able to transfer into your area of interest. At Dun & Bradstreet I got experience in project management, market research, competitive analysis, product development, product management, pricing, and technology. I was also given management responsibility, first for a department of four, then for thirty-five. I was given training in management and in conducting presentations. I got lots of writing experience everywhere I worked.

You can voluntarily expand your on-the-job responsibilities in most companies. Make known your interest in task forces and initiate projects. If you aggressively seek learning opportunities on the job, you'll find them.

Acting as Understudy and Stand-in

If you are working for an employer, you may wangle a chance to act as assistant or stand-in for someone doing interesting, profitable work. Someone in a hot area often needs help or someone to handle things when they're on vacation or on the road. Politically you must present yourself as wanting to help them because you're interested and want to learn, not because you're gunning for their job. This can be a very worthwhile technique because people good at handling hot areas tend to get bored, get recruited, get rich, or just get out—and when that person does, you may be next at the plate.

Working Part-Time and Moonlighting

Both part-time work and moonlighting represent essential transition techniques for the multipreneur, so they will be covered in detail in chapter 10. This book was researched and written mainly during moonlight hours. Both part-time work and moonlighting—as well as project work as an independent contractor—are ideal learning vehicles because you earn while you learn.

This technique works because intelligent, educated, mature, skilled people can get hired into areas on a part-time or project basis by virtue of these qualities and their general business skills, rather than on their experience in a specific area. If the employer knows that despite your lack of experience you can do the job, she will let you do it. You learn how, while collecting the money and a work sample or reference.

Underpricing Yourself
Want to learn something new and get paid for it? Underprice yourself. If you can afford to forgo the income, this can be a great way to enter a new field. Yes, you may have to take several steps back to learn a new line of work, but then—particularly if you're experienced and interpersonally savvy—you will take three steps forward relatively soon.

Note that even if you have twenty or thirty years in the workforce, it can be worthwhile to consider a lower-level job in the business you want to pursue. While it may take a younger person five years to get somewhere, you will probably make real progress in two or three years. And if you love the work, it will be worth it. Incidentally, if you are young, the danger lies in the opposite direction. Young people often underprice themselves for too long or take too many entry-level jobs and stay in them too long. The result? Instead of three years of experience, you get one year of experience three times.

Volunteering and Internships
Another way to apprentice yourself is volunteer work or a paid or unpaid internship. If you want to break into theater, television, film, or a helping profession, such as social work or counseling, volunteer work or an internship can be a great way to learn. Also, you "pay your dues" and exhibit the sincerity that entry into such work typically requires. Many motion picture directors and assistant directors started as "gofers" (as in "go for coffee and doughnuts, go for more film stock"), and most social workers and psychologists have done community or hospital volunteer work. Along with job knowledge and skills, you acquire valuable contacts this way.

Be wise, however, when using this technique. First, you must address the obvious issue of whether you can forgo some or all of your income for an extended period. Second, there is the matter of what, exactly, you will learn. Many volunteers and interns find themselves doing endless grunt work and learning little or nothing. For this technique to succeed, you need clear agreement up front about what you want to learn and what you're willing to do to learn it. You have to trust the people you're dealing with. Also, be sure to meet with the person who'll be supervising you. Someone three layers up can paint a rosy picture while the floor boss runs a sweatshop. Whenever possible, talk with someone who has volunteered or interned at the place you are contemplating.

Fake It 'til You Make It

I asked Boston-based television producer Marge Heiser how she learned her craft. She replied: "You fake it 'til you make it." In a new work situation, if you act the part sincerely (that is, "fake it"), people will take you at face value. You will be in learning mode, naturally, because the situation is new to you, so you will quickly absorb new information and skills, which will enable you to "make it" in that profession. In this context, "faking it" does not mean pawning yourself off as something you are not. Admit that you don't know something instead of screwing up due to lack of skill or experience. In the best sense of the term, you "fake it" by leveraging your existing knowledge and skills and taking your cues from the environment and from those around you.

Fake it 'til you make it is the remedy for those situations in which you know you can do the job but lack the experience. And it can be exhilarating. When I first became an executive recruiter for a small midtown search firm in New York, I didn't have one day of experience. For "training" in this firm, you just watched how the other recruiters worked. The orientation was, "There's your desk. There's your phone. Get to work."

In those first days as a headhunter, I was astonished to find that when I called a potential candidate for an opening, she didn't say, "Ha! I know you're not really an executive recruiter. You sound like you were sitting in a bank's marketing department last week. Don't waste my time." Instead, candidates believed I was a recruiter because I called them and told them I was, then I described the job opportunity I was pitching and asked about their interest and qualifications. How could they know I was faking it? They couldn't, although I was certainly a better recruiter after five hundred cold calls than I was after five.

If you are committed to learning a skill, don't ever let the feeling that you're "playing the part" interfere with your progress. It takes skill, energy, and heart to play a role convincingly. We've all seen people who pride themselves on their substance but fail in business because they can't be bothered presenting themselves to the world and interacting with the people in it. If you ever feel funny about faking it, think about this. In medical school—yes, medical school—there is a saying, "See one. Do one. Teach one," referring to operations and other life-preserving (and life-threatening) procedures performed on human beings. Often medical students have the opportunity to see the procedure only once, do the procedure once, and then teach a student in the class behind them how to do it. Business is not brain surgery, perhaps, but the situations are analogous.

The Instant Expert

One of the best ways to become a true multipreneur is to develop the ability to become an "instant expert." You can be sure there will be many times when you'll have to learn something fast—typically about a skill or a business—so that you can hold your own at a meeting, make a deal, write a proposal, or not get snowed by someone. Often, whether I've been on staff or on my own, a boss or client has asked me to look into something that was quite unfamiliar to me and I've had to learn about it quickly, or I've had to design my own crash course to get myself up to speed for a project or presentation. The process of becoming an instant expert is a learning process that can be structured based upon what is generally known about how we learn. Assuming that you are intelligent and open to learning, you can reasonably expect to become an instant expert in just about any area in a matter of hours or weeks, depending upon the depth you seek and complexity of the topic. The ability is invaluable to the multipreneur.

The term "instant expert" may strike you as an oxymoron, but an instant expert is not a real expert any more than instant coffee is real coffee or an instant shelter is a real house. An instant expert is someone who has taken the time to learn about something specific, usually for a specific business reason, and has used this learning time to maximum efficiency. A real expert is someone who has spent years in study or practice, or both, in a relatively limited area. A true expert is the ultimate specialist, which is hardly the role of the multipreneur.

On new assignments, which you will continually face as a multipreneur, becoming an instant expert can help you talk and write more convincingly, because you will have prepared as efficiently as possible, thereby positioning youself farther along the learning curve.

As a liaison, the instant expert is extremely valuable in business. Experts are typically accused of having knowledge that runs a mile deep and an inch wide, of knowing more and more about less and less. Generalists, on the other hand, are often accused of running a mile wide and an inch deep, of knowing only a little about a lot. The multipreneur can bridge the gap between the expert and the generalist and do so by acting as interface, translator, facilitator, and implementor. As a multipreneur you'll need the ability to ask questions, get answers, do research, and synthesize the results, that is, make it your own and use it in your own way.

Here is an example: When I was fresh out of grad school and into the lending officer training program at Manufacturers Hanover Trust, they gave me an odd assignment. I was asked to do some research on beaver farming. An executive from a large corporate client had been sitting next to our president at a fund-raiser and had asked him about beaver farming as a tax shelter. The client had been approached by a guy selling such tax shelters. Our president offered to look into it, and the task was assigned to me.

Within a week I was probably New York City's reigning expert on beaver farming (admittedly a dubious distinction). I had spoken with various people: a woman in southern New Jersey who ran a beaver preserve, several fur ranchers out west and in Canada, and a couple of tax specialists. I had spent hours in the library. I had visited William Entrup American Raw Furs down in the fur district, who had me handling coyote, raccoon, fox, bear, and, yes, beaver pelts.

In my naive desire to show how thoroughly I could tackle a project, I wrote a seventeen-page double-spaced report on beaver farming. A while later I realized that I could have summed up my findings in one sentence: "Beaver farming makes money only for those *selling* beaver farming tax shelters." I mention this example because it shows how fast one can become well versed in even the most obscure subject.

Note the process of synthesis I went through. I had a specific purpose and a product—a final report—to deliver. That fact directed my efforts and research. So when the furrier Bill Entrup started talking about trappers in Canada, I could steer him back toward fur farming, because trapping can't provide a tax shelter. My purpose also dictated that I shape the information in a certain way and add my own opinion. Although nobody I interviewed in either fur or finance knew anything about beaver farming as a tax shelter, I became knowledgeable enough so that I could wholeheartedly recommend against the proposition.

Perhaps you can recall a time when you had to become an instant expert in your career. No doubt you rose to the occasion. As you go through the following sections, you might ponder that experience and see how this material applies.

While it is important to develop your own method for rapid knowledge acquisition, here is a general framework, followed by two more specific frameworks, one for learning new skills and one for learning about a new business.

A Framework for Learning Rapidly

The following general framework offers, in a logical sequence, several techniques for learning:

- Access print and electronic databases.
- Read what you need, actively.
- Interview experts.
- Make it your own.

Crash courses should begin by accessing a vast print database—like your local library. With so many specialized areas changing so fast, accessing an electronic database is also often essential. As noted earlier, however, these can be pricey, so prepare before you go on-line, and watch your return on expenditures. Also, find out quickly where the most highly specialized sources of information on your subject are located. There are often libraries or rooms of libraries—and entire museums or institutes—dedicated to single subjects.

Depending upon your subject, you may quickly find that not

much has been written on it, in which case you will have to dig deep, perhaps into scholarly journals or specialized magazines or newsletters. Or you may find that huge amounts have been written, in which case you must quickly narrow down the material to what is essential. Decide what your approach will be and eliminate anything irrelevant. (This is what journalists do.) If very little has been written on the subject, locate the live experts fast. Try to find out why so little has been done: Is it a very new area, product, process, company, or industry? Is it new to this country? Does it inherently lack intellectual interest or commercial possibilities? Has it already proven unworkable or incredible?

Talking with experts helps tremendously, even if the topic has been well covered, because the problems and challenges in an area are always changing. If you ask, experts will generally tell you whom else to approach as well. The process of interviewing experts heightens your confidence, partly because the conversation brings the subject to life. Also, you will often find that patterns or conclusions you arrived at intuitively are supported by someone who has spent years studying the situation. Of course, having your ideas contradicted can represent even more of a learning experience.

After you've completed your research, let it simmer at least overnight, longer if time permits. Allow time to reflect upon what you have found, then think about how best to assemble it. Part of making material your own is blending it with your existing knowledge and experience. One of the best ways to synthesize information is to write about it. Others include talking it over, preparing a presentation or proposal, or making a recommendation or decision based upon the information gathered. Remember, however you go about it, it is important to make the material your own so that you can apply it with confidence to your situation or assignment.

To help you further develop the facile mind that you need in order to become an instant expert on command, I'm going to suggest two additional, more specialized frameworks, one for learning a business skill and one for learning about an industry or company or department. They represent frameworks for learning rapidly and for identifying and understanding the essentials in a situation so you can quickly locate opportunities and solve problems.

The Instant Expert Approach to Skills

Becoming an instant expert in a skill requires you to quickly learn the basics. If you grasp the basics, you can then either build upon them to achieve the expertise you need or at least deal more effectively with people who are skilled in an area. This framework rests upon the concept that success in any skill depends upon diligent execution of the basics and that failure results from either not knowing or not practicing those fundamentals. When you are learning a skill or learning about a skill, you should therefore

- identify success
- define technique
- act the part

Identify Success
The best starting point in learning about a skill is to recognize success when you see it. How do you know when the skill has been effectively practiced? What is the measure of success? In skeet shooting, it is broken clays. In golf, it is low scores. In sales and marketing, it is growing (or at least stable) revenues. In finance, it is properly funded assets and profitable operations. And so on.

To identify finer measures of success, question yourself and your models. Your models are those who successfully employ the skill you want to learn or learn about. For most business skills, the measures of success tend to be fairly evident, meaning objective rather than subjective. A salesperson either does or does not close sales. An accountant either does or does not keep the books properly. An information system either does or does not maintain information and deliver reports timely and accurately.

But the measures of success are not always quite so clear. Advertising people once became so enamored of "creativity" as a measure of success that David Ogilvy felt compelled to coin the phrase "If it doesn't sell, it isn't creative." Senior managers find themselves constantly redefining the measures of success: Is it high market share? High sales? High profits? High cash flow? High stock price? High volume of new products? Some combination of these?

For many business skills, it is in the planning process that you define how you will measure success. Thus people will—or at least should—spend time up front to define, for example, the characteristics of sound product development, of a useful accounting system, or of a company's mission. This represents time well spent.

Again, to identify the measures of successful application of a skill, you must question yourself and others. What is the objective? How do we know it has been reached? What are the characteristics of high performance? Of low performance? What are the earmarks of a professional approach? What are the hallmarks of success?

Define Technique

The process gets trickier here. First, as noted, you must find and observe models of success. Then you must discover what they do— that is, *how* they achieve their success. You have to do this at the proper level of detail, fine enough to be practical, yet not so fine as to be overwhelming or confusing. For example, if you want to become an instant expert at golf (yes, it's impossible), you need to define technique beyond "Hit 'em straight," yet you must ignore the ten things people will tell you to do with each part of your body.

The problem is that often even truly skilled people are not aware of how they achieve their results or, if they are aware, they're not good at explaining it. They are just not good self-observers or teachers. In this case, you have two choices. Either find models of success who are good teachers or become good at observing models of success and asking intelligent questions. I suggest you do both, but concentrate on observing good models and asking good questions.

The fact is that you will not be able to closely observe or personally question all of the people with all of the skills that you may want to learn about. Fortunately, in many areas—for example, in writing advertising copy, making films, delivering sales presentations, and managing others—after you have identified the measures of success, you can readily find the work of good models all around you. You can read good advertising copy, see good films, witness effective sales presentations, and watch what good managers do when they interact with their employees.

Such examples of good work are of most value to the practiced eye. You must observe details and analyze them carefully. To develop a practiced eye, you need to understand the relationship between action and result. With that, you can see what works and what does not. Good ad copy is crisply written, speaks to the reader, and holds his attention. It positions the product clearly and represents it well. Bad ad copy is mushy or pompous, talks down to or past the reader, or bores or confuses him. A good salesperson is friendly but professional, organized, and knowledgeable about her product, uses questions to learn about the customer's problems, and presents what she is selling as the solution. Bad salespeople depart from this model.

In this step you must discover the basics—the fundamental techniques—of the skill you seek to learn and how those basics are applied. It is not enough to hear "Hit 'em straight" or "Write clearly and speak to the reader." You have to learn *how* it is done. So in your discovery process, keep asking yourself and your sources, "How?" You must learn that the guy who hits 'em straight keeps his eyes on the ball, the club face parallel to the ball, his forward arm straight, his back arm relaxed, and his feet evenly positioned. You can't just hear "Write clearly and speak to the reader." You have to learn that sell copy relies on nouns and verbs rather than adjectives and adverbs and on short rather than long sentences and emphasizes a benefit for the reader rather than a feature of the product.

Once you grasp the basics—the techniques that lead to success— you are halfway toward your goal. Thus the instant expert works hard to discover and learn, to the degree required, the basics. This is the foundation for instant expertise with regard to a skill.

With any skill, many people hope to ignore the basics or try to get past them quickly and get on to the fancy stuff. This doesn't work. One idea underlying the instant expert approach is that it takes less time to firmly grasp the basics than it does to discover, consider, mess around with, and ultimately discard everything but the basics. Typically, when people by-pass the basics, stubbornness or laziness plays a role. Diligent application of the basics requires faith and hard work. Many of us find the search for a shortcut more engaging, or we enjoy using the excuse that natural talent, rather than faith, work, and the basics, dictate success. Becoming an instant expert is not exactly easy, but it is often necessary and always fulfilling.

Act the Part

When it comes to skills, the real difference between the expert and the instant expert is time. Both know the basics—neither the measures of success nor the fundamental techniques are secrets. However, presumably the expert has spent years practicing and applying the basics. He has more experience (and, yes, perhaps more talent) than the instant expert.

How much practice do you need to become an instant expert? The answer depends upon your goal, motivation, and time. If you can act the part convincingly—for example, on your job interview or project proposal—you may well get to practice and get paid for it. Haven't most of us learned many of our skills on the job? If you practice enough so that you can speak confidently and act the part before it is casted, you'll get the part. In determining what to practice, reflect upon the role models who have the skill you want to learn or learn about. What do they do? Where do they focus their attention and efforts? How much time do they devote to various aspects of the skill? What kind of planning do they do?

That last question is key. Just as success with any skill depends upon application of the basics, planning represents a basic in the exercise of any skill. Successful salespeople plan their sales calls; successful managers plan their meetings and workdays; successful performance appraisers plan each appraisal. Planning will enhance your chances of success with any skill, while lack of planning will hurt those chances.

The instant expert uses learning time more efficiently than the person with a willy-nilly approach. One big difference lies in the amount of planning the instant expert does. Identifying success, defining technique, finding models, and practicing all amount to planning. No actor—on a stage or film set or in business—tries to act a part without preparation.

The Instant Expert Approach to Understanding a Business

Let's assume that you have to learn not about a skill, but about an industry, a company, or a department. You may need to learn about the telecommunications industry or about Microsoft or about your client's sales division. In essence this is a research task, and there are ways to organize yourself for undertaking it. The following points represent a framework for learning about an industry, a company, or a department (a framework I've learned mainly from credit, industry, and competitive analysis):

- Identify the inputs, outputs, and tasks performed (inputs and outputs).
- Discover who does what and why (players and teams).
- Learn how money is made (drivers and transactions).
- Find out what has changed over time (history and changes).

Inputs and Outputs
Start by researching the fundamental business of the industry or company: What do they do? Try thinking about this in terms of inputs and outputs. For an auto manufacturer the inputs are steel, aluminum, copper, fiberglass, plastic, rubber, and fabric or vinyl or (if you're lucky) leather, as well as human inputs in the form of engineering, design, labor, and so on. The outputs created are cars, trucks, and minivans. Any business or business process essentially takes inputs and creates outputs, thus adding value.

The advantage of thinking in terms of inputs and outputs—or I/O, as economists say—is that you get a firm grasp of process, of value added, and of the chain that leads from raw material to product to market. Right off, you see that a business is dynamic rather than static. This has implications. For example, the price, the availability, and even the nature of the inputs can change, and this will somehow affect the output. The amount of value added depends upon the degree to which, and the manner in which, the inputs are transformed. A company that buys and distributes steel without fabricating anything from it adds less value than the automaker. The I/O concept also reveals the importance of the suppliers upstream in the process and the other adders of value downstream.

You may be thinking, That's fine for manufacturing firms, but what about service firms? What inputs do they process? They are processing intellectual inputs: data, ideas, information, knowledge, maybe even wisdom. The entire knowledge industry (information, publishing, education, finance, consulting, engineering, and design) along with the entertainment industry, the professions of politics and government, and the classic professions (law, medicine, architecture, and accounting) and many business services industries (training, advertising, sales, and marketing) take people's ideas, talent, knowledge, experience, and creativity—even their personal qualities like compassion and enthusiasm—and organize, transform, package, and sell them.

Of course, the outputs are information, publications, books, films, research reports, new systems, software, training programs, design concepts, management methods, insurance policies, resolved legal actions, cured patients, and so on. The value added amounts to the improvement in performance, competitiveness, and financial and human well-being realized by the customers and clients of firms in these industries.

Players and Teams

The players are the people in the business. To really get to know an industry or company, you have to know the roles people play and the individuals who play those roles. In an industry, who are the major companies? Who are the innovators, the CEOs, and the other leaders? Who has succeeded, and how have they done it? In the microcomputer industry, for example, to know about founders Steven Jobs and Steve Wozniak at Apple and Bill Gates at Microsoft and to know who is running these companies when the founders no longer are is to know a lot about the microcomputer business.

The same is true for teams. Who does business with whom? Who owns whom? Or wants to? Who wants to sell whom? Where are the rivalries? Who are the domestic and foreign competitors? What makes a great team, that is, a great company, in this business? What happens when a team breaks up or a new team is formed?

Drivers and Transactions

To understand any business entity, you have to understand how money is made. This gets you into *how* inputs are transformed into outputs and into what drives the growth and profitability of the industry and of the companies and people in it.

How and why does money change hands? Who gets what from where? Ask Cicero's basic question: *Cui bono?* Who benefits? Who gets rewarded? Rewards, in the form of money, prestige, power, security, improved operations, and opportunities to use their intelligence, talent, and energy—but most of all, money—represent key drivers for managers, employees, customers, suppliers, and stockholders of a business.

Competition is another driver. On what basis do the companies in an industry compete? On what basis does the industry compete with other industries? In certain industries novelty is a competitive advantage. In others it isn't a factor. Some companies are driven to produce the highest-quality product, others to be the low-cost producer. The fashion industry is driven by design and image. The copper business is driven by the need to employ productive capacity (the more they employ, the lower their costs per pound of copper). Most businesses have more than one key driver: for example, the auto industry is heavily driven by novelty, quality, cost, design, image, and capacity.

The drivers of a business find expression in transactions. To find and understand a transaction, simply follow the money. Money changes hands in exchange for benefits and rewards. To get benefits, someone has to do something at some stage of the business process. That's when a transaction occurs and moves the process along.

History and Changes
By viewing the industry or company historically, you see how it responds to challenge and how the various elements can change. How have the inputs and outputs changed? Have the players and teams changed? Have the determinants of how money is made changed? What's new? The history of many industries and companies is determined by technological change. Technology has fostered the moves from handwork to machine-made products, from small shops to mass marketing, from industrial enterprises to knowledge industries. Societal changes (such as increasing levels of education), government regulations (such as trade regulation), and international developments (such as wars) all have profound effects on industries and companies, none of which can be understood without a historical context.

With this framework you can ask the right questions, find the right materials, and discover the relevant facts needed to understand any business entity, from the American auto industry to the mailroom in your firm.

Learning as Competitive Advantage

It is now widely recognized that in our environment of constant change, in today's marketplace, real, sustainable competitive advantage can be realized mainly, and perhaps only, by learning continually. This means that any elements that a person or business can acquire—knowledge, technology, equipment, processes, rights—now confer only a temporary advantage in the marketplace. In a sense, choosing not to learn continually is choosing to place yourself at a competitive disadvantage. It is choosing failure. Each of us is either developing or stagnating, moving forward or slipping backward, becoming smarter or getting stupider. The ability to learn continually determines the difference.

part three

The Practices
of Multipreneuring

6

Act Like a Producer

If you want to maximize your added value, you've got to learn to act like a producer. Do I mean that you should get an Armani suit, grab a table at Spago, and start calling everyone "baby"? Of course not. You must simply develop a producer's ability to put things together creatively, profitably, and with minimal downside risk. If the name of the game in the 1980s was Other People's Money, it has now become Other People's Talent.

The model of "producer" being used in this context is the independent producer of films, plays, books, software, conferences, or events. While many such people operate as traditional business owners, they share a common characteristic: they take an idea from concept to market and do so with financial, human, and tangible resources brought together for that particular project. A producer does not generally finance the production, does not have a large permanent staff, does not have much in the way of tangible assets aside from an office, a telephone, and a Rolodex. Rather, the producer locates the financing, hires the talent, and rents the needed equipment or space or "jobs out" the printing of the book or duplication of the software, as well as the distribution. Given the fact that much of today's production activity creates intellectual content, the producer is a true intellectual capitalist.

The Job of the Producer

The producer assumes five essential roles:

- idea generator and visionary: creates or finds saleable ideas, envisions the final product, and communicates that vision to others
- planner and scheduler: identifies the steps necessary to realize the vision
- talent scout and resource manager: locates, recruits, and oversees the people and materials needed to bring the project to fruition
- financier and deal maker: structures an arrangement so that everyone gets paid and any financial backers have a good shot at a decent return
- controller of quality and budget: balances technical against practical demands and artistic against commercial demands to ensure a successful project

While many producers work solo, production teams and strategic alliances between producers are also common. Such a team, which is most often two people, will divide the production duties in keeping with their strengths. Typically, one takes care of the financial and deal-related aspects such as financing, budgeting, accounting, and negotiating the distribution deals, rights sales, and payments to those involved with the project; the other partner supervises the creative talent and ensures the quality of the project itself. But, again, many producers do handle it all as one-person operations.

The Manager Versus the Producer

Today, a producer can work as a full-time manager within a company, as an independent contractor or part-timer, or as a bona fide supplier. No matter where you work in relation to a company, to truly maximize your value added you should be able to act like a producer. This is especially true if you are an independent operator rather than an employee. But it is also true if you are in the core of a company as an on-staff manager, because the economic rationale and lack of structure are facts of business life regardless of where you work.

Compare the characteristics of the traditional manager with those of the producer-intermediary or "intellectual capitalist":

Traditional Manager	Producer-Intermediary
Works within rigid structure	Works with minimal structure
Oriented toward role in the company	Oriented toward specific project
Power comes from the organization	Power comes from expertise and relationships
Compensated with salary and bonus	Compensated with fee and a piece of the action
Usually works with in-place resources	Usually works with best available resources

The traditional manager can find herself hobbled in today's economy. When organizations are in flux, her reliance on structure and her orientation toward her role in the company can lead to an identity crisis. When power is derived from an organization's structure, a manager is in a precarious position, since that organization can also remove her power. Also, many traditional managers succeed because they can work within the political structure of an organization, acting as buffers and not making waves—skills that provide minimal value outside the company. Although managers derive some income from incentive pay, bonuses are usually a small part of their total compensation and are often not closely tied to performance. Managers are used to having resources at their disposal, which magnify their power. That's part of the fun of working in a large organization. But when resources are cut, the traditional manager can wind up impotent and frustrated.

In contrast, the producer-intermediary is well suited to today's economy. The producer works with minimal structure, at least in his organization, within which he has a role that can be approached flexibly because that role is to complete the project. The traditional manager's role is to focus on the project *and* on "organizational issues," "interdepartmental concerns," and "the charter of the organization." Like the traditional manager, the producer depends upon relationships and connections but, knowing how ephemeral they can be, develops broad networks. A big part of the producer's job is to leverage off the marketing, distribution, or financial resources of a company—without becoming its prisoner. That flexibility and expertise are the source of his power. Since the producer lives on fees and generally funds his own benefits, he is more inclined to deliver on time and on budget.

While the traditional manager and the producer-intermediary operate differently, the border is starting to blur among forward-thinking managers. Why? Because managers on staff at companies of all sizes must act more and more like producers. Open-architecture corporate structures, fluctuating professional roles, team-oriented management, and the trend toward performance-based pay all dictate the need for managers to get results on budget with minimal resources hard-wired into the company. Another driver is the changing nature of the workforce, with its corporate nomads, executive temps, independent contractors, and just-in-time workers. To manage these people productively and profitably, you need the skills of a producer.

The Skills of the Producer

Despite the multifaceted job of the producer, the skill set underlying the practice is straightforward.

Conceptual Thinking Skills

Whether he generates ideas or discovers them, the producer must be able to work with ideas. This calls for the ability to take a concept and visualize how it can be expressed in a product, service, or event that will serve a need people will pay to have met. There are techniques for generating ideas, including brainstorming and free association, but the ability to visualize commercially viable outcomes can be more difficult to learn.

Fortunately there are lots of models of success in various forms of production. You can readily see good (and bad) movies, books, concerts, software, videos, video games, and so on. You can pick up on how the final product should look and learn how best to express your idea. The distribution channels always need good product, and the people in those channels will tell you what they are looking for (although they often don't know exactly what they want until they see it). Thus a producer must never forget the power of an idea. New York City–based book producer Roseann Hirsch sees it this way:

> You have to be creative to come up with ideas that are salable. I guess that is the hardest part, but it's also the part I like best—coming up with good ideas that make good proposals. I work hard to stay on top of the market. I think all the time about what might make a good proposal. Actually, in a way I never stop working on that.

Planning and Organization Skills

The true producer should be both creative and organized. She should be able to use her right-brain conceptual skills at the idea-generation stage and then move on to the left-brain practical task of bridging the gap between concept and result. This calls for gauging market demand, planning, scheduling, budgeting, and assessing resources.

Gauging market demand is essential. In fact, you must determine the marketability of the project before anything else. Conversations with others and a survey of similar or substitute items can help, as can *concept testing* the idea. (In a concept test, you either slap together a prototype that embodies the concept and show it to prospective buyers or investors, or you explain the concept and get reactions to detailed questions about it.)

Once you have determined the marketability of a concept, the scheduling and resourcing become an exercise in project planning. Excellent courses and books are available on how to do project and business plans. The essential thing is that you indeed do such a plan, not just for yourself and your project team, but so that you can properly approach potential co-venturers and sources of financing. It is also essential to go about this creatively rather than solely "by-the-numbers." As television and industrial film producer Rebecca Miller has found:

> Planning—knowing how long something will take and how much it will cost—is important, but it's not just a matter of laying down time frames and dollars on paper. It's a matter of finding creative solutions to getting something done. For example, if (as an executive producer) you usually hire a line producer, a director, and a crew, but you have a very small budget, sometimes you have to find all those talents in one person or get someone who brings his or her assistant along. There are also a lot of technical issues having to do with the compatibility of different equipment formats, such as those used internationally and those we use in the United States. How creatively you resolve these issues will impact the entire project.

People Skills

A producer must work well with others, as a collegial leader more than as a manager. She has to assess people's personal qualities—reliability, intelligence, judgment, detail orientation, perseverance, congeniality, honesty, and character—as well as their skills and bring together people with a variety of skills and personalities to build a motivated team. Political and media consultant Todd Domke has this to say:

> You have to view every freelancer, vendor, and associate as an artist, as having the sensibilities of an artist. You want them to be creative and to take pride in their work. In the early stages, you have to encourage them to come up with whatever they think is best. If you have firm ideas, express them clearly and diplomatically. Then, while they're doing their work, encourage them but try to stay out of their hair. It's a matter of pride and creative freedom. If possible, have interim milestones where you check their progress and

direction, but don't cramp their style. Finally, when the work is finished, let them know they've done a great job if they have. If they haven't met your needs or achieved the desired effect, try not to be utterly aghast. Instead, recognize your role in the mishap. Calmly redirect their efforts and help them along. You have to think of them as working partners on the project, as associates and colleagues.

These people skills are hardly foreign to traditional managers, but exercising them in the context of a freestanding, perhaps one-shot project rather than in a company presents new challenges. The best producers create a sense of partnership as well as possibilities.

Financial and Negotiation Skills

In structuring the project so that it will work financially, you must create, first on paper and then among the involved parties, an arrangement to pay all workers and suppliers, either during the project or upon or after completion. You must also ensure that any investors get a return. Aside from knowing the requirements and costs, figuring this out requires realism. As book producer Roseann Hirsch explains it:

> It's necessary to add 10 to 15 percent aside from the production fee and the advance and the royalty arrangements to cover extra expenses. For example, you might have to pay more for photos than you planned because new rare material is now available. You can count on things like that happening. You don't want the extra expense to come out of your fee, and you really can't go back and ask for more money. It's better to anticipate it at the beginning.

If you seek investors, you must hone your sales and negotiating skills, such as understanding investor motivation. Individual investors in films, plays, fledgling companies, joint ventures, and speculative software, publishing, and multimedia projects are in a sense gamblers. They seek glamour, excitement, special treatment, or bragging rights. They want tax write-offs and a shot at outrageously high returns. For corporate investors—that is, companies who finance speculative projects or ventures—these motives are tempered by wanting an early look at new concepts, products, and technologies or exposure to futuristic thinkers in their industry. This is especially true in the media, software, publishing, and technology businesses.

In structuring the deal, the goal is to pay everyone working on the project fairly and, if necessary, give them some upside potential from the back-end payout. You may be better off paying those doing the actual work as an expense and saving the back end for yourself and any backers. If you doubt that the back end will be large or you can't completely trust the accounting practices of another involved party, you should get the money up front. Structuring joint ventures, strategic alliances, and similar arrangements is a field unto itself. In such cases, have someone help you, preferably the right attorney— meaning one who can do, rather than kill, deals.

Supervisory and Managerial Skills

To bring your concept to market, you must follow through, supervise the work, manage the process, troubleshoot the inevitable difficulties, and keep the project on track. The quality of the final product depends on the hundreds of details that add up to quality. These details, and particularly cost control, also dictate the financial success or failure of a project.

Managerial effectiveness begins with a sound project or business plan agreeable to all parties. The plan must include milestones and measures of quality. At the milestone dates, you keep the project on track by checking whether what was supposed to be done was done and done to specifications. Would it surprise you to learn that, as straightforward as that sounds, this is not usually how project management occurs?

When things are not going according to plan, the producer must not simply sweat. She must act, which may entail replacing someone, renegotiating deadlines, respecifying deliverables, or taking remedial action as specified in the original agreement, such as fee reductions for work not completed to specs or on time. Obviously, from the contractual standpoint, the better you have specified deliverables and time frames, the better your position if the project heads south. Of course, no contract will completely preserve you from the wiles of those to whom you job out work.

While many people are drawn to the role of producer because of the creative dimensions, you must realize that managerial skills are key to the producer's ability to "make it happen." You have to be able to be both creative and managerial, right brained and left brained. Says television producer Rebecca Miller:

> You really need one foot in the creative world and one foot in the world of logistics. It's a creative business, but it's also a logistics business. It's a challenge to make sure that the logistics of a program don't eat me up and that I maintain a fresh approach. There are a host of logistical problems and decisions involved in getting a show on the air, but I'm also responsible for the look of the program, the music, and other creative aspects. Some of the details can be mundane, like arrangements for the crew's transportation and lodgings and so on, but, like anything, there's a trade-off. To have creative control, or at least creative license, it is worth it to be totally eaten up by logistical details for three days a month.

Find Out What You've Got

Let's assess your capabilities in each of the five skills that a producer needs. Please indicate whether you agree or disagree with each of the following statements.

	Agree Strongly	Agree	Disagree	Disagree Strongly

Conceptual Thinking Skills

1. I get so many good ideas I never worry about running out of them.
2. I've noticed that I get ideas and then see that someone has done something very similar a year or so later.

	Agree Strongly	Agree	Disagree	Disagree Strongly

Conceptual Thinking Skills
(continued)

3. When people criticize an idea of mine, I listen objectively.
4. It is easy for me to see how my ideas—or those of others—can be turned into products, services, or projects.
5. People come to me for ideas.

Planning and Organization Skills

6. When I plan, I do it on paper.
7. When I plan, I detail each step in the process and how and when it will be done.
8. I've been told that I am detail oriented.
9. I have experience in some phase of market research.
10. I have written project or business plans that have worked well.

People Skills

11. I have had responsibility for hiring people and have made bad as well as good hires.
12. I can work with and respect the competence of people whom I do not like personally.
13. My history is one of confronting difficult people rather than of avoiding confrontation.

	Agree Strongly	Agree	Disagree	Disagree Strongly

People Skills (continued)

14. To me, people's psychology and motivations are key factors in their business performance.
15. I have built and led successful teams.

Financial and Negotiation Skills

16. I understand the financial aspects of investments, venture capital, joint ventures, and/or strategic alliances.
17. I have done budgets for projects or businesses.
18. I have demonstrated that I can operate on a shoestring and still grow a product or a business.
19. I understand how revenues break down into labor, materials, space and equipment costs, taxes, and profits.
20. I have successfully sold a product or service.

Supervisory and Managerial Skills

21. I have initiated and completed major projects.
22. I have been asked to troubleshoot others' projects.
23. I am known for being organized and keeping good records.
24. People have told me I am excellent on follow-up.

	Agree Strongly	Agree	Disagree	Disagree Strongly

Supervisory and Managerial
Skills (continued)

25. For any business goal, I have
    milestones, interim
    objectives, and contingency
    plans.

To Score Your Self-Assessment:
Give yourself four points for each "Agree Strongly," three points for each "Agree," two points for each "Disagree," and one point for each "Disagree Strongly." For any given skill area, if you score between sixteen and twenty, you probably are fairly well developed in that area. If you scored fifteen or less, you should develop in that area or those areas or get a partner who has those skills.

A Playbook for a Successful Production

A walk through the stages of a project will help you see what's involved in acting like a producer and and may help you develop a few worthwhile business ideas. At each stage below, you should consider one of the two following projects:

Take a skill of yours and produce a software program to train others in that skill.

Or

Plan to produce a conference on a topic that you know well.

Stage One: Generate the Idea and Visualize the Outcome

What business skill do you know so well that you could build a software course around it? What topic of interest to you could support a conference? If you have no ideas, you can generate some through brainstorming. When brainstorming, shoot for quantity, not quality—that comes later. Look for a need. Look to needed skills or hot topics in your field. What developments are affecting people in your line of work? Look to the past. There have been training sessions and workbooks on virtually every known business skill. Might one of them work as software? There have been conferences on every topic that ever got hot (in fact, conferences raise a topic's temperature). Do you have an idea for one that would work for a sizable audience?

Once you have a decent idea, you must envision the final product. Would the software be a simple text-on-a-screen package or a full-blown multimedia product? Would the conference run a half day, one day, or two days? Who would be your market? How would people benefit? Could the idea support an audiotape? A videotape? A newsletter? How would you position it in the market? Would the software need regular updating and subsequent releases? Could the conference be held in more than one city? Would it be an annual event? A one-shot deal? Could it spin off a membership association of some kind?

Who might invest in such software or sponsor such a conference? Who has a good mailing list? Who goes after your target audience with a product, service, or publication that would be complementary? Who would benefit by underwriting the software or conference?

To develop an idea into something salable, you must ask yourself—and answer—such questions.

Stage Two: Plan and Organize the Project

There is a gap between the idea and the result that must be bridged, plank by plank. You must plan and organize the resources—financial, human, and tangible—needed to produce the project, in this case the software or conference. Training software requires a syllabus, programming, and documentation. You need people to develop the course and program the computer-based training package. A conference, any event, requires an agenda. You also need a venue—an auditorium, corporate retreat, or hotel facilities. You have to recruit speakers. All of this costs money. If you could create the software syllabus or write the conference agenda yourself, you'd save money. If you could get space on the cheap, you'd save money. If you could get instructional designers or conference panelists who are local and want the experience or exposure, you'd save money.

How will you market this software or conference? Direct mail? Advertising? This may be where a sponsor comes in. Marketing expenses mount up fast, but if you can get a corporate partner who is already going to your target market regularly (for example, with a magazine or newsletter), you can cut marketing expenses drastically by piggybacking. Corporate partners can also act as a concept test or a sanity check. For example, if no software publisher or retailer would take on your project, why are you so sure it is a good idea? If no association or publication would dream of sponsoring your conference, what makes you think people will pay to attend it?

A good plan includes every step and a time frame and dollar figure for each one. Never fear too much detail at this stage. Also, remember Rebecca Miller's advice for this stage: It's about creative solutions, not just numbers.

Stage Three: Use People Skills to Build a Team

For the software, you would need an instructional design consultant, a programmer to run the course-authoring software (the software used to create the instructional software), a designer for the packaging, and perhaps a copywriter and a marketing coordinator. For the conference, in addition to speakers, you'd need a marketing coordinator, an on-site facilities coordinator, someone to process registrations and cancellations, and someone to answer questions. Or you could perhaps pick up some of these roles yourself or have a venture partner pick them up.

How would you build a team? First, you need a clear, compelling vision to share. Second, you need to be clear about how you intend to bring the vision into reality. If you can show people a vision and show them how they can play a role and profit, you have a basis for approaching them and motivating them. You must also size them up and check them out, communicate what they have to do, and secure their commitment.

Stage Four: Structure a Deal and Secure Financing

Unfortunately, the expenses on a project usually come due before the revenues are realized. This creates cash-flow problems. So you must try to speed up the receipt of revenues and delay the payment of expenses. If you get up-front money in the form of deposits, good-faith payments, or advances, you speed up income. If you get your subcontractors to work for delayed payment or to take a (small) piece of the action in lieu of a portion of their fee, you slow down outgo. Whenever possible, any cash infusions or progress payments from customers, investors, or sponsors should be timed in advance of the payments you must make to subcontractors. Otherwise you must finance payments from your own resources, which can include credit lines or even credit cards, or you wind up with extremely unhappy subcontractors on your hands. No matter how convincing or charming you are, you must pay people as agreed or big trouble, including legal trouble, will find you.

A shoestring mentality helps. It is tempting to think that you need a cool address, fine furnishings, spiffy cars, and high-end restaurant meals in order to do business. You don't. Instead you need to cut out all extras. Pinch pennies. Project an image of cheapskate on everything that does not directly affect the quality of the production. This provides three benefits: first, people won't even ask you to spring for half the stuff they would if you acted like a big spender; second, they will adopt your shoestring mentality when it comes to spending your money; third, when you do spring for something they'll appreciate it because they didn't expect it. Caution: When it comes to items that affect quality, spend what you must. Craftspeople, technicians, and professionals become frustrated and disgusted when forced to work with faulty equipment or shoddy materials.

You must get written estimates from subcontractors and time income and outgo realistically. Also, include a fudge factor of about 10 percent (meaning cut revenues by 10 percent or raise expenses by 10 percent) and see if the project is still a moneymaker. If the project and the investors or sponsors can bear it, try highballing on expenses at the outset, then come in lower and return a portion of the funding. If they ever get over the shock, they'll throw money at your next venture.

The image of cheapskate-who-can-deliver will serve you well. But be realistic about what things cost, or you will suffer cost overruns, which never sit well with investors or senior management. They will accuse you of lowballing them up front or of managing things poorly, and they'll be justified. You can't go back to them for more money without looking bad and, perhaps, having it come out of your end.

Stage Five: Supervise and Manage

The first step here is to review the first four stages. Were your idea and vision sound? Did you plan and organize properly? Did you spec out the job in sufficient detail? Did you establish milestones and progress payments so that you could periodically check the subcontractors' work and take action if necessary? Did you assemble a team equal to the job? Did you establish credibility, motivation, and high expectations? Was your budget and financial plan sound? Did you plan for "the expected unexpected"?

If the answers are "yes," all you would have to do now is manage the day-to-day, which should be easy since you have a sound concept, a good project plan, the right people, and sufficient financing. But it won't be easy. There will always be fires to put out, but at least you will not have started any of them.

Project unflagging enthusiasm for the project and calm control of the business and everything will be fine. Finally, listen to people at all levels. Many traditional managers forget that the people doing the work tend to be good judges of a project. If they tell you something is screwy, follow up on it. Not always, but usually, there is something to it.

Common Problems Producers Face—And How to Avoid Them

Since the following problems result from a failure to practice the basics of the producer's craft perfectly, theoretically they can be avoided—but only theoretically.

Conceptual Problems

The most common conceptual problem is not recognizing and discarding a bad idea quickly enough. You can waste months, even years, pursuing the wrong ideas, banking on only one idea, or pursuing an idea after its time has come and gone. Problems will also arise if you fail to visualize how the concept would work as a moneymaking venture.

How to Avoid Them?
Know the market and watch the money. If there is no money in an idea, it'll become apparent pretty quickly. Get input and listen to it. Concept test ideas. Visualize what could go right and wrong with a project. It is okay to vacillate for a while. Neither pessimism nor

optimism should rule when you are deciding to undertake a project. Above all, ask, "Would people pay for this?" If you know your market, you'll get good ideas. Book producer Roseann Hirsch at times finds herself ahead of her market:

> Very often I fear that I know something is salable and editors don't. This is probably because I had years of magazine experience before I went into book packaging, and that gave me a good sense of what people want to read and what will sell. For example, I wanted to package a book on the New Kids on the Block when they were hot, and I tried from June to October that year to sell it to a publisher and got nowhere. Finally, in October a teen magazine I was publishing at the time, *Dream Guys*, got about one thousand letters on the New Kids over one weekend. At that point, I told the editor at the publishing house, "Look, you've just got to move on this. Come on!" So she brought it up again at the next editorial meeting. Luckily there was a salesman there whose granddaughter had mentioned the New Kids the other day. That was all they had to hear. So I got a deal the next day, after five months of pushing.

Organizational Problems

Lack of organization leads to operational problems of all kinds: missed deadlines, inadequate equipment, scheduling difficulties, poor record keeping, and, the worst, trouble with the IRS.

How to Avoid Them?
First, if you are disorganized, find someone who is organized. The world is full of people who can keep you organized, which is the function of a secretary or assistant. Second, you must plan realistically, which nobody can do for you. Finally, recognize that disorganization often stems from committing to do the impossible with the hope that you will somehow find a way to pull it off. New York City–based conference producer Alexandra Scott at International Business Forum, who works with freelance conference producers, concurs:

This is the critical issue in the conference world right now. There are a lot of start-ups, but they are not all making it because they don't have the organization and infrastructure to make the conference really happen. They can do the creative side, but they can't deliver. You need workbooks, systems of working with the registrants, registration, and name tag software, policies about how you work with speakers, systems of follow-up, and so on. The number of details is amazing.

People Problems

People problems include a depressingly broad range of bad hires and difficult individuals: the prima donnas, renegotiators, hold-up artists, undependables, people who can't or won't deliver, those whose enthusiasm fades or who can't take constructive criticism. Then, pepper the pot with overwork, deadline pressure, and tight finances. It's enough to make all but the outrageously ambitious forget about acting like a producer.

How to Avoid Them?
If possible, have someone else interview a candidate for an important role in a project. Hiring is difficult enough without a sounding board. Get references, check them if you have time or think you should. When you do check references, let the person you are calling know how important this hire is and that you are relying on their opinion as a professional—then listen carefully.

Always ask for and inspect work samples. Even if they are unrelated to your project, they'll indicate the person's level of professionalism. Sloppiness tends to be obvious, as is poor writing, badly done graphics, or dull, mediocre work. A sample will also help you gauge the person's daily-rate league.

Do everything that you can in writing, no matter how clear you think it is or how well the other guy seems to understand what you're saying. I've learned this the hard way. Even a simple letter agreement from you will help your case if the person spends a week going in the wrong direction, then hands you the deliverables and a bill. If you have nothing on paper, just try cutting his fee or not paying him.

Almost all the producers I spoke with felt that the best way to avoid people problems is to work repeatedly with people you know and trust. Some of them do this to the point that they almost have a stock company, to borrow a term from the theater. Todd Domke, however, has a different system. He prefers to work with new people often:

> I like to go to new people, for several reasons. To an extent it is caused by the demands of quick turnaround or because my client or an associate wants to use a certain person. Sometimes price dictates it. There are real benefits to moving around. You learn new things from new people. You expand your available resources. You often wind up in a more competitive position, because sometimes suppliers can take you for granted. Soon the price goes up without your really being aware of it and, for that matter, without conscious intent on their part. They begin to assume that you won't mind and that you pass it on to the client anyway. That's not the kind of relationship I want with my suppliers. There is kind of a quality control built in if they don't take the work for granted and they are aware that they face competition for your business on things like price and timeliness. The control is in their wanting you to come back again.

Profitability Problems

Here you have cost overruns, absorption of costs, underpriced projects, overhiring, and being run ragged by various parties. If you and your backers are not making money, look to your budget and your cost controls. If you stand to lose money, look to your original deal. You did remember to pay yourself a healthy production fee as well as a back-end percentage, didn't you?

How to Avoid Them?
You must plan, budget, and negotiate costs up front and on the project itself. Remember, in business today there are simply too many people chasing too many projects that are only marginally profitable, perhaps inherently so, due to low value added, high competition, or lousy odds of success. If a project is inherently only marginally profitable, you will see it if, and only if, you cost it out properly—and discount the myth of ancillary benefits.

Ancillary benefits (that is, something other than money) can tempt you to take an underpriced job as a producer. If such temptation arises, ask yourself how likely you will be to realize those benefits. The sad fact is that ancillary benefits—typically "bigger and better things down the road"—usually do not materialize. I suspect that this is because if a deal makes financial sense on its own merits, nobody has to drag up the issue of ancillary benefits. So if the other party focuses on the ancillary benefits you will reap, the rip-off flag should pop up. The ancillary benefits probably exist only as ammunition in the other party's battle for a lower price. Also, if you work for too low a price because you were bought off with ancillary benefits, you still peg yourself at that low rate and may never overcome it with that client.

There is also the fundamental issue of making sure you get paid for the work you do, as a producer or in any other capacity. Notes Todd Domke:

> You have to have something in writing. This has to be as specific as possible. For example, if your client is a start-up company, you may have to drop your fee initially in order to reflect the reality of their cash flow, and then raise it as they grow and their cash flow improves. You have to have this understood, and in writing, to begin with or they will resent it when you raise your rates later. It's also wrong to think that because a client has a lot of money he can be trusted to pay. A client may have all that money because he is stingy about paying. Be particularly suspicious if someone is reluctant to sign a contract or if you hear things like "You know I'm good for it." If somebody tries to put things on a personal level, it's a sign that there may be good reason to have a written agreement—or to get your money up front or COD. You can't be shy about this issue. It is not about trusting someone personally. It is about the way you do business.

When a Manager Should Act Like a Producer

If you are an independent operator, clearly the reason to act like a producer is to exploit a large, genuine opportunity that you cannot exploit yourself. But what if you are an on-staff manager with in-company resources at your disposal? When should you act like a producer?

If you are on staff as a manager, the major reasons to act like a producer are to

- cut costs
- learn about a new area
- move into new areas while minimizing risks
- vet employees or build a trial team

Many on-staff managers now act like producers to *cut costs* through outsourcing. If you can cuts costs while maintaining or improving quality by going outside, your company will thank you, perhaps in dollars or increased responsibility, and you will gain valuable experience in project production.

Acting like a producer is a great way for a manager to *learn about a new area* without hiring people or purchasing resources. Even just investigating an area, you'll meet freelancers and vendors who will teach you about technology, costs, time, and benefits. Undertaking a project with them will teach you even more.

Acting like a producer helps you to *minimize risks* associated with moving your employer into a new business or technology by doing so without buying equipment and hiring employees. Do you think you need an in-house public relations firm or fax-broadcast capability? Why not hire some freelance PR people or a fax service bureau and see how it works? In a year you can decide whether to bring it in-house or discontinue it.

Many independent contractors would jump at the right opportunity to join a company. The manager who acts like a producer can *vet employees or build a team* from this pool of people. He or she gets to know more people than the manager who just interviews and hires from the pool of full-time-job seekers. Acting like a producer can help you find good employees when you need them.

Whether you are on staff or an independent operator, you should act like a producer when it makes economic and professional sense—and avoid the role of producer when it does not. If, in any capacity, you run across an opportunity large enough, you just might take the practice "act like a producer" to the maximum level and start a virtual corporation.

Building a Virtual Corporation

An open-architecture or "virtual" corporation represents something of a formalized production arrangement. Such a business has no full-time employees except for the president and a small core, if that. A virtual company may function largely in cyberspace, with many members or associates never meeting in person.

The term "virtual" indicates that the arrangement seeks to repli-cate the results, if not the workings, of a "real" company. Virtual companies grew out of the corporate partnering/strategic alliance trend of the 1970s and 1980s and the outsourcing and independent contractor trends of the 1980s and 1990s. Ideally a virtual cor-poration embodies the principles of multipreneuring—providing cost-effective means of adding value and managing risk through a productive, flexible resource. Virtual companies can be platforms on which experts of every stripe work to maximum efficiency, doing what they do best. Virtual corporations minimize risk by avoiding the debt burden of purchasing plant and equipment and the structural costs and legal responsibilities of hiring actual employees. Such a company can even be created to exploit a short-term opportunity, with all players knowing they are in a three-to-five-year business.

At their best, virtual corporations offer

- rapid response and state-of-the-art quality
- high-level experts, managed into a team
- intense, project-focused effort
- technology-enabled communications and other techno-logical capabilities
- coherent corporate image, with fewer expenses and ad-ministrative burdens

A virtual company does not attempt to bamboozle anyone. Most admit their status, positioning it as an advantage. ("We bring together the best available resources for each assignment." "Our flexibility enables us to respond rapidly to your needs.") Some virtual companies may try to appear larger or more successful than they are, but that's customary for actual companies of all sizes.

For the multipreneur, a virtual corporation can provide a company identity, a structure, and, if it is an actual incorporated business, legal protection and tax advantages.

A company identity can help you do business in a way that independent contractor status cannot. Much of the advantage lies in the way you think about yourself. A company identity may lend focus to your efforts and to the way you present your capabilities to the public. Of course, a d/b/a, rather than a virtual corporation, might have the same effect. The designation d/b/a means "doing business as." Your status becomes "Joe Smith doing business as Renegade Consulting Associates." With a d/b/a you get to call yourself Renegade Consulting Associates or whatever. In most states you must register a d/b/a with your city or county clerk in order to use that name, get a business checking account, and so on. I once had "the Gorman Group" as my d/b/a. I was the Gorman Group, although I would occasionally hire freelance designers and research assistants. You cannot use the term "Corporation," "Inc.," or "Corp." in your d/b/a—those designations are for legal corporations—but you can say "Associates" or "Group."

Frankly, calling yourself a virtual company doesn't mean much unless you actually have one in place. That means building the concept of the business, the flow of projects, and the network of relationships that constitute a true virtual company. But you have to start somewhere, and if you get a better start by thinking of yourself and presenting yourself as a virtual company, do so.

A structure enables you to do business better by formalizing things. Remember what structure does for productivity? Sound methods of dealing with those to whom you subcontract work can boost your productivity and project quality. What is meant by sound methods? Pricing policies and rate schedules, standard forms and letter agreements, quality-control practices, standard policies for dealing with late deliverables from subcontractors, standard technological interfaces that others must use if they're going to work with you—those are sound methods. This structure can truly improve your dealings with customers and subcontractors, and it can even improve the way you present yourself.

The legal protection and tax advantages of a corporation are available only to legally incorporated businesses. If your virtual company is a d/b/a, you will not have these advantages. As you may know, a corporation is a legally defined "person" apart from the owners and employees. It can be sued, and it can pay taxes. The decision to incorporate can be made only with the help of an attorney and an accountant, neither of which I am. Some businesspeople I know are so afraid of legal action that they would never operate an unincorporated business of any size. Others think it doesn't matter, that in any legal action everyone involved in a business will be sued. Incidentally, when applying for bank credit, incorporation tends not to matter. A bank insists that owners of small businesses be personally liable for the borrowings of their companies and will insist that you sign a personal guarantee. From the tax standpoint, ask an accountant. From a legal standpoint, an attorney can form a corporation for you for several hundred dollars.

A virtual corporation can be the de facto result of your efforts as a producer. The virtual corporation basically represents a strategy of a multipreneur or entrepreneur outsourcing to the maximum degree possible.

Do You Want to Produce?

The practice "act like a producer" can boost your multipreneurial career and earnings to heights you may not have thought possible. Aside from adding significant value to whatever kinds of projects you do, this practice will help you learn new skills, form new professional relationships, and have more of a financial stake in projects. Given today's economy and its lack of structure, its focus on intellectual capital, and its rapidly evolving technology, the producer-intermediary may well emerge as one of the key professionals in business in the next ten to twenty years. Many multipreneurs are sure to be in their ranks.

7

Market Hard, Sell Soft

Selling is the toughest job in business simply because (1) people resist parting with their money, and (2) you open yourself to certain rejection by asking them to part with it. Nobody likes rejection, yet it's intrinsic to the sales process. In fact, when this dynamic is absent—for example, at a movie theater box office—we don't even think of the seller as a salesperson. A salesperson must persist in the face of rejection in order to close sales. Closing is, of course, the crucial, final step in the sales process and the one that nonsalespeople think they can't handle because that is where both resistance and risk of rejection are highest.

Resistance can take various forms. In business-to-business sales, resistance most commonly takes the form of bureaucratic inertia. Why should the company do something new when it is comfortable? Why should someone make a decision when it might be wrong? Why should someone spend money when budgets are tight? Then there are buyers who like to be courted or chased, who test and challenge the salesperson, who make him jump through hoops to get the sale. Nonsalespeople hate these games.

The distinction between salespeople and nonsalespeople is deliberate. "Salespeople" can—in return for compensation based on commissions—pick up the phone, get appointments, close sales, and make a good living. "Nonsalespeople" can't do these things.

Salespeople see overcoming the prospect's resistance as a challenge and a game. When she makes the sale she wins. When she doesn't make the sale, she loses—and she hates losing.

The salesperson takes a certain approach to sales and has a certain relationship with the prospect. Most multipreneurs don't have this approach or this relationship. In fact, most would rather avoid the process entirely. Take a look at what some multipreneurs say about selling:

> One of the greatest difficulties is having to make cold calls. I'll tell you, the minute the thought of cold calling comes to you, it just kills you.

> It's painful. The sell is painful. The phone calls, the rejection. You submit a proposal and you don't hear from them. You call and they say it's buried in the pile on their desk. They say they'll get to it next week; they never do. That's all part of the selling process.

> I very rarely throw myself out into the world of looking for work because, basically, I hate it. I do it, but not very often these days. It's frustrating.

> I kind of recognize that the only way I am going to get any work is if somebody knows me. I am never going to sell very well.

> I realized early on that if my business had to survive through telephone marketing and cold calls, I wasn't going to last long. I had to come up with a plan fast.

How do these five people make a living as multipreneurs? They do it through what I call the practice of "market hard, sell soft." They use marketing to define, package, and position what they are selling. They use networks to get referrals. They use a soft sell to present their products and services and to close. With such methods, although rejection still occurs, it is generally perceived as far less personal.

If you are—or aspire to be—a multipreneur, you don't need to be a great salesperson. In fact, if your core skill is selling, you'll probably add the greatest value and thus earn the greatest return by selling for someone else or being an independent sales rep. If you're a stellar seller, you certainly can become a multipreneur, and you may do extremely well. But multipreneuring is in its way as difficult as selling and very different. For example, if you excel at sales, you may find certain aspects of multipreneuring, such as creating the deliverables, unappealing. True salespeople are a breed apart. But then so are multipreneurs.

Before exploring selling, we should define a few key terms. "Marketing" means selling to groups; "sales" means selling one-on-one. Marketing tends to be more strategic and passive in nature, while selling tends to be more tactical and active, but both are complementary and each must support the other. Finally, soft selling is not no selling, but rather the natural follow-up after effective marketing has paved the way. "Market hard" prepares the way for "sell soft"—yet the fundamental dynamic in selling won't go away.

Market Hard

Often when people leave an employer to become independent contractors, they think the phrase "I'll sell my services on the open market" represents a strategy. It does not, for several reasons. First, "your services" have largely been shaped by your current employer's needs. Why would these services have much value on the open market? Second, you haven't yet packaged and positioned these services to differentiate them from those of others selling similar services. Without differentiation, your broadly defined services as a market researcher, financial analyst, industry analyst, copywriter, or whatever are a commodity item. Third, since you are selling a commodity—something largely indistinguishable from others of its type—you've basically positioned yourself, by default, as a freelancer. This does not represent a multipreneurial approach.

To get beyond the "I'll sell my services" concept, begin by answering two questions:

- What am I selling: what is my actual product or service, and how does it add value?

- Whom will I sell it to: what people in what organizations will I approach?

Most people working the open market answer these questions the hard way, which is through trial and error, over too long a time. To some degree, that's unavoidable. However, you can reduce the time spent on trial and error by answering these questions as specifically as you can, up front. Here's how.

What Am I Selling?

Don't define yourself as "selling your services," but rather as selling a core skill that adds value in a *specific, readily apparent way*. Think back to chapter 2. Reconsider how you add value. Look to the business processes you can affect for the better. Look to the money you can help someone make or save. *That* is what you are selling. Ways to package and position this will be examined later, but it is essential first to confront this question and develop a solid answer to it.

I've done this correctly, and I've done it incorrectly. In 1986 I founded a business called the Creditech Corporation with the aim of consulting to the credit departments of large companies. The goal was to help these companies improve their use of credit information and their credit approval processes. There were several problems. First, my core skill was in information product development and product management, not credit management. Second, the process I was trying to affect, while important to credit managers, was viewed by most businesses as a necessary evil rather than essential. Third, I did not have a specific method for consulting to credit departments, but rather a vaguely defined mission of "gathering information, examining the efficiency of the process, and recommending improvements." Creditech was doomed from the start.

When I did this the right way a year later, as an information product development consultant, I considered my core skill, which was developing information products. I determined how I could add value, which was to create something that someone else would sell. And I looked at how my prospects would make money and save money, which, respectively, was by selling what I developed and by not having me on staff. This led me into the business of writing industrial reports for information companies and business publishers. For these companies, creating reports represents an essential process since they sell them to their clients.

If you answer this question honestly, you will come up with something you believe in. Without this knowledge and belief, you have no foundation. With Creditech, my foundation was so shaky that in order to have something to sell, I soon took on the task of selling credit management software as an independent rep, when I had no real interest in doing so. This compounded my problems and prolonged my involvement in an area I should not have been involved in at all. It pays to take the time to define what you are selling and to do so in terms of an activity that your clients view as essential and to which you feel fully capable of adding value.

Whom Will I Sell It To?

You have to define whom you will sell to in very specific terms. Not just in terms of company name; you want individuals, their names, titles, addresses, and telephone numbers. All this goes into your marketing database.

You want to make sure you are selling to the right person. This is not always easy. As you are probably aware, the individual who uses your product or service may not be the person who would approve the sale. In this area, trial and error are the best teacher. Also, stay flexible regarding your market. You may find that the market you originally targeted is not ideal and that you should be selling to an entirely different one. For example, consider what Michèle Van Buren of Cayuga Communications in Newburyport, Massachusetts, found:

> When I first targeted the corporate relocation market, my service was designing orientation programs and materials for employees who were going to be transferred. My target market was originally the people in the companies who were responsible for helping the employees through the relocation process. I did mailings and cold calling. I got a few responses and had some meetings, but I didn't generate any real business. Then, because I had started writing articles for the industry publications and started meeting people in the industry,

people became interested in me as a communicator. Those most interested in what I could do were in the relocation service business—in firms that sold relocation services to corporations—rather than in the corporations themselves. This was a market that I hadn't looked at before, but they came to me. They helped me define what I was doing, because they asked me for the specific marketing communications and public relations services I could provide.

Don't chase every project that looks vaguely like it might relate to your area of expertise (although some people make a living doing so, with a lot of wear and tear). You should, however, be sensitive to what the market tells you.

How Multipreneurs Really Get Business

Without a doubt, the major source of business for multipreneurs is referrals, whether from clients, contacts, or formal or informal networks. A lot has been said and written about networking, and lately the practice has fallen into a bit of disrepute. The sense of mutual exploitation that underlies a lot of networking has worn the practice thin. Also, some people have found themselves so inundated with requests for informational interviews, courtesy interviews, and sales calls from friends of acquaintances of contacts, that they don't make the time for them anymore. On the other hand, people get referrals all the time from their networks of friends, associates, contacts, and, of course, clients. The question is: What works and what doesn't?

Multipreneurs use three types of networks to help them in marketing their services:

- swap meets
- formal networks and associations
- informal networks

Swap Meets

Swap meets (often called networks, although in a sense they are not) have been used by salespeople for some time and can be either set up by a group or organized by someone in the business of setting them up. In the latter case you pay a fee, generally ranging from $20 to $40 per month, to meet once or twice a month with other professionals in noncompeting businesses to exchange names and information. The fee covers the administrative costs of setting up the swap meet and the rent for the meeting space. Typical members include a management consultant, a communications consultant, a computer salesperson, an equipment salesperson, a financial planner or insurance salesperson, an advertising salesperson, a photocopier salesperson, and so on. Typically there are ten to fifteen members. Peter Lowy of Business Communications Strategies in Westwood, Massachusetts, uses a swap meet as an intelligence-gathering tool:

> The value of this kind of network depends on what you are selling and who's there at the meeting. The one I'm in is very efficient and wastes no one's time. Not everyone shows up every time, but there are always at least eight of us. I've gotten leads, and I've given them. Now and then I'll hear about interesting things going on at a company that can give me something to work with when I approach them. This isn't the only tool, or even the only networking tool, I use. But it seems worthwhile so far.

Formal Networks and Associations

Formal networks such as monthly city or regional business breakfasts or those set up for women or minorities can also be valuable. You often have the opportunity to hear inspiring speakers or learn useful information and maybe get a chance to speak before the group yourself. Unlike swap meets, these are networks in the more traditional sense in that you meet people and get to know them because of shared interests. There can be a subtle dimension to getting out the word about your business in this environment. There is a time to whip out your business card and a time not to. In other words, it often doesn't pay to network aggressively in these venues, but rather to come to know people gradually over time.

Depending upon your business, industry associations offer a major plus or a major minus in that you will meet people only in your industry. If they are the people you are trying to market to, that's great. If they are your competitors, don't waste your time.

Michèle Van Buren offers this perspective:

> Most of my business develops through personal contact at industry meetings and conferences. I joined the regional association for relocation professionals in New England and became active in it. This year I was elected to an officer post. I also produce their newsletter, which has introduced me to a number of people and given me a chance to show what I can do. Getting involved in the organization, rather than just paying your dues and showing up for the meetings, is important. That's how you really get to know people.

Joining an association represents an excellent way to learn more about anything, including the industry itself and the people in it.

Informal Networks

If you work as an independent operator for a while, you will ultimately see that your personal network of clients, friends, acquaintances, associates, and contacts is your most valuable source of referrals. This is natural. If you get business through a swap meet, you either create a satisfied client or not. If you meet people through formal networks and associations, you either enter their orbit or bring them into yours, or not. In contrast, your informal, personal network of friends, associates, and long-term clients, some of which can originate in other networks, has a more personal stake in your success.

Building and maintaining a personal network is essential for the multipreneur and goes beyond networking as a marketing strategy per se. When you are a long-term employee in a company, you have a ready-made social system. When you are a multipreneur, you make your social system—or fail to. As you've heard, working as an independent operator can be lonely. Networking represents a survival skill in more ways than one.

As political and media consultant Todd Domke points out:

> If you think of networking as this technique and as a means of getting ahead in business, I don't think you're going to be

terribly successful because that suggests circulating like someone who wants to be popular. You wind up being thought of as a social butterfly or as superficial or as opportunistic. The first thing is to be genuinely interested in people. Second, realize that if you are close to people who have so-called networks, you end up with as good a result as if you were networking all the time. There are people who, because of their type of work or years of experience, have a huge number of contacts. If you do good work for that person and they like and trust you, their contacts open up to you. They want to introduce you because you've become a friend or an associate or someone they like and respect.

Despite business being so competitive and profit oriented, there is still time for personal relationships. In the average person's day, two or three hours may be devoted to forging personal relationships. An independent also has to devote time to relationships, to being interested in what others are doing, how they're doing, seeing if you can help. Just the payoff in learning can justify this use of your time, learning about their business and what they do, their personal lives, their likes and dislikes, their social life and family life, sports and hobbies.

Even in mercenary terms, this way you have more people who are interested in you and who know about you. So when opportunities that affect your business come to them, they'll think of you. If you are just a work function to them, you won't come to mind. Instead they will do the favor for someone whom they do have a personal feeling for. Perhaps a corollary to the golden rule is this: If you are interested in people, they tend to be interested in you. If you're interested in helping them, they will likely feel similarly toward you. If you think this way, you will be part of many networks, some of them not really known to you—friends of friends, associates of associates—without consciously trying.

There is the world of networking, and then there is the world of genuine interest, genuine respect, and genuine relationships and friendships. Business comes from both purely professional relationships as well as from personal relationships, so it is wise to cultivate a wide range of both kinds of relationships.

To Market, to Market: The Prospects, the Offer, the Positioning

The Prospects

In answering the question "Whom will I sell to?" you define your prospects in terms of both the overall market—for example, the banking industry—and specific entities—for example, banks with assets of at least $10 billion—and specific people—perhaps retail branch managers. After you have your information, load it into a database on a personal computer. Sure, you can use index cards (a great tool, very portable), but there is a compelling reason to use a PC: the ability to manipulate and search the list to target specific mailings to specific people. The key thing is to have accurate information in an easy-to-use form. Although you can buy fancy software for the purpose, a spreadsheet like Microsoft Excel or Lotus 1-2-3 works fine. The value of a database depends on the accuracy of the data. If you use an old industry directory, your data will be dirty. Get on the phone and update it. Don't be shy about doing this. If you've never done phone work, it will be a gentle introduction. Secretaries are used to such calls and usually give the information freely. When they ask why you need it, just say, "I'm So-and-So from Renegade Consulting and we are updating our mailing list." (Go on, say "we"—it sounds better than "I.") Once in a blue moon you'll get the prospect on the line. Tell him the same thing. Sometimes they even express interest. Most people are nice on the telephone.

The Offer

The problem with offering "your services" to the market is that most people want to buy not an amorphous blob of services, but rather solutions to their problems. If you try to sell yourself as an industry analyst or a market researcher or technology consultant, you're offering an amorphous blob of services. If instead you offer, as an industry analyst, a "competitor tracking service" or, as a market researcher, a "market-feedback report" or, as a technology consultant, a "local area network audit," you offer a potential solution. Even if you never actually sell it, the fact that you have it (a) sets you apart from those who don't, (b) gives you something concrete to use as a door opener, and (c) lets the prospect react to a specific proposal.

When I left Dun & Bradstreet to start the Creditech Corporation, I pitched an "audit of your credit approval process" to six large companies. I sent them a letter and followed up with a phone call. The credit managers at each of the companies took my phone call. Three of them had me in for a visit. Unfortunately, I hadn't thought through my "credit approval process audit" very well and was thus unable to sell it. In other words, I didn't know what the hell I was doing. The point, however, is to illustrate the power of a specific offer: using one, even someone who doesn't know what the hell he is doing can get solid appointments with prospects.

The "audit" is a time-honored way for consultants to offer something specific. Simply take the expertise you are selling and think of how you would do the first-step assessment. The doctor does a physical, the dentist takes X-rays, the consultant does an audit.

Peter Lowy of Business Communications Strategies states:

> I use a communications audit to assess the power of companies' communications across various constituencies. This service gives me and my potential clients solid information about their communications program and sets the stage for BCS's approach. This approach states that you must target each constituency of a company—customers, prospects, competitors, suppliers, investors, employees, and the media—with specific but coordinated messages if your communications program is to achieve its goals. I use an audit to find out whether this is happening or not for a potential client.

Your door opener must grow naturally out of your approach. It can't be something "stuck on." It must be a concrete expression of what you are doing. If at all possible, charge a fee for any audit, survey, assessment, or other door opener you use. The fee should reflect one to three days of your daily fee and take about that long.

The Positioning

If you don't consciously position yourself, you'll be buffeted about by the need to generate revenue. You'll take on projects above or beneath your capabilities. You'll try to be all things to all people. You won't understand what work should be custom and what should be off the shelf. You'll overprice yourself sometimes and underprice yourself at others. Positioning helps you—and others—know where you are.

Positioning must be done with an eye toward the competition and the business realities you face. When I started in business writing, I realized that freelance writing for magazines and newspapers paid too little for my needs, yet it would provide a useful credential. So I decided to do only a few articles for reputable publications—just to position myself as a professional writer—and then forget about that business. Then when I pitched my writing services to companies, I positioned myself as serving information content firms. I had experience in product development and knew the information business. (My "offer" was to do new product concept testing.) I positioned myself as "an information product development consultant" instead of "a writer" because people will pay "a consultant" more than "a writer." I dressed as well as or better than my prospects, and I priced myself high, because I felt I was worth it and I needed the money. By positioning myself in this way, I lost some projects, but I didn't mind because I wound up working on higher-level assignments for higher fees.

Like a good multipreneur, I developed multiple positions from which to market my services. One was public relations writer. With no experience, I was paid $2,500 for three days of speechwriting. After a while I hit upon a lucrative specialty—industrial reports—so I positioned myself as "a report author" and did better with the information firms than I had as a product development consultant.

Once you have identified your prospects, defined your offer, and established your positioning strategy, grab your tools and start marketing.

The Big Ten: Basic Marketing Tools

Hundreds of books have been written on marketing and marketing tools. If you are new to marketing, read those books. What follows is a nickel summary on proven marketing tools. It's best to try at least several of these to see which work best for you in your particular business. Also, when several tools are used together, they support and reinforce one another.

Contact Plan

Decide who in your marketing database is going to get what message and when they are going to get it. Also decide what follow-up you're going to do. Your prospects should hear from you every six to twelve weeks, that is, four to eight times a year. Here's one way to do it: Prioritize your prospect list according to likelihood of purchase. Take the top third and mail to them in month one and call them a week or so later. Repeat this on the second third of the list in month two and on the third third in month three. If you can't prioritize them or you'd rather not deal with all of the lower-likelihood prospects in one month, randomly divide the list into thirds.

However you do it, do it. This should be an automatic process. Over time, regular effort will yield results, often in unexpected ways. People get used to your presence and approach. They see that you are going to be around and they come to accept you, simply because of regular exposure.

Product and Service Descriptions

For almost any business, you need a written description. Effective brochures briefly describe what you do, the benefits to your customers, your qualifications, and how the prospect can get in touch. However, you can also do some positioning with a section on "how we work with clients," discussing how you specify a project, outlining typical time frames, describing who does the work and how you assure quality. You can list prices for products, but not for projects, which are priced accordingly. You can indicate your price range by referring to your reasonable rates, if you are at the low end, or, at the high end, your intense focus on quality and your customized approach.

Include generous margins, blank space, headings, and bullets. If you need a writer and a designer, hire them but don't go overboard on production values. A good copy shop or quick printer can give you a range of options. Tell them you want to go cheap, then work your way up. To get ideas and to see what works, look at others' literature. I don't believe in going the high-end, four-color route unless you are selling a high-quality product and have deep pockets. I'm not convinced that many people actually read marketing literature, no matter how well done it is—they're usually too busy. A brochure is more a proof statement that you exist as a business. For you, the thought process that goes into creating it may be the most valuable part.

Sales Letters

Keep sales letters short and focused. My formula: First paragraph, dramatize a problem ("Surveys have shown that information companies grow most rapidly through new products. But how can you tell the good ideas from the losers?"). Second paragraph, present the solution ("A quick, inexpensive concept test is the answer. I have concept tested new products for several major information firms"). Final paragraph, request action ("If you want new product ideas that generate revenues, please call me").

Client List, Endorsements, and References

If you have permission from clients to name them on your client list, do so. I've seen client lists included with marketing literature I've received unsolicited in the mail. Endorsements are nice, but their value is proportional to the credibility of the endorser. Remember, you need permission to use an endorsement. And you must have references, which you should supply upon request in the sales process.

List of Recent Engagements/Work Samples

A list of recent engagements ("recent" tends to be liberally interpreted) can be a real credibility builder. This list does not have to identify the client except in vague terms ("Designed and installed guided missile system for a major investment bank"). Work samples are trickier. If your work was public—for example, an advertising campaign or a published study—there's no problem. Otherwise you have to respect client confidentiality and get permission. Keep track of your work samples and let any client who takes them know how important their return is to you.

Advertising

Advertising in the press or broadcast media is expensive, not due to the cost of a single ad—although they aren't cheap—but because the repeated buying needed to build recognition is so expensive. For most business services, direct mail and public relations work better anyway. But if you have a targeted product or service and a publication in which you believe it is worth advertising, go for it—but go easy. Certain mail-order items sell very well this way, but mail order is a business unto itself—one that is open to the multipreneur but shouldn't be addressed here.

Promotional Items

A promotional item is anything of value that you give away to your prospects and customers. Items such as pens, mugs, and calculators strike me as good-luck talismans for the givers rather than reminders to call for the receivers. Complimentary newsletters are the rage, thanks to the PC, the laser printer, and the apparent belief that people have time to read them. I only glance at them. The most interesting are those with survey results or interesting bullets ("Five Ways to Handle Customer Complaints").

Public Relations

PR includes all the tools for gaining media exposure to potential prospects, generally without paying for that exposure. You can hire an expensive PR firm, but if you have the time, the talent, and a product or service that would benefit from PR, it is worth your efforts—or those of a freelance PR person—to get media exposure. A few guidelines:

- Carefully target the publications and media you wish to appear in; if a medium doesn't reach your target audience, it is useless.
- Send the managing editor or editor of the section in which you want to appear a query letter stating what you want to write about, how long the article would be, why the readers would find it interesting, why you are qualified to write it, and when you could deliver it.
- Avoid the most common errors: (1) failing to read the publication and understand the editor's needs, (2) pitching obvious "puff pieces" for your business or articles that pontificate rather than deliver value, (3) underestimating the amount of work involved in writing a good article.

Usually you'll receive only token payment for an article, if that, and you won't get any business from it, really. The value of the article is as a reprint that you send to your prospects ("in case you missed the most recent issue of *Linoleum News*"). One good guide to the print market is *Writer's Market*, published annually by Writer's Digest Books.

The broadcast media and the better cable venues are tougher to break into. Write or call the producer of the program you are interested in appearing on. Writing a book helps you get on, but only if it is newsworthy or unique.

The press release is a staple of public relations. Essentially it's a one- or two-page write-up of something newsworthy, such as a product release, findings of study, or a summary of remarks at a conference. Thousands of press releases spew out of editors' fax machines every day. Many of them are poorly written; few are newsworthy. Give it a shot if you have something truly exciting to report and know how to write.

Despite the hurdles, PR of some kind should be part of your marketing plan. When you publish or appear in the media regularly, you acquire that ephemeral designation of "expert." Several people I know are PR juggernauts. They are highly quotable while giving reporters what reporters need: reinforcement (usually) or a contrarian view (sometimes) of the slant on the story. They also enjoy the exposure, and it shows.

Speaking Engagements, Conferences, and Forums

Public speaking builds your credibility, gives you exposure, and broadens your horizons. After several appearances you can include in your literature the phrase "So-and-So frequently speaks before business groups." You'll meet people at conferences, which, by the way, you attend for free if you are on a panel. If you have some speaking experience and a flair for it, getting a spot on a conference panel is one of the few things that is easier than you might think. Of course, doing the prep work and delivering an interesting presentation is not. You must be interesting, exhibit your expertise without parading it, and keep things focused and snappy. If you use slides or overhead transparencies, keep them simple, uncluttered, and few.

Scorched-Earth Cold Calling

Everyone sees cold calls as part of sales rather than marketing. But since marketing is selling to groups, I see sitting down and calling twenty, thirty, or forty people as a marketing tool, not one-on-one selling. (After all, it's called tele*marketing*, not teleselling.)

Aside from a phone, you need two things: (1) a list of company names and people's names, titles, and phone numbers, and (2) an offer. Be sure you have a *complete list* before you start cold calling or you will break the flow by having to get numbers from directory assistance or names from receptionists. Consider your offer and write out exactly what you are going to say. Use all caps or, if you have the font, small caps so it will be easy to read. (I write a script even for two-question market research calls.)

Dial, identify yourself, and ask for the person you want. If the secretary asks what it's about, tell her. She'll usually say the person is in a meeting and ask for your number. Don't give it to her. Tell her you are unreachable. Tell her anything, but don't leave a number.

Why? Because you will not get a callback, which is depressing, or you will get a callback at a bad time, which is embarrassing. Don't leave messages. Don't ask about or take notes on people you can't reach. If you ask the secretary about the best time to call, the prospect will usually not be there anyway, and if he is, he won't take your call if he's not in the mood. Just keep moving to the next name. Have at least twenty names to hit. Keep it to an hour or so. Cold calling is draining.

There are two great things about cold calling. First, do it enough and it will undoubtedly increase your confidence and your ability to talk on your feet. Second, you will get people on the line who hear your offer and then say, "That sounds interesting. Tell me more." That's when you move from marketing hard to selling soft.

Sell Soft

Selling is the process of transforming hot prospects into customers. The soft sell process is straightforward and based upon the principles of traditional selling:

- Qualification
- Needs assessment
- Proposal
- Negotiation
- Close

Qualification

Here's advice from communications pro Peter Lowy: Talk with people who know what you're talking about. Explain what you are selling. Listen for feedback that indicates that your prospect understands. If they don't, explain it again. If the prospect seems unable to grasp what you are talking about, move on. Don't waste a lot of time trying to educate people.

In fact, beware of those who want a free education ("Hey, we're just talkin', right?"). Let them try getting a free consultation from their physician or attorney. Of course, you walk a fine line in this area. You must show enough expertise to prove that you have it, but not give it away. The best way to handle those who want free expertise is to avoid answering questions specific to their business. When the conversation heads that way, offer to make a formal proposal ("Jim, that's a question that I could answer only after looking into the situation. I'd like to put a letter proposal together for you so I can do that").

To qualify properly, you must ask two questions in some form: Do you have the money? Can you make the decision to purchase? (Remember, your prospect has expressed an interest or a need.) Here are some variations on the first question:

- How soon would you want to make this purchase? Is it in the budget?
- Right now, I am taking on only substantial projects—in the low five-figure range, minimum—and from what you tell me your need would fall into that range. Does that present a problem?
- As a first step, I'd have to survey your operation. That takes about two days, during which I'd need access to some of your key players, plus about a day to write up the results for you. This costs about $2,000. (Then clam up until you get a response.)

If you are new to business or have not held a high-level post, you might think the nice thing to do is to pretend that money is not on everyone's mind and try avoiding so crass a subject. Don't waste your time with such thinking, and never let it dictate what you say. Money is on everyone's mind all the time. Go ahead, talk about it. But quote a range, unless you know exactly what you'll charge or you're selling a product with a set price.

The easiest way to phrase the second question—Can you make the purchase?—is to ask the following:

- Do you have the authority to engage me (or to purchase the product)—or would someone else be involved?
- Who else would be involved in the decision to engage me?
- To whose budget would my fee be charged?

Such questions enable you to avoid making the same presentation five times. You have a right to know who's who on the client side, and they have the same right regarding your shop. Prospects will usually tell you who's who when you ask. Most people in business are honest, but thanks to corporate politics and conflicting motivations many are not straight shooters. But don't limit yourself. Deal with 'em all. Just go in armed with questions that get you the information you need in order to be able to sell—and get paid.

Needs Assessment

After qualifying your hot prospect, you must assess her needs along two dimensions: the nature of the need and the timing/intensity of the need. Again, questions like the following are your tools:

Nature of the need:
What parts of your operation are affected by this situation?
What would you consider an ideal solution? Give me a wish list.
What have you tried in the past? With what result?
Which employees are affected by this, and how?
What departments and areas are affected and should be involved?

Timing/intensity of the need:
How long has this need existed? Is it now urgent? Why?
Are you losing money while this situation goes unresolved?
Has senior management directed that this be fixed (studied, purchased)?
Are there issues of legal liability here?
When would you like to see this completed? What is your time frame?

By necessity, these questions are generic. They indicate only the kinds of questions you should ask, along with the questions that are specific to what you sell, such as "Do you use IBM or Apple?" or "How much exporting to Asia do you think you'll do next year?"

Proposal

The proposal begins when you say words to the effect of "Jim, having heard about your needs, I'd like to submit a proposal." If you've been talking with a prospect long enough to understand their problem, tell them—don't ask—that you will submit a proposal. The worst they can say is, "Oh, please don't go to that trouble." Which means (1) they don't want the delay of a proposal, (2) they don't want to do business with you, or (3) they are not sure. To determine which it is, say, "I always sell by proposal. It's not a big deal for me to put one together, and it will be short so you can evaluate it quickly." If they still don't want to see a proposal, leave or get off the phone. But mention that if they change their minds and want to see something from you, it won't cost them anything. You will eventually sell to a lot of people who previously said "no" repeatedly.

Unless you are selling to the government or a regulated industry, you don't need a long proposal. If you are responding to an RFP—request for proposals—you must address every point in the RFP, no matter how many pages it takes. However, a letter proposal can literally run one page, although two to three pages plus some exhibits, like a list of clients or past projects, is more realistic. Anything longer than five pages or so will look better with front and back covers and a GBC binding (the usually black plastic devices that work like spirals). Attach a brief cover letter. Depending upon what your prospect tells you, either submit a copy just for her or one for each person making the decision.

Here are the basic elements your proposal should include (this assumes some kind of consulting assignment; adapt it to your needs if you sell other services or a product):

Proposal Outline

1. *Introduction*, stating purpose and scope of project
2. *Tasks*, stating the work to be performed

3. *Time frame*, stating when you'll perform the tasks
4. *Responsibilities*, stating what you *and* the client are responsible for
5. *Compensation*, stating your fee, any percentage payments, and billing arrangements (including when you will be paid and an up-front, good-faith payment)
6. *Conclusion*, mentioning that you believe that the project will achieve the client's goal and that you appreciate their consideration

If you include these elements, you can't go wrong. Each element is, of course, subject to negotiation, which is detailed in step four. That is why it's called a proposal. By definition, a proposal is negotiable and subject to the other party's conditions. (He: "Will you marry me?" She: "Yes! After you've made partner at the firm.")

Negotiation

When you write your proposal and cost out the job, you have to decide what is negotiable and what is not. Most things in your proposal should be negotiable, subject to lower limits and to give and take. Lower limits means that you have a minimum price, time period, and level of quality for the project. Give and take means that you are willing to make trade-offs. If you lower your price substantially but agree to devote the same amount of time to the project, what, exactly, have you negotiated? If you agree to do the job faster yet at the same level of quality that more time would have ensured, you may be setting yourself up for failure, and, again, you haven't negotiated anything. Negotiation is give *and* take. Many independents fail at negotiation because they are desperate for the work (and show it) or they believe they have no power to negotiate. Act as if you want the business but will do fine without it. If you have the right prospect, project, and proposal, your position is stronger than you think. So act as if it were stronger. After you see the results a few times, you'll become an even better negotiator.

In my experience, the best sales, the ones for projects that turn out to be the best all around, happen fast. The prospect has a need, and you can meet it. You know it. They know it. So things move

Proposing Proposals

Unsolicited Proposals

The value of unsolicited proposals depends on your business. In publishing, business writing, consulting, and many business services, they can be a great sales tool. They are simply detailed offers: an executive search firm sends proposals to act as screener and reference checker for human resource departments; a business publisher distributes proposals for a multi-client study of personal banking services in the ten richest U.S. markets; a writer submits a book proposal to an editor; and so on. Some businesses expect unsolicited proposals, but they can also work in situations where they're rarely used. If you are going to submit unsolicited proposals, be certain you know your market and prospects, or you will waste time and look foolish. And be sure to follow up.

Multiple Proposals

Multipreneurs need multiple proposals out in the market at all times. Believe it or not, some independent operators put out a proposal, then wait for it to be accepted or rejected. If it is rejected, they then move on to developing the next one; if it is accepted, they wait until they finish that project before floating another proposal. They usually feel they can focus only on either selling or fulfillment, or they are afraid that multiple proposals will lead to too much work. The truth is, if you can't sell and fulfill business at the same time, you doom yourself to the feast-or-famine, roller-coaster income pattern that spouses and creditors find so unsettling. If you get too much work, that's good. Either act like a producer and get subcontractors or stall and juggle and work fourteen-hour days. Unless you have reached your financial goals or feel headed for a nervous breakdown, there is no reason not to have multiple proposals and multiple projects going at all times. That *is* multipreneuring.

forward. Oh, they might not like the wording in this part of the proposal or they may want the deliverables a little sooner or they may try to hammer you down on price a bit. But overall, things move forward. They want to do it, so they do it.

The deals that drag on drag on for a reason. The reason is usually that the prospect is either too conflicted or disorganized to make a decision, or the decision is negative and they lack the ego strength to tell you. Some deals that drag on finally happen, but more often you get dragged through three meetings, five drafts of the proposal, and twenty phone calls for nothing. Large and even midsize companies have people on staff who want to keep busy, and one way for them to do that is to waste your time.

Requesting a proposal can also be a prospect's way of getting free work from you. If you submit a detailed project plan, you've given them a detailed project plan—for free. Cut your losses when you sense terminal foot draggers or a fishing expedition. Here's how:

1. Have an expiration date of thirty days on all proposals. During the thirty-day period, keep in touch and be help-ful. As the expiration date looms, work with the client to get closure. After that date, don't initiate contact, but don't write them off, either. If they're not interested now, they're not.

2. Ask frankly about the barriers to moving forward. Ask which section or provision they're uncomfortable with: Is it price? The deliverables? Your qualifications? Ask what you can do to raise their comfort level.

3. Be stingy with information—not to mention work—that they would have to pay you to receive. You cannot win them over by giving them free work or advice. It will in fact work against you.

4. Never become angry, petulant, or miffed if a proposal is not moving forward or is turned down after a long wait. Yes, it's frustrating. But you will get nowhere by even obliquely implying that they are bozos. Just walk away and come back another day.

5. Never, ever, ever count on anything. Never sit waiting for the phone to ring. Never bet a cent that a proposal will be

accepted until it is and you have the signed agreement *and* a good-faith payment. Never make any material change in your status—don't turn down work, buy equipment, promise work to a subcontractor, ease up on other sales efforts, or change your plans—because you have a proposal on someone's desk. Until you have an agreement and good-faith money, you have nothing.

Yes, it can be rough out there. The world is full of people who will run you around when they don't know what they want, make an agreement, then ask for more work for the same money, have five people edit your deliverable and ask you to reconcile their conflicts, then pay you sixty days late because they know you're not a major supplier. But then there are those who know their business, can make a decision and tell you what it is, give you good and timely feedback on your deliverables, then personally make sure you get paid promptly. The world is full of these types, too. To find enough of them to make a living you have to market hard, but when you do find them you can sell soft and successfully.

Close

When it comes, the close comes naturally. You hear things like "I've signed off on it, and so has Jim. We're getting a check cut now and we'll FedEx it to you this afternoon." It's a great feeling. If you have known it, congratulations. If you have not, please know that getting your business well defined in your mind, getting your prospects well defined in your database, getting the needs well defined by the client, and getting the project well defined in your proposal are the keys. The rest is just businesspeople talking business.

8

Exploit Technology

If you've successfully avoided dealing with technology for most of your business life, you may have noticed recently that it's harder than ever. Today, technology is integral to many business functions, and as a multipreneur, you must learn to live amicably with technology because it is driving many, if not most, of the opportunities in business. As Boulder-based publisher and teacher David Rye tells those who attend his how-to-run-a-business classes:

> It's a serious handicap not to be computer literate now. The longer you delay, the more difficult it will be to keep up with your competition. But even before you learn how to use a computer or whatever, you need the right mind-set.

Tuning in to this mind-set is not necessarily easy for many of us. New York City–based electronic publisher Michael Wolff marvels at those in publishing "who want this technical knowledge and these capabilities, but refuse—and in fact are even afraid—to get their hands dirty." Michael believes:

> In any transitional period, such as in the movement from theater to movies or from radio to television, there are some people and companies who just don't make it. There is no

law or logic that dictates that people doing "X," which is significantly different from "Y," should make the transition to doing "Y." In business there is a process of natural selection that actually determines who survives.

The technology shift is a reality that calls for the kind of evolutionary process described in chapter 1, by which people either will or will not adapt to the survival requirements of the new economy. Technology consultant Steve Childs of ChildsPlay in San Mateo, California, sees it like this:

> The ability to learn technology is a matter of motivation. If someone is more afraid than they are motivated, they will only scratch the surface. They will only learn to change their screen savers. But if they are really motivated and determined to learn something useful, they'll push through the pain and get comfortable with technology.

Can your motivation outweigh your fear? How much do you really need to know in order to exploit technology? How, exactly, do you go through the process of learning technology? What's involved? What help is available? These questions, among others, are explored in this chapter.

Why Bother?

Multipreneuring itself has become possible because of the technology-driven diffusion of work. Now that the tools to create work and exchange information can be anywhere, we can work anywhere. Also, in the postindustrial economy, intellectual content represents both input and output for knowledge workers. Given this, the diffusion of technology enables the knowledge worker to become truly independent. For example, now that we can run our own databases and marketing campaigns, we can reach the market directly in ways that were impossible before the personal computer. The personal computer has made it possible for knowledge workers to be independent businesspeople in the same way that people who work with their hands—bricklayers, carpenters, electricians, roofers—have always been able to be independent.

There are two types of opportunities created by technology: opportunities to do business and opportunities to increase your productivity. "Opportunities to do business" refers to the fact that technology has created an environment in which those who understand technology, how it works and what it can do, can use that knowledge to create projects, ventures, and businesses. "Opportunities to increase your productivity" means that by using technology in your business, in your office, and in your attaché case, you can increase your professional productivity.

You can take advantage of these two types of opportunities only if you know how to exploit technology. Notice that I did not say "only if you know how to program a computer" or "only if you know a bit from a byte." In fact, to take advantage of opportunities to do business you do not even need a hands-on capability, although it certainly doesn't hurt. You do need to understand how technology works and how it adds and creates value. To increase your productivity, however, you need a hands-on capability. But even for that purpose, you do not have to understand programming or know a bit from a byte. You need only to know how to work the software to do what you want to do.

What if you are a technophobe? What if you've tried to learn how to use a computer and failed? What if you wish the Internet would just go away? Take heart. The time has come when a businessperson who can't deal with technology is seen much like a suburbanite who can't drive a car. You don't have to like technology (any more than you have to like cars), but you do need to be able to use it. If you really want to make it as a multipreneur and really make some money, you need to exploit technology.

What Technology Does

Except for a relatively small group of technologists, people want technology for what it can do, for the benefits it delivers. Actually, only a small portion of the business community, let alone the general population, cares about understanding the arcane workings and language of technology. By the way, technology, for our purposes, means information technology (IT). IT includes computer, audiovisual, and communications technologies that use data, information, and images in some way. This is technology for creating, capturing, maintaining, manipulating, and communicating information. The term "information" (or "content") includes data, knowledge, and expertise—and entertainment—as well as the subset business information. Business information focuses on financial, market, industry, competitive, product, legal, pricing, and performance information, as well as specialized categories such as design specifications and industry-specific areas such as health care information.

What does IT do for us? Because it places so much information management power in the hands of the individual, IT, especially the personal computer,

- levels the playing field in many businesses
- creates new ways of combining things
- creates new learning tools
- enables us to work in new ways

A Level Playing Field

IT levels the playing field because information is now a resource comparable to other forms of capital (land, labor, machinery, money), and IT and the openness of our society have made information and the ability to manage it widely available. If you work with information, you have the equivalent of a factory on your desk and you are the plant manager. Go on, go up against the big boys. The only thing that's bigger is their factory—and it's not much bigger. Don't be intimidated by the size of the competition when you set out to develop a technology-based business opportunity. Even a small company with limited funding can afford large amounts of computing power. Also, you can use IT to exploit the advantages of small size: the ability to move quickly, focus on a niche, and price competitively thanks to low overhead.

Journalist-turned-electronic-publisher Michael Wolff believes:

> Technology bequeaths advantages such that the playing field
> is not only level, but that I have an advantage as a player.

What is appealing about information technology is that it gives you control. If you are a writer working with a large institution, one of the first things that you lose is control. Desktop and electronic publishing technology gives that control back to you. I can perform functions that previously justified the existence of large publishing houses, and I can perform them with just a few people and for a lot less. While they may still have an advantage in print distribution, that is changing rapidly as electronic distribution becomes the wave of the future. This brings it all down to an issue of talent rather than size.

Of course, for the field to be level and to gain any advantage, you must be able to use the technology or at least be able to understand its capabilities.

New Ways to Combine Things

Many businesspeople prosper by combining things—ideas, information, processes—in new ways to create applications to meet new, and old, needs. Think about the bar code system. The electronic ability to identify things, such as products at the supermarket checkout or trucks rolling through a tollbooth, not only speeds up the process, but also creates new information to fuel new processes. At the supermarket, if you count how many boxes of cornflakes (and scores of other items) you sell when you run special offers on them, you know a lot about which incentives work and which products people purchase together. And you know it immediately. If the consumer buys by credit card, debit card, or check, you can even know who buys what. At the tollbooth, bar codes not only automate toll collections, speed up traffic, and reduce emissions—they also reveal what trucks of what size are using what routes and when they are using them.

Combining things in new ways, whether made possible through bar codes or a "fifth medium" of an interactive, real-time, integrated, audio-text-image box, represents a major means by which IT adds and creates value. To exploit these opportunities, you don't have to use technology in a hands-on sense. You simply have to understand the processes that technology can enhance and *how* IT can enhance those processes.

New Learning Tools

Because IT centers on information, it provides new ways of learning. Take vast databases, for example. They can be searched on simple key words and represent an incredibly powerful research tool. This power is especially important given that the volume of human knowledge is doubling about every seven to ten years. What good is all that knowledge in books, newspapers, magazines, newsletters, and research papers unless you can access it? Without search-and-retrieval mechanisms, you're drowning in an ocean of information. With such mechanisms you can quickly find and learn exactly what you need to know.

The computer can also act as instructor and teacher. According to Professor Roger Schank at Northwestern University's Institute for the Learning Sciences:

> We work with artificial intelligence and multimedia and are building essentially intelligent teaching programs. They are not computer-based training because CBT is usually lots of quizzes and text on screen and we don't do that, or even believe in it. These are simulated environments in which you practice a skill by having the program look and feel *exactly* like the thing it is trying to teach you. We have stored up to a thousand different video stories in the program, each story a minute or two long, indexed to various failure points. When you make a mistake, one of the stories pops up on the screen and tells you what you should have done and what you ought to think of doing. You can engage in a little simulated dialogue with the experts until you understand what you need to know and then go back to the simulation.

While an in-person teacher or trainer is sometimes essential to a learning process, in many situations the portability and standardization of IT-based instruction are overwhelming advantages. However, business has barely scratched the surface when it comes to exploiting these new-media learning tools, partly because the costs of production are still high for true multimedia, which incorporates text, video, sound, and graphics.

IT as a learning tool already enables the process of becoming an instant expert. Here's one small example of its power. Suppose you want to learn about a noteworthy person. Simply access a large database of periodicals (one good one is ABI Inform's *ProQuest*, a compendium of over eight hundred periodicals) and search on that person's name. You will find any articles she was mentioned in, as well as any she has written. (It's tempting before, say, a sales call to do such a lookup and then, when you are introduced, say, "Gee, it's great to finally meet you. I remember your article in the winter 1990–91 issue of *The Journal of Applied Linguistics*. I just love your work." The trouble is, a lot of us are on to this tactic. Still, I suppose it's flattering).

New Ways of Working

IT enables you to work, either on your own or with others, in new ways. Despite the diffusion it fosters, IT has the balancing effect of enhancing the team approach by heightening interactivity. The ability to work on a plan, design, report, budget, or survey and to share the results immediately can outweigh the disadvantages of geographical distance and lack of personal contact. You get instant access to expertise, rapid response capability within the team, and faster review and approval (or disapproval) from clients. All of which speed turnaround and increase team productivity.

In some cases the tools have created more speed than most of us can handle. Clients' approval processes, for example, often remain mired in bureaucracy. Some of this results from human nature and reflects the time people need to get comfortable with a decision, but a lot of it is vestigial. Some people take three weeks to review a report because they have always taken three weeks to review a report. So you send work via E-mail or FedEx to someone stuck in a time warp. It can be frustrating.

However, people are adapting and will continue to do so. Competition, if nothing else, drives this need to adapt. Meanwhile, fortune will favor those who can quickly locate and develop information and expertise and apply it to clients' needs, who can cut turnaround time, and who can budget, schedule, plan, design, cut and paste, and blend contributions interactively. Shouldn't you be among them?

Exploiting Technology: A Primer

Let's look more closely at using technology to create business opportunities and to increase your productivity. Michael Wolff has managed to do both, finding that involvement with technology changed his entire approach to his profession, which was author, and to his product, which was books:

> In the desktop and electronic publishing business I became involved with other people who were interested in the technology's possibilities and began to see writing as information production and collaborative process. I therefore moved from being a single practitioner to being involved in a collaborative process. It has turned out that our value added [at Michael Wolff & Company] is really the ability to straddle the two worlds of writing and technology. Our value is the ability to speak to both sides, the creative/author side and the technology/distributor side, so that we are, among other things, an interface between publishers and electronic distribution. In the process, we've had to rethink the nature of "a book" because technology has changed its limitations. For example, it used to be easy to protect the property, because who could go out and reprint the book? But now, because the on-line medium is a reproductive medium, a book can be reprinted instantly. So when we put our books on-line, they can be scarfed down by anybody. But we can also update them on a minute-by-minute basis so that if you scarfed it down ten minutes ago, you already have an old product.

To create business opportunities, you have to learn *about* technology; to increase your productivity, you have to learn *to use* technology. This distinction is important. *To create business opportunities*, you do not have to know how to actually use the technology—but you must know enough about it so that you can apply it to business situations and processes in order to add value. *To increase your productivity*, you have to know how to use technology on the job so that you can do what you want to do and do it better, faster, or cheaper. Both of these processes involve rethinking process, activity, role, and product, as they did in Michael Wolff's case.

To create business opportunities by exploiting technology, you must understand the process that you would be enhancing and the way the technology could work within that process. In general, situations amenable to IT solutions are characterized by

- large volumes of information to be accessed, processed, or maintained
- dynamic information (meaning that it changes often)
- information that people need in order to do something important to them
- inadequate current methods of accessing, processing, maintaining, or representing the information—that is, the technology can make the task involved easier, faster, or more accurate

Airlines, financial institutions, and government agencies are great users of IT because of the volume of information they must handle. Much of that information is dynamic. The information is important because airlines, financial institutions, and government agencies conduct transactions involving money. The methods formerly used to process the information may have been adequate but were certainly not as efficient. More to the point, IT creates value: the airlines can run frequent flier programs, financial institutions can offer new services such as ATMs, and the U.S. government can (more or less) keep track of 250 million people and an annual budget of over $1.5 trillion.

However, it is not a good idea to put, say, your recipes on a database. Why not? Because the process of looking up recipes in an index card file box is straightforward. What's the added value of being able to search on "chicken" or even "chicken and tarragon"? The costs and the stakes are such that it takes more trouble to create and maintain that database than it does to use the index cards. On the other hand, if you put something as complex, time-consuming, and calculation-intensive as your tax returns into a good software package, you then have added value.

To increase your productivity, you have to be able to work the software. You can't use word-processing, graphics, or E-mail software in your business unless you (or someone you hire) know how to work it. With many software packages, you can easily learn just enough to do what you want to do. That typically gives you a small portion of the total functionality of the software, but at least you are more productive with it than you were before.

Let's examine ways of exploiting technology, first for business opportunities and then for productivity increases.

To Develop Business Opportunities with Technology

The person who can see the business opportunities presented by technology is not necessarily a techie—at all. Rather it is someone who can, on the one hand, grasp the business situation or process and, on the other hand, know enough about the technology to see how it could be applied to that situation or process to somehow make it more efficient or more effective. Technology consultant Steve Childs sees it this way:

> Such people don't get stuck in their own particular discipline. If you never pick up a magazine in a category outside your area or never leave your comfort zone, you lose the incremental value associated with crossing disciplines. The habit of being able to come at things from different points of view helps you to create new solutions. This happens because you can look at a lot of seemingly disparate pieces and see how they can fit together in new ways, either to enhance something or to extend your reach.

Would you describe such a person as creative? I would. But while creativity often comes as a result of inspiration, insight, and intuition, it is even more often the product of hard work. The work lies in:

- analyzing the current situation or process
- understanding the capabilities of the technology
- focusing on what the technology can—and can't—do in the situation
- developing a cost/benefit profile and an implementation plan

Analyze the Current Situation or Process

Ignoring this first step or giving it short shrift creates misery down the road. A sound technological solution, let alone a true technology-based business opportunity, demands that you first examine the current situation or process in depth. Doing so will reveal opportunities as well as a lack of opportunity, which is so often papered over with talk about "educating the marketplace." Doing so will help you avoid implementing a technological solution for a nontechnological problem that doesn't exist. People—smart people—have lost millions with such "solutions."

A genuine opportunity grows out of a genuine need. Sure, opportunities have come from creating needs or meeting needs that people didn't know they had. Overnight delivery services are often cited as an example. But that's not the way to bet. Consider: The major reason that personal computers were so quickly adopted in business was that they enabled people to do two grueling, time-consuming, error-prone, but very necessary tasks: word processing (a/k/a typing) and spreadsheet calculations. In fact, before the proliferation of the spreadsheet program Visicalc in the early 1980s, the personal computer was viewed as having all the business utility of a ham radio. To this day, the main tasks performed on the PC are word-processing and spreadsheet functions.

Look at the business situation or process, whatever it is. In doing so, you will identify needs. Be sure you

- examine all aspects of the situation and process: investigate inputs, outputs, equipment, manpower, work performed, costs, timing, and (key point) relationship to other processes
- talk with the people doing the actual work: those who

    are doing the tasks and using the current system can
    point out practical ways to save time, effort, and money
- flowchart the current process: a visual representation of
a system or process can help you grasp it quickly and
firmly and make it easier to present to others

In other words, understand the situation before you start trying to
improve it.

Understand the Capabilities of the Technology

With a firm grasp of the business situation, you can now turn to the
technology. Your goal is to understand its overall nature and relevant
capabilities. You want to know a lot about what the technology does
and a bit about how it does it. You do not generally have to concern
yourself with real technological details. As with a car, you want to
know how far it can take you, what it can carry, and how fast it can go.
You do not need to understand the technical specs. You do, however,
have to understand a technology's unique capabilities because they
typically add significant value to the process, provided they are
properly applied.

Be very aware of the "rethinking" involved in exploiting technology. Consider the approach of Michael Wolff & Company. Their goal
is not simply to distribute books through electronic media, but to
"rethink the book" in light of that technology:

> We ask ourselves, "What is the property of this medium that
> makes it thrilling to its users?" One of the things we tell
> publishers is that it is not really a reader's medium. In the
> electronic medium, text is the thing that draws the fewest
> people. It is an applications medium. It has to *do* something.
> The property of this medium is to change things, to shorten
> them or reproduce them or separate them. It also provides
> instant and direct communication. That last element is a
> really interesting addition to traditional media because you
> don't have to go through the provider. You can go directly
> from one mind to another. So these are the kinds of things
> we are looking at and trying to isolate and integrate.

There are, of course, practical, implementation-related questions that always arise when you move toward a technological solution. Typical questions to be addressed include the following:

- What operating systems will this run on?
- What hardware and software purchases are essential to achieve functionality?
- How long will it take to learn to use the system? How easy is it to use?
- Will this interface properly with the technology now in place?
- What are the options regarding speed, storage, ease of use, and cost?
- What kind of flexibility is gained *and* what is lost by using this technology?
- How will introducing the technology change the situation or process?
- How will the people in this process be affected?

Finally, keep up on developments. At a minimum, keep abreast of the technology news in the general press. Read material at the level of the "Executive Computing" column in *The New York Times* and the "Technology" pages in *The Wall Street Journal*. By doing so, you'll get ideas and, over time, come to understand how technology works. It will not make you a techie, but you'll learn the buzzwords, which will help you communicate with techies, who can be reached through the right mix of tech talk and Standard English.

Focus on What the Technology Can—and Can't—Do in the Situation
After you have your facts in hand, you must compare both sides of the equation—the business side and the technological side—and assess the opportunity. You must fully understand the process you are trying to improve or replace and what the technology can and can't do.

You must understand the entire picture because that is your role, not the role of your computer consultant or the technology vendors. You are the buyer, and "buyer beware" holds true. The vendors are not out to rip you off or to you sell you something just for the hell of it. They want you to be satisfied. But they generally believe in what they are selling, so they'll take your order and fill it. So if you want to put all of your Aunt Tilley's 1,241 chicken recipes onto a CD-ROM disc complete with photos of each dish in various stages of completion and then try to sell it, nobody is going to stop you. The CD-ROM service bureau will ask you for your file and the job specs and ask how many you want them to press from the master. Then they'll work out a delivery date. They'll also expect to be paid even if you find that Aunt Tilley's recipes on CD-ROM don't sell because the installed base of CD-ROM readers in kitchens is minuscule or because your Aunt Tilley can't cook. Be sure to resolve such issues up front.

Develop a Plan

Once you have a true opportunity that you are reasonably sure can be exploited through technology, you have to write a project or business plan. The key elements of the plan include a cost/benefit analysis, a marketing plan, and an implementation plan.

The *cost/benefit analysis* is crucial. Too often a technological solution adds capital costs and ongoing expenses far in excess of the marginal added value realized. Here are some key questions to answer in your plan:

- What is the total cost of the current system, over three to five years, versus the total cost of the technology-based solution over that time?
- What is the payback period, the point at which the savings (or added earnings) on the new system outstrip the costs?
- What is the added functionality of the technology-based system? What is revolutionary in terms of capabilities, speed, or savings?

To minimize the up-front investment, use rented or leased equipment, service bureaus, or a corporate co-venturer's existing resources. Investing in new technologies, or getting others to invest in them, carries high risks. You often need deep pockets to succeed. Today, new IT gets commercialized so quickly that it rapidly finds its way to service vendors who hold themselves out to implement projects based on that technology. So if you have an idea and a plan, you can contract with a multimedia production shop to make a multimedia disc for a shopping mall directory, an instructional or promotional program, or any other application. Given this, wouldn't you be crazy to invest in (or ask someone else to invest in) this equipment and the people to operate it just to implement a multimedia project? Service vendors don't work cheap, but they're a lot cheaper than buying everything they provide. Also, if they're hungry and business is slow, you may be able to cut a good deal with them.

The *marketing plan* is the second essential element in the project or business plan. Many products or services, including worthy ones, get funded and developed but are not successfully brought to market. Why? The most common problems are

- incompetent marketing efforts
- insufficient distribution resources
- insurmountable competition

Incompetent marketing efforts range from poor positioning, packaging, or pricing to the astonishingly common mistake of thinking that because the product is so great, the world will beat a path to your door. The most successful technology products—those of IBM, Apple, Lotus, and Microsoft—had the benefit of superb marketing programs, even if the companies faltered at times. Marketing is as important as technical excellence to the success of a product, often more important. The marketing program must be properly conceived, properly funded, and properly targeted to the audience. (Regarding the latter, many technology products rely on reviews in the trades and the opinions of consultants; many licensing arrangement–based products for teenagers offer a fleeting opportunity.)

Distribution resources are essential because you can have a great product and great promo and press, but if people can't easily purchase your product, you are doomed. Your doom will arrive when someone with the right distribution system "knocks off" your product and captures the lion's share of the market. If, for example, you need to have the OEMs (original equipment manufacturers) in your distribution chain and you don't have them, you may be killing your product. If mail order or retail shelf space is the way to go, you'd better be able to go that way. Services do not require distribution. They require delivery. If you have a technology-based service, you have to be able to deliver it. You need extremely reliable contractors or a corporate co-venturer with the people, the communications infrastructure, and (key point) the billing mechanism to deliver the service properly.

Your business or project plan must also include an implementation plan: the tasks to be completed, who will complete them, with what resources, and when.

You must have a credible, competent team in place. Whether you are acting like a producer on a freestanding project, starting a virtual company, or seeking capital for a corporate start-up, you must have a team and you must be realistic and forthright about their qualifications. Do not place people on your team because they are your friends. Seek people with complementary skills—technical, marketing, distribution, financial, and organizational. Finally, ask yourself: If I were objectively judging the ability of this team to execute this project, would I believe them capable?

The pace of technological change, the power of information technology, and the diffusion of resources—many of the things that create the opportunity to act like a producer—also create the opportunity for multipreneurs to exploit technology. You can do this through projects, joint ventures, and entire businesses, but only if you clearly comprehend the business situation, the technological capabilities, and the planning dimensions.

To Increase Your Productivity with Technology

As is the case in using technology to create business opportunities, you do not have to be a techie to increase your business productivity. You do, however, have to learn how to use technology to do what you want to do.

If you are a technophobe, if you are a current or former manager who has avoided the keyboard, if you are computer illiterate and extremely busy, you may recoil at the very thought of learning to use a computer. I've experienced those situations myself. I did not even learn to type until, in my thirties, I taught myself from a book of touch-typing exercises. But I've also experienced the productivity boost that technology confers on the knowledge worker. No one who has learned to use the computer for a task they regularly need to do would ever go back to their old method. It's that simple.

To increase your productivity by using technology, you must

- overcome your fears and learn "the rules"
- know what you want to do and what the technology does
- get the right equipment, software, support, and service
- find the best way to learn the skills
- use your new skills and stay current

Overcome Your Fears and Learn "the Rules"

IT is simply a tool for working with information, yet it intimidates people more than most tools. There are several reasons for this. Some people, particularly high-level executives, simply cannot or will not relate to a keyboard. They don't know how to type or feel that keyboards are for secretaries and data entry clerks. Such attitudes can be charitably described as Neolithic and indeed are fading fast. (Touch typing, by the way, can be learned in about four weeks of practicing a half hour a day.) Other technophobes fear that they will break the "expensive computer" or somehow screw things up. The former fear is groundless. Just watch grade-schoolers use computers. They don't worry about breaking anything; they simply do what they want to do. The latter fear—that of screwing things up—is more realistic, as those of us who have turned off a computer before saving our work can attest.

The real fear that we call technophobia may simply be a fear of having to learn and obey "the rules." It is fear of the effort involved, a fear that it is too hard, a fear, perhaps, of "the rules" themselves. The rules are simply the protocols, the language, that the computer understands. Unfortunately, while the rules are logical, they are not intuitive, and your ability to follow the rules determines whether the computer will do what you want it to do, whether you will lose your work, and whether you can access information. Two things are at work here—your knowledge of the rules and the user-friendliness of your software. The rules often seem Draconian, enforced with reprimands such as "bad command or file name" and "fatal error," but while software can still be unforgiving, things have improved to the point at which you will be asked if you really want to close a file without saving it. In fact, some software will save your work automatically at regular intervals.

The rules amount to a new language. How did you learn English? By sitting down and learning rules, vocabulary, and grammar? No. You learned English by speaking it, by asking for things and either being understood or not. When you learned to drive, you were given a brief orientation to some rules and probably had to pass a written test, but you learned the rules of the road by driving. With technology, the best way to learn the rules is by using the computer and the software.

Know What You Want to Do and What the Technology Does

In any work situation, the tool you use depends upon the task. Unfortunately, technology is not as simple as the workbench tools that we all know, partly because the intellectual tasks that these tools help us perform are newer and not as straightforward. For example, there are many ways to define the operations involved in word processing or creating spreadsheets or designing graphs and charts, and features such as ease of use, service, support, and compatibility across brands can vary widely. As Steve Childs notes:

> People have to say to themselves, "I want to get this done and I know I can get it done by using a computer, but I'm going to have to invest some time in that." They have to hunger for something better. They have to recognize that the power is right there in front of them and realize that they have to get something done and that they can do it—and then they just have to invest. They have to stop frittering away their productive powers and start investing in greater production for tomorrow. It really is an issue of attitude and approach.

Start with the tasks you want to perform. Word processing, with a mail merge function, represents the bare minimum for the multipreneur. (Mail merge enables you to write a letter once and merge it with a list of names and addresses, invaluable for marketing your services.) The two most popular word-processing packages are currently Microsoft Word and WordPerfect. Beyond word processing lies desktop publishing systems, such as PageMaker, Ventura, and QuarkXPress, which offer formatting and layout capabilities unavailable in word-processing software, but which also take longer to learn. If you are using an IBM or IBM-compatible personal computer, it pays to have Microsoft Windows because it is so easy to use and so widely used.

The next level of necessity would include an electronic spreadsheet such as Excel or Lotus 1-2-3. A graphics package is also useful if you need to create charts and graphs from numerical data. Excel includes a good graphics package. Popular freestanding ones as of this writing include Harvard Graphics and PowerPoint. A database management system can be useful, but you can create simple databases in Excel, and Lotus 1-2-3. If you want to communicate with other computers or use E-mail, the Internet, or remote databases (that is, those outside your computer), you will need a modem and communications software. A modem can be either internal or external to your personal computer. Many PCs sold today come with an internal modem. Get 14,400 baud (a measure of speed) or faster and an easy-to-use communications package. In fact, you may want to get a fax modem so you can receive faxes via your personal computer. Then there are a slew of other specialized software tools ranging from office management software for maintaining your accounts receivable to specialized software for statistical analysis or architectural design.

One age-old question for many people was whether to purchase Apple or IBM technology. The big advantage of Apple's Macintosh technology was that it offered an icon-driven, point-and-click, drag-and-drop means of interacting with the computer. Traditionally IBM had more of the business market, thanks to its large installed base of mainframe computers, while Apple had greater share in the creative and educational communities. IBM and IBM compatibles still hold more share in the business market (except for desktop publishing and multimedia applications, in which Apple has an advantage), but thanks to Microsoft's Windows technology, such computers have had icon-driven, point-and-click mouse technology. This technology is a must, as much for flexibility and functionality as for ease of use. Also, more than 70 percent of business PCs have Windows, meaning that many of your clients and subcontractors use it, so sharing files will be easier if you use it, too.

The rest comes down to peripherals, the most essential of which is a printer. Get a laser printer if you can afford one. They are now the standard for business use. You could go with ink-jet, but they are slower and the prices of laser printers are falling. Color printing is where it gets more expensive. If you do a lot of presentations and enjoy using 35-mm slides, you might consider a device that takes pictures of your screen on film that can be developed at a regular processing shop, which will also mount them. One such device is the Polaroid Digital Palette.

Obviously an entire book could be devoted to this subject, and many have been. Let it suffice to say that many, perhaps most, of the tasks that a multipreneur working with intellectual content will perform will be performed better, easier, and faster with the right equipment. Choosing the right equipment begins with an inventory of the tasks you will have to perform, the frequency with which you will perform them, and the speed and quality at which they must be performed.

Get the Right Equipment, Software, Support and Service

Call it a lingering vestige of yuppiehood, but I believe in buying the best of anything that you can afford. I believe that the open market being what it is, differences in price generally reflect differences in quality and service. I also have come to believe that when it comes to technology, faster and bigger—with respect to calculation speed and memory size—are worth the extra money. Unfortunately, I didn't realize this before wasting hundreds of hours with slow machines and cumbersome software. Get up-to-date equipment. Don't overbuy insanely, but if you can afford it, overbuy a bit. That way you'll stay current longer.

I also believe in support. Lemons exist, and if you get one, it helps to have an outfit that stands behind its product. Thus I've always avoided the "gray market." Support means you have an 800 number (or at least some number) to call for help. You're able to purchase upgrades to the software at a deep discount, and you stand a better chance of getting useful documentation. Do look for a warranty, and use it when you need it.

Find the Best Way to Learn These Skills

Most people prefer muddling through software to any form of structured learning, even reading the user manual or using the tutorial programs that come with many packages. According to one survey, some 60 percent of the questions asked on vendors' help lines are answered in the first ten pages of the user manual. Muddling through has the advantage of being very hands-on, and you will get hands-on experience early in the learning process, but keep a good guide handy. The best guide may not necessarily be the one that comes with the software, which may be confusing, incomplete, or too complete. Try several ways of learning software and see what works for you.

When learning new software, technology consultant Steve Childs combines a structured approach with muddling around:

> I just bought Windows for Workgroups. I know it is going to improve my PC's performance, but I won't touch the software discs until I have looked over the manual carefully. I read software manuals. I don't read them cover to cover, but I look at what the software does, what it's capable of, how to install it, how you can really mess something up, and then I'll decide to load up the software and start muddling around. Nowadays, Windows software and Macintosh and all these help-assisted software packages and integrated tutorials really leave you with no excuse for not learning something. People say they're too busy, but if they think about it and if they hunger to improve their productivity, they take whatever help people have given them and use it. The help is there. There's no question about it.

Another good way to learn to use software, as noted in the section on developing business opportunities, is to ask others for help. Those who know can show. The best way for them to do that is with you, not them, sitting at the keyboard. To avoid using others as your memory, which will annoy them, write down what they tell you to do as you do it. Finally, consider taking a course. They tend to throw a lot at you, but if you learn well this way, you should definitely consider it.

Use Your New Skills and Stay Current

If you buy only the software you will use regularly, you'll have no trouble following the advice "Use your new skills." Staying current also means that when new equipment gets a lot faster, when the software gets a lot more functional or easier to use—or when your workload increases or becomes more complex—you should review your hardware, your software, and your skills. You may find that an upgrade to any, or to all three, could make your life much easier and more enjoyable.

One final word: As you work on a computer, always, always, always, always, always save your work often and, at the end of the session, make backup copies of all files you changed. Keep these copies elsewhere, off site. I speak from experience.

Get Technical

When it comes to technology, you can run, but you can't hide, and for the multipreneur, some of the greatest opportunities lie in developing technological solutions to process problems and technological means of leveraging, packaging, and distributing intellectual content. And to boost multipreneurial productivity, IT *is* the solution. Says consultant Steve Childs:

> You have to focus on the value of technology in handling information more effectively and in creating understanding more quickly. The question is, "Do you want to make money or not? Are you trying to communicate or not?" If you do want to make money and you do want to communicate, then don't be phobic, because the value is so much greater than the perceived cost.

For most multipreneurs, technology means one thing: opportunity.

9

Take Care of Business

Many businesspeople who try to establish themselves as independent operators fail not because they lack sales, technical, or interpersonal skills, but because they ignore certain business realities. Your career is, among other things, a business, so you should run it as a business. This chapter addresses the most important housekeeping details of running a multipreneurial career. It therefore represents something of a counterbalance to the previous chapters, which focused on broad career management principles and high-level business skills. Yet in a sense, the ability to run your career as a business also represents a high-level skill that encompasses aspects of planning, management, and financial analysis. Unless you take care of the business side of your career, you will be wedded to an ad hoc way of getting things done. When you have that side of your career well in hand, however, you will have the administrative details under control and you'll be able to pursue your main endeavors free of the worry that some important detail has been overlooked.

Some people make taking care of business look easy. They tend to be organized, detail oriented, left-brain dominant, and grounded in reality. Yet this does not describe everyone drawn to multipreneuring. In fact, I believe that while many of us will become multipreneurs, those most intensely drawn to such careers will often be disorganized, big picture, right-brain dominant, and driven by imagination. Both types can succeed as multipreneurs, but this chapter is included especially for the latter.

Just what does "take care of business" mean? Any business has what are known as front-office (or line) functions and back-office (or staff) functions. If you are a full-time, "permanent" employee, your employer takes care of the back office. If you are a multipreneur, it's your responsibility (along with everything else!).

The major back-office functions of a multipreneurial career include

- facilities management
- financial management
- benefits management
- business and household support
- legal, business insurance, and tax matters

Let's take these one at a time.

Facilities Management: Home or Away?

After you've worked in a company and then leave to become an independent contractor, you'll realize how much "business" was taken care of for you by your employer. Aside from salary and benefits, the area where this realization hits hardest is in facilities. You suddenly realize that the furnished office, the telephone, the computer, the fax machine, the copier, and all those supplies didn't get there by themselves. Now you have to line these things up yourself.

Here are the basics:

- office space and basic furniture
- telephone, telephone answering and fax equipment
- computer equipment, modem, and software
- copier or copy services or both
- sundry office items and supplies

Office Space and Basic Furniture

You have five options for getting office space: an office in your home, a turnkey office, a sublet (or desk space) within another business's office, an office you rent, or an office condominium. The home office has so many pros and cons that it is treated separately later in this chapter.

The turnkey office supplies most of what you need for a base fee plus variable costs such as telephone and use of the copier. Executive Suites and HQ Business Centers are two big chains in the business as of this writing, and there are local outfits everywhere. This arrangement usually provides furniture, telephone, utilities, a shared copier, and (two real bonuses) a shared receptionist and shared conference room. You also have neighbors, mostly other independents. The disadvantage, in terms of the space itself, can be cost. Long term, it is generally cheaper to rent or sublet your own space, although adding the receptionist and a conference room might swing the advantage back to the turnkey office.

Subletting space, which is what I do, is a great arrangement. It's often hard to find small offices through real estate agents because they earn relatively little on them and thus tend not to handle them. But a business with spare space wants to see it used. The price of a sublet will often beat that of either a turnkey or directly rented office. You'll have neighbors because you'll get to know the people you sublet from, if you don't already know them. (By the way, networking is a great way to find an office sublet.) You'll probably have to outfit it yourself, but you may find furniture and even a phone line in there already.

In many cities the commercial real estate pages and the Yellow Pages list "Desk Space" for rent. This can mean a separate office or, literally, a desk in an open office filled with other people. I did this when I had the Creditech Corporation. Aside from the desk and a phone, I got an address, a mailbox, and an answering service, which are all also available apart from the desk as a "business identity package." While turnkey office providers offer such packages, you can assemble a business identity all on your own—all it takes are business cards, letterhead, a business phone and answering machine (or answering service), and a post office box.

A rented office is, of course, where the commitment gets heavy because you have to arrange for and install everything and sign a lease. Thanks to the overbuilding of the late 1980s there is still a glut in some areas, but nobody would call office space cheap. The commitment is even heavier with an office condominium or co-op, which you actually own.

Skimp on furniture, especially if you'll most often meet at client sites, restaurants, and hotels. Project an image with your clothing instead of furniture. But don't suffer with uncomfortable stuff or with poor lighting. Just go the secondhand, want-ad, flea-market, garage-sale, close-out, liquidation route. If you are in a business in which your clients have to visit you, you will have to pay more attention to your office interior. Many multipreneurs do see clients in their home-based offices, and as long as the space is clean, orderly, and comfortable this generally presents no problem.

Telephone, Telephone Answering and Fax Equipment

I've had telephone numbers that end in 00 (332-3600). They are nice and look good on a business card—and, at least in Massachusetts, it didn't cost extra. I simply asked for one. Would I pay for one (or for a number like 3030 or 8080)? Certainly not more than a few bucks a month, but my business doesn't depend on people remembering my number. My business never required an 800 number, either, but if I were selling something direct, I sure would have one. Car phones are nice, but the value depends on your business.

As to other phone-related items, I like answering machines more than answering services. Answering services add the human dimension with all its incompetence and unpleasantness and, in my experience, little of its warmth or personal service. (Granted, this is an expatriate New Yorker's provincial view.) Even if the service is polite and competent, with an answering machine or the phone company's voice mail you can get more business done because people are more inclined to leave detailed information or answers to your questions on a machine rather than bother a real live person to take it all down.

Clients typically expect you to have a fax machine. From an integrated phone/fax unit you have both functions on a single, split line, which saves money. I recommend a fax for most multipreneurs. Don't forget to consider a fax modem if you are buying a computer. E-mail has grown rapidly in popularity, certainly within companies,

---

How Big Should You Try to Appear?

Many sole practitioners worry about how large they should make their businesses appear. This may mean more to the practitioners than to their clients. The matter reaches comical proportions when people buy tapes for their telephones that produce "office noises in the background" so people on the other end hear the doings of a bustling company. (Yes, it's true.) Others agonize over whether living on Deer Hart Lane rather than Washington Street, which sounds more commercial, will hurt business. Still others overspend to put on a front.

This energy, time, and money would be better spent on finding ways to add value for your clients. People everywhere have noticed that the world of work has changed radically and that many talented, productive people work in one-person offices or home offices. The best way to handle the home office situation, when it comes up, is to position it as a lifestyle choice ("I like having my work close at hand, because I get ideas 'round the clock") and as an advantage for your client ("Without the overhead, I can keep my rates reasonable"). If you have an actual business office, be proud of it regardless of its size. Many of the people you deal with will envy you.

Ultimately you have to do what makes you and your clients comfortable. I've hired independents who work out of their homes when I was on staff and when I was an independent myself. As an independent, I've had the "look bigger" setup at times, and I've worked out of my home. In reality, neither cooking up ruses to look bigger nor admitting to home work will make or break you. What you say on the phone is a hell of a lot more important than anything you could have going on in the background.

but less so between companies since there is still neither one standard software nor a way for all E-mail software to interface easily, although this is changing quickly.

Computer Equipment, Modem, and Software

In general, when I'm in the market for a technologically oriented product or service, I find friends who do their homework and comparison shop. Then, with modification for my needs, I do what they did in terms of equipment, price, and place of purchase. This works for me and saves time and shoe leather. (See chapter 8.)

Copier or Copy Services

I know people in home offices who own their copiers, but I personally don't want the expense of purchase, the hassle of supplies and breakdowns, the copy-quality problems, or the tedium of hand-feeding 350-page manuscripts. I need a copier with a good automatic feed, and they are expensive. With so many copy services in my area, their hours, prices, quality, and service are quite competitive. In today's business climate you're apt to find a Kinko's or another chain in smaller towns and cities across America, not just in the big metropolises. However, if your taste or business dictates that you get a copier, get one with a good warranty and service contract.

Sundry Office Items and Supplies

Get what you need in the way of paper, envelopes, labels, folders, markers, paper clips, organizers and such at a warehouse-type store like Staples, where the items are discounted. Buy more than one box of envelopes so you don't run out five minutes before a client meeting or a FedEx deadline.

Pros and Cons: The Home Office

For anyone, the home office decision hinges on your working situation, living situation, and temperament. If you live alone, have the space, meet at client sites, and don't mind having your worklife and personal life under one roof, you're the ideal candidate for a home office. However, if you have a spouse and children (or roommates), have little space, work mostly at home, and like a clear demarcation between your working and nonworking lives, you will suffer in a home office.

I like having an office outside my home, but that may be because I spent years in corporate life, always having an office to go to. Also, my family can be a real magnet for my attention. Perhaps because at some level I am always thinking about work, I like physically separate working and nonworking environments. When I worked in an office in my home, I enjoyed it, but I also spent half my time on the road as a corporate trainer. Most everyone I know who works at home enjoys it. Many have been doing it for years.

The major "pros" of working at home have to do with cost and lifestyle, but mostly cost. Work-and-technology consultant Joanne Pratt and CPA Larry Elkin each put the cost advantage of a home office, as opposed to renting an office, at about $10,000 a year. According to Hastings-on-Hudson, New York–based certified public accountant Larry Elkin:

> A lot of people focus on the tax deductibility of the home office and miss the big picture. The deduction can be hard to get unless you see clients there and use it for no personal purposes. But even without deducting a fraction of the utilities and of the depreciation and maintenance on your home, the advantage is huge. You're going to be paying your rent or mortgage anyway, you're going to be heating it anyway, so on a cash-flow basis—and cash flow is critical in a new business—you've got no incremental cost. You have a lot of avoided costs. And all your marginal costs of maintaining the office—the second phone line, the fax line, and your equipment and supplies—will be as deductible as they would be anywhere.

You also have no broker's fees, no commute, and minimal lunch expense. Many also like the convenience of the setup and the closeness of family. Political and media consultant Todd Domke is among them:

A lot of my work is about ideas. And you get ideas in the shower, shaving, reading the newspaper, running an errand. So a lot of times when I get an idea, a division between my work and home life would act as a barrier in a way. I don't need a clear line between my worklife and my nonworklife because in the kind of work I do, that line doesn't really exist. Sometimes I have to work evenings and sometimes weekends. In some campaigns I get very little time off, and if I do get a little time, I can have dinner with my family. If I have to work long hours, I can at least tuck my daughter into bed. This arrangement helps me feel integrated, not as though I have a dual life.

Historically this is how most people lived. Before the twentieth century, most people worked in businesses or shops or on farms adjacent to home, so there's nothing odd about it. Yet the advantages of working at home mean nothing if you can't be productive and make a good living. Thus the major "cons" of working at home revolve around family management, time management, and minimizing personal business during work hours, which can be tougher when you're working at home.

Facilities management is about giving yourself every chance of success. Our tools and workspaces have a lot to do with our day-to-day reality. Within your budget, do all that you can to make that reality pleasant, productive, and supportive. To take care of business on the facilities management front, outfit yourself with a real office either at home or elsewhere. You need a place to think, plan, write, calculate, reflect, and work.

Financial Management: Get a Grip

Financial management is about planning and controlling to plan. Accountant Larry Elkin points out:

The underlying mistake—everything else becomes symptomatic—is failure to plan, including failure to make up a budget and a cash-flow schedule. Ask somebody in month one of their start-up what their total expenditures will be for the first twelve months and most of the time you'll get a blank look and an "I don't know." How much are you going to spend on equipment? How much on furniture? They don't know. This thinking assumes no constraints. It's important to remember this is not the corporate well, where you can go to the treasurer and say, "Cut me another check." That thinking can kill you.

If you are on staff in a company, or recently were, you first have to know what you were earning. The calculation involved is minimal. Most of us know our gross income and take-home pay or can readily get those figures from our tax records, specifically from form W-2 from employers and form 1099 from clients. Also, add any income from savings, investments, rents, alimony, and child support as well as capital gains, gifts, and inheritances, although you usually can't count on capital gains, gifts, and inheritances as ongoing income.

The important number in this calculation is your total dollar income rather than your take-home pay. It is tempting to think in terms of matching your take-home pay without an employer. After all, that is what you have been living on and using to pay your bills. But thinking in terms of your take-home pay excludes the matter of income taxes and the self-employment tax. Such thinking leads many self-employed individuals to fail to make estimated quarterly tax payments, which the IRS requires because there's no employer to withhold taxes. If you do not pay quarterly estimated taxes, you owe them all by April 15 the following year—plus a penalty in the form of an interest charge calculated on the dollars overdue and the days outstanding. This is an expensive way to finance your business since the interest on a business or home-equity loan would be deductible, while the penalty is not. On federal taxes, the interest rate floats. On state taxes, also due quarterly, some states have floating rates and some have fixed rates. Either way, it gets expensive.

You will probably have to do some figuring to understand your annual expenses. The table on page 215 shows suggested percentage-of-income levels for typical expenses at various incomes. So that you don't fudge when filling in the blanks, ignore the suggested levels

Ideal Budget Percentage Allocation

Status Gross Income	Single $30,000–$40,000	Married, No Children $50,000–$75,000	Married with Children $75,000–$100,000	Your Allocation
Taxes	16–18	19–21	22–24	_____
Child Care	0–0	0–0	6–7	_____
Debt Payment	4–5	3–4	1–2	_____
Insurance	6–7	6–7	6–7	_____
Housing	17–18	16–18	14–16	_____
Transportation	4–5	4–5	3–4	_____
Utilities	3–4	3–4	2–3	_____
Clothing	3–4	3–4	3–4	_____
Contributions/Gifts	2–3	2–3	2–3	_____
Dues/Subscriptions	1–2	1–2	1–1	_____
Education	1–2	1–2	2–3	_____
Entertainment/Hobbies	5–6	5–6	5–6	_____
Food	7–8	7–8	7–8	_____
Household	5–6	4–5	3–4	_____
Medical	2–3	2–3	2–3	_____
Personal Care	2–3	2–3	1–2	_____
Vacations	3–5	3–4	2–3	_____
Mystery Cash	1–1	1–1	1–1	_____
Savings	8–10	9–11	8–10	_____

Source: Shires Financial Group, Little, CO

Notes:

- These percentages are ideal. Most people spend more on taxes (due to poor planning) and on debt payments, housing, and transportation.
- These percentages are ranges. For each income level, the low percentages total 90%, while the high percentages total 110%. This allows for flexibility and personal spending priorities.
- To equate these percentages to monthly dollar expenditures for the three income levels, use the monthly income figure of $2,900 for the $30,000–$40,000 level, use $5,200 for the $50,000–$75,000 level, and use $7,300 for the $75,000–$100,000 level, then apply the monthly percentages to these amounts.

until you have figured out what you are spending. Notice that if you are currently or were recently employed, two of these categories— insurance and medical expenses—might relate to employer-paid benefits. If so, enter only the amounts you paid through deductions and out-of-pocket for your life, disability, and health insurance as well as any unreimbursed medical and dental expenses.

You must know how you are spending your money. Keeping a written record of everything you spend for a month or two is—when coupled with your tax records, pay stubs, and checkbook—the best way of knowing this. Absent the discipline to do this, you must take an unemotional look at the amount of cash you go through and where it goes. Think carefully. Food bills (especially take-out and restaurant meals) add up fast, as do cash payments to baby-sitters and other household help. Video rentals (and late charges) and other accouterments of modern life insidiously boost your cost of living. According to Scott Shires of Shires Financial Group in Littleton, Colorado, even a close accounting will leave you with a "mystery cash" category—money that you simply cannot trace.

Given that our national saving rate is below 5 percent of income and consumer debt outstanding is well over 15 percent of income, a few words on debt are in order. In business—and remember, the goal is to run your career as a business—you take on short-term debt to finance the purchase of short-term assets and you take on long-term debt to finance the purchase of long-term assets. The inventory loan is the classic short-term business loan. The company borrows $50,000 to buy raw materials—say, fabric and thread and buttons—makes the product (its inventory)—say, evening gowns or kids' togs—sells them for $100,000, and pays back the loan. A mortgage is the classic long-term business loan. The company buys a factory for $2 million and finances $1.5 million of it with a mortgage. The company then uses that factory to make products that it sells, and it uses part of the proceeds to pay off the mortgage.

Unfortunately, many households take on debt to finance a lifestyle, to buy restaurant meals, furniture, or cars that they could not otherwise afford. Using long-term debt to finance short-term expenditures is dangerous. From the standpoint of financial prudence, the vacation loan is the worst idea ever conceived. Many households permanently maintain levels of credit card debt, which in effect amounts to long-term debt financed at exorbitant rates.

American Express is smart to point out the benefit of its card (technically a T&E—travel and entertainment—card, not a credit card) carrying no monthly balance. You incur short-term T&E expenses every month, and you should pay them every month. In general, credit card debt can be deadly, but some installment debt makes sense. Car loans are a good example. The interest on them is no longer tax-deductible, but at least the life of the loan matches the life of the asset: you take a five-year loan to finance a car you will drive for five years. That's different from paying for a trip to Hawaii two years after taking it. Keep the relevant time frames in mind when you use debt, especially credit card debt. CPA Larry Elkin notes:

> A lot of these [one-person] businesses are being funded with credit cards. I don't suggest it, although I can see as a practical matter how it can happen in the short term. The question is: Can you honestly say that you are dealing with a short-term situation? Do you have a contract to do some work? Do you know that you can do the work? Do you know when you will be paid? Can you say that you have a thirty-day or forty-five-day wait? If so, that is a rational decision. You can see the end of the tunnel. That is very different from saying, "I'll just pile it on until the whole thing collapses."

Aside from a budget, the most useful tool in a financial plan is a cash-flow schedule. To create one, simply lay out your monthly *cash* income and your monthly *cash* expenses, month by month for a year. Then, for each month, subtract the expenses from the income. For each month, the result will be positive (a cash overage) or negative (a cash shortfall). This puts your cash income and outgo on a monthly basis so you can manage them on a monthly basis. Note the use of the term "cash." You have cash when an invoice is paid, not when you send it out. The cash-flow schedule pulls together several important elements:

- your sources of income *and their timing*
- your recurrent monthly expenses (your monthly "nut")

- your nonmonthly expenses *and their timing* (quarterly tax payments, summer camp tuition, holiday gifts)
- your cash overage or shortfall *on a monthly basis*

The object of the game of Cash Management is to maximize the number and size of monthly cash overages and to minimize the number and the size of monthly cash shortfalls. Timing can be essential in this game. When you get a shortfall (also known as negative cash flow), you must finance it. How? By drawing on savings or selling off investments, if you have them. If you don't, or if you would rather not touch them, and if your credit is good, you can finance shortfalls *temporarily* with credit cards or a credit line (preferably a business or home-equity loan or line of credit so that the interest is tax-deductible). Whether it is really temporary depends upon cash overages in later months. If you consistently run cash overages, you have positive cash flow. You're ahead of the game, and if you stay there, you will emerge a winner.

There is also the option of reducing your expenditures. (Yes, I'm serious.) Can you cut out the health club or go to a less tony one? Should you sell your car and get a cheaper model? What about that food bill? How about a vacation close to home, or at home, this year? Movies instead of concerts? Board games instead of movies? Basic cable instead of premium? No single trapping of middle- to upper-middle-class life will break you, but together they add up to a lot that is nice but not necessary. Adopting a "financial siege mentality" can be very useful during a start-up period or a rough patch.

To have a grip on your finances is to have a grip on reality. The way to get and maintain that grip is through information. Whether it is on a computer, in a ledger, or on pads of paper, information is the key. Keep track of everything. This simple skill will keep you grounded in reality.

Benefits Management: Be Your Own Benefits Manager

Ideally you need a self-funded package of benefits that will provide for your needs regardless of your terms or length of employment. You certainly need such a package if you prefer or are forced to work as an independent. Although most medium and large companies still offer good-to-excellent benefits, most will continue to cut costs by reducing the value of benefits and shifting more of the cost onto employees. Many employers will keep people off the payroll by hiring independent contractors. There is little motivation to add another person to the head count when that person will require group life, disability, health and dental insurance, a savings incentive plan, and a retirement plan. Few companies will be growing fast enough to play candyman with benefits. Thus we all should learn to be our own benefits managers.

The talk about "portable benefits" is encouraging but so far has just been talk. Under such a system, workers would have their own benefit plans that follow them from employer to employer and into periods of self-employment or unemployment. Employers who offer benefits would simply subsidize some or all of the cost of this package. The idea has its merits and its drawbacks, not least of which is the potential erosion of current benefit packages. Any way you look at it, packing your own benefits makes sense.

Pack Your Own Benefits

Under the circumstances, a self-funded, self-contained benefits package sounds like a great idea. But how do you do it? And what are the costs? They can, as you might imagine, add up, but you can control costs if you carefully choose your benefits and plan with foresight.

The planning begins with understanding what you have, or had, with your employer. Don't assume that you know what you had. If you were employed, you may have been in savings incentive and retirement plans. You should always know the value of your vested benefits in such plans. You also typically had life insurance, disability insurance, and either health insurance or membership in a health maintenance organization (HMO) or preferred provider organization (PPO)—all at group rates. You may also have had dental coverage and, in some progressive companies, health club memberships or children's day care. Did you have a company car? Also, don't forget paid vacation, holidays, and days off. Identify each element in the plan.

What your employer was paying for your benefits is irrelevant.

What is relevant is the amount that you must pay to cover your needs going forward. If you have identified each element in the plan you had while employed, you can then prioritize. Some benefits may have been necessities, others useless. If you are young and childless, for example, life insurance is less of a priority than if you head a family.

The next step is to assemble your own package of benefits. The following discussion assumes, perhaps unrealistically, that a major priority of yours will be short-term, emergency savings equal to six months of your take-home pay. When you have that taken care of, the following five elements represent a basic, self-funded benefits package:

- health insurance
- life insurance
- disability insurance
- long-term/retirement savings
- days off and vacations

The more of these areas you address on your own, partially or completely, the better. A blanket of basic benefits, and the ability to patch any holes that appear when you leave an employer, will let you navigate more freely. Paying for this as an independent has become more practical because when employers cut benefits and shift costs, they narrow the gap between what you pay in the group plan and what you pay on your own. However, the gap remains substantial. To calculate the cost of security, you must shop, learn the pricing and offerings, and then allocate money to this expenditure. If you used the budget table offered here, you have a head start on understanding your finances. After this analysis, which costs you nothing out-of-pocket, comes the hard part: buying—and paying for—your benefits. The following guidelines should help.

Health Insurance

For health insurance, an HMO or PPO will be less expensive from a given insurer than an indemnity plan, which allows you freely to choose your physicians. If you can afford a traditional indemnity plan such as Blue Cross/Blue Shield, wonderful. Be aware, however, that because they are not as cost-effective, they are becoming prohibitively expensive. HMOs and PPOs are cheaper because, as "managed care" organizations, they provide greater procedural and cost control than physicians' private practices. They contract directly with hospitals and labs to provide a caseload, with agreed-upon fee and cost schedules. An HMO typically provides its physicians and other caregivers with salaries, benefits, and offices. A PPO typically contracts with caregivers who are in private practice and does not pay their salaries or benefits or provide offices. However, the PPO does provide them with patients at agreed-upon fees and costs.

In a PPO, look for the ability to "go out of network," a feature that lets you choose physicians not on the list of providers under contract to deliver services through that PPO. This feature is subject to some provisions, but it gives you some flexibility. In an HMO, the ability to go out of network is usually more restricted.

Be selective in choosing an HMO or PPO. Their strengths, weaknesses, and levels of service can vary wildly. If you have a special need of any kind, selectivity becomes even more important. Check out the reputations of the hospitals to which the practitioners in the HMO or PPO admit their patients. In health care the key, of course, is always getting the most competent care you can and being comfortable with your caregivers.

When you leave an employer who has been providing health insurance benefits to twenty or more employees, you have a legal right under the Continuation Health Law, which is part of COBRA (Consolidated Omnibus Budget Reconciliation Act), to continue those benefits for eighteen months and in some cases longer. You are no longer subsidized by that employer, but you remain in that group plan, which generally yields a cost advantage to you for the level of benefits you had. This is usually the next best thing to having your benefits paid by the employer.

Another strategy is joining an affinity group, such as an industry or professional organization. Affinity groups represent a "group" from the standpoint of the insurer. I used one called the Massachusetts Businessperson's Association when my rights under COBRA ran out after I left Dun & Bradstreet. I found it expensive but worthwhile. However, the results of my research on affinity groups was mixed. While I ran across multipreneurs using affinity groups, not everyone believes they offer the best deal. Accountant Larry Elkin states:

I've become wary of affinity groups [as places to get benefits]. People tend to think that the affinity group has gone out and shopped the market for the best deal for its members. In many cases, I don't think that's true. Rather, it seems the affinity group has been approached by an insurance company that has said, "We'd like to market to your members. If you give us your membership list, we'll give you a royalty." The fact that a group allows its name to be used in connection with an offer does not—repeat, does not—mean that it is the best deal.

Larry goes on to note that getting health insurance for something approaching reasonable rates without joining a group plan is becoming more practicable.

This is an extremely fluid area that is changing dramatically. More and more jurisdictions are creating so-called community ratings. In effect, they are requiring companies to take on all comers in a community in what amounts to a kind of group-rated cost structure. Compared with not having this system, the young, healthy person who gets insured in one of these jurisdictions will probably pay a bit more, while older persons will actually pay a bit less and in effect be subsidized by the younger members.

However you do it, get health care coverage.

Life Insurance

Most of the books and articles advise buying life insurance strictly for the insurance coverage, not for "investment features." This translates to advice to buy only term insurance. Term insurance just provides a payment—the policy amount—to the beneficiary upon your death. Whole life and other forms of cash value insurance have an investment feature in that some of the premium (which is higher than that for comparable term insurance) goes into a tax-deferred investment fund where the cash value builds up. After the value builds, it can be borrowed against or paid to you, or you can stop paying your premiums and keep the insurance in force (because the future dividends will pay the future premiums). Other forms of cash value insurance include universal life and variable life, which offer various premium adjustments and investment choices. Term insurance offers a lower premium in the early years, but this rises with your age. Cash value insurance has a higher premium, but it's fixed at the time (that is, age) you purchase it.

The reasoning behind the advice to buy term insurance is that the policy amount is a straightforward number, and the price is actuarially derived given your age. Also, term coverage is relatively cheap during the typical child-rearing years of life. Meanwhile, not even actuaries can gauge future investment returns, and the pricing of investment features is all over the map. Thus many experts believe you'll do better buying term insurance and investing the extra money that you would have spent on a cash value policy. This assumes, however, that you will invest the money and not spend it.

I have about 20 percent of my total coverage in whole life, partly to force some long-term savings and partly because I like having a flat, albeit higher, premium (rather than the increasing premiums of term policies) and a policy that ultimately gets paid up and has cash value. When I get older and the term insurance gets expensive, my children will (I hope) be self-supporting and I'll drop the term, keep the whole life, and get into some serious estate planning (or serious spending, depending upon my mood).

Term insurance from an employer is generally priced a bit below what you'd pay on your own, but unless you are senior management you're usually limited to a multiple of your salary, about five times including some supplemental coverage. I have coverage of 8 times my annual earnings, reasoning that if I die and the proceeds are invested to yield 10 percent or so consistently, my income will be almost replaced. I believe in carrying your own life insurance, even if you are insured by an employer. To make your decision, consult an insurance professional or financial planner.

Disability Insurance
Disability insurance is an income replacement device. If you become disabled (partly or completely, depending upon the policy) through sickness or accident, the insurance company pays you a monthly income for life. The insurer wants to make certain that you cannot

profit by becoming disabled, so typically you are limited to 60–70 percent of your gross income and to one disability policy at a time. The 60–70 percent figure is meant to equate with one's typical after-tax income. If you are self-employed and become disabled, the monthly disability benefit payments are tax-exempt. If you are employed and your employer has been paying for your policy, your benefit would be subject to taxes. Either way, your earnings must be documented.

Disability insurance is expensive, particularly if you are not in a group plan. Nonetheless, I wouldn't go without it. As I've gotten older and witnessed some of life's more vicious vicissitudes, I've become a believer in this financial product.

Long-Term/Retirement Savings

The suggested approach to funding your living expenses in old age can be summed up in two words: Start saving. The single biggest mistake people make in this area is waiting too long to start saving, thus losing years and years of the power of compound interest. You may be familiar with the Rule of 72: If you take an interest rate and divide it into 72, you get the number of years that it will take to double a given sum. So at 10 percent, compounded, your money doubles every 7.2 years. At 5 percent it takes 14.4 years. This means that if you invest $50,000 at 10 percent and you have 15 years to go until you retire, that $50,000 will grow to about $200,000 upon your retirement. *But* if you have 30 years to go until you retire, it will grow to about $800,000. Invested at 10 percent, the $800,000 would throw off income of $80,000 a year, which is more fun to live on than $20,000 a year.

However you do it, you must save regularly and aggressively for your retirement. Since I know you can read, I know you are not counting on Social Security (unless you are sixty years of age or older). Neither should you count on your children or other relatives.

There is another option: Keep working into old age. Already there have been articles and loose talk about the baby boom generation not retiring. The reasons? The supposedly eternal youth of this crowd (oh, please), the lack of long-term employers to provide pensions, and the impending bankruptcy of the Social Security system. If you want to work until you drop, that's your decision. But while being wheeled from the shady side of the porch to the sunny side of the porch every afternoon isn't my idea of fun, neither is having to work to pay my bills at age seventy-five. There must be something in between, and while I earnestly hope that I'll have the physical, mental, and financial health to be able to find out what, for me, that is, the financial part requires saving and investing.

Many, many books have been written on investing. In a sense the genre is akin to weight-loss books. Everyone knows what to do, but nobody wants to do it, so they are always open to alternatives that promise quick, painless results. We know that to lose weight you must exercise and eat a balanced diet that limits total calories to the level needed to decrease your weight. Everyone knows that. Everyone also knows that to retire with a million you calculate what you need to save regularly given your age and a reasonable rate of return. Then regularly save that amount and monitor your investments. Never touch that money, and invest only in solid real estate and high-grade securities, emphasizing stocks for long-term appreciation, and in well-run mutual funds. That's it! Unless you are a professional money manager or trader, the rest is hooey. But listening to hooey is easier than saving money.

Be sure to take advantage of any tax-deferred plans available to you. As an independent, you will have income derived from professional fees. Given this, under current tax law you can, and should, start a Keogh plan as soon as possible. Of course, many of us think that we can't afford to do that, but actually we cannot afford not to. According to accountant Larry Elkin:

> The tax laws drive you so hard toward Keoghs and similar plans. If you've got a successful business—by the time you figure out your federal and state taxes and the self-employment taxes, which are 15 percent on that first $65-odd thousand and 2+ percent indefinitely now because of the Medicaid tax—your marginal tax rates can be very high. So the ability to shelter money in Keogh-type plans is very attractive. Where the strategy falls apart is in cash management, actually putting the money away. But I submit that if you are talking about putting aside 15 percent of net self-employment income, which is your typical limit, and you're

getting a tax subsidy for that, we are really talking about less than 10 percent of your income on an after-tax basis. Although people will cry about it, most of us have enough freedom in our budgets to handle that kind of commitment if we plan for it. If you don't, it hurts not only because you deprive yourself of a cushion in retirement or if something happens before retirement, but because you pay higher taxes every year along the way.

Finally, never pass up free money. A woman I knew at a company I've worked for stunned me one day by revealing that she did not participate in the savings incentive plan (SIP). (SIPs are tax-deferred plans that many companies have set up to encourage their employees to save and invest.) This SIP, like others I've participated in, allowed you to deduct up to 6 percent from your salary and place it in one or more of four funds. Then the company matched each dollar you contributed with seventy-five cents. By choosing not to be in the plan, the woman passed up $450 for each $10,000 of salary per year ($= \$10,000 \times 6\% \times .75$). Since she was earning $40,000 she was forgoing $1,800 every year she was there. It was free money! Right now you may be thinking that she needed the 6 percent of current income and couldn't afford the deduction. Wrong. She had no dependents, no husband, no kids, no aging relatives, no big rent, no cocaine or Bergdorf Goodman habit, no exorbitant expenses. She also had either no financial acumen or a feeling that she didn't deserve part of her total compensation, or both. Never pass up free money.

Vacations and Days Off
Granted, vacations and days off may not hold the priority you should assign to the above benefits, but assign them some priority. First, they are, or were, part of your compensation from a full-time employer, so if you are trying to match the benefits of such a setup, time off should be part of the deal. Second, only time off can assuage the mental, emotional, and creative fatigue you will naturally experience if you work hard at intellectual pursuits. Perhaps you are, or can be, one of those guys or gals who operates from the deck of a Colorado cabin in the sky and who takes chunks of vacation time each day, mountain

biking, rock climbing, or trout fishing. But if you are a city-bound grind, you either have to move to the Rockies or take vacations and days off. Third, if you have a family, you sometimes, of necessity, have to put them after your customers, prospects, and subcontractors, which of course is not where they belong. Vacations and days off provide time to put the people you care about most first. Finally, there is the issue of deserving it. You do deserve a vacation, don't you? Even beasts of burden get the yoke off now and then.

Business and Household Support: Get What You Need in Order to Succeed

As a multipreneur you have two choices: either go crazy trying to do everything yourself or find people to help, including

- accountants and attorneys
- part-time file clerk, secretary, or office manager
- secretarial/transcription services
- librarians and information-on-demand services (such as Find/SVP in New York City)
- repair people on service contracts
- household help (day care provider, cleaning/cooking person, lawn care service, shopper, handyman)

Before you say, "Obviously, this guy thinks I'm made of the long green, the big bucks, the do-re-mi," please know that I don't think that. But part of running your career as a business is realizing up front that division of labor still makes sense. After reaching that conclusion, you have to revisit questions such as: Where do I add the most value? Are there tasks that must get done, but that I cannot or will not do or do well enough? What is my time worth versus what I must pay someone else to do these tasks? What earnings can I achieve with the time saved?

You shouldn't take on financial commitments that you can't handle, but you have to think in terms of the support you legitimately need in order to succeed and still have a life outside your work. Notice I said "legitimately need." When you are starting out, unless you are in very good shape financially *and* in terms of your flow of business, you do not "need" even a part-time secretary, let alone a full-time one. You don't need a salesperson or an on-staff office manager. Proceed with caution and at a measured pace in this area, but do proceed. Whenever I've hired the right person for the task, it has always been worth the money.

Legal, Business Insurance, and Tax Matters: Cover Your Assets

In any company or professional services firm, the legal department or outside counsel draws up the contracts, sees to insurance needs, and otherwise keeps the outfit from running afoul of the law, while the accounting department takes care of tax matters.

Unlike many businesspeople, I don't believe that you need a lawyer at your elbow every step of the way. Yet you must make sure that your business is legal and legally protected. Keeping your business legal extends beyond the obvious measure of staying out of illegal businesses. It entails things like dealing with licensed professionals (try going after an unlicensed plumber or electrician who messes up), avoiding the gray and black market when you buy equipment (try getting service and support), and respecting copyright and patent laws (try getting sued for violating them).

I believe in letter agreements rather than lengthy contracts. Even in a letter agreement, there can be two potentially sticky subjects: nondisclosure/noncompete provisions and provisions regarding proprietary material. A nondisclosure provision states that you will not pass on information given to you by your client. These provisions are fairly standard and shouldn't send you running to an attorney. Many clients require them. They are merely trying to protect themselves. Noncompete provisions are different and less common. When you sell a business, a noncompete provision will prohibit you from having a similar business in a region, or even at all, for some period. Such provisions are at times part of severance agreements. A noncompete provision could be a condition of doing certain work or creating a line of business for a client or co-venturer. Be careful about signing anything that can limit your ability to earn a living. Get legal advice on this one.

Provisions regarding proprietary material can be tricky, as can the issue of what materials belong to whom. Are your notes and background research materials yours or your client's? How much of your "approach" to a project is proprietary in the legal, rather than marketing, sense of the term? Who owns the copyrights and subsidiary rights to work you create? Here is another area in which legal advice can be necessary, depending on the money, time, effort, and potential involved in the project. If you think this doesn't matter, think instead of how you'd feel if you did six months of very specialized work on something for a half-decent daily rate and then that something went on to make, literally, millions and millions of dollars. It happens. Protect yourself.

When you begin an independent career or a business, you materially change your status, so you should reconsider your property and casualty insurance coverage. If you have computer equipment in a home-based business, it may not be covered for fire, theft, and water damage under your homeowner's or renter's policy. (Check your policy.) Since standard business property and casualty insurance is so cheap, you may as well get some.

On tax matters get the proper guidance from an accountant who is right for your needs. If you subcontract work or have employees, be certain that every form is filed and every detail covered. A big benefit of going independent is that you can deduct as business expenses many professional expenses that you could not deduct as an employee. These can include phone calls, professional publications, supplies, and so on. Save your receipts.

Avoid thinking you can spend like a sailor because the expenses are deductible. If your marginal tax rate is 30 percent and you spend $10,000 on deductible items and activities, you are still $7,000 lighter, and that's if you can deduct it all in one year. Again, it pays to have taxes prepared by an accountant (and not a self-styled "tax preparer").

Not being an attorney, insurance broker, or accountant, I cannot dispense legal, insurance, or tax advice, but merely convey my own and others' experience and opinions. This section is here to raise these issues and to suggest that you get the right professionals to take care of, or to show you how to take care of, these issues.

Going About Your Business

Business does not take care of itself. Your office, finances, benefits, support people, and legal, insurance, and tax matters will not take care of themselves. Get the right things in place, preferably before launching a multipreneurial career or at least early on in the game.

By planning ahead, you will have a suitable office. You will have a financial plan and a benefits package. You will have people to call for help. You will have your legal, business insurance, and tax matters squared away, and you will have the proper paperwork for your banker, your accountant, and your clients. You have the peace of mind that comes with being on top of things because you devoted the time and effort to planning and to putting things in place.

···

part four

The Transition
to Multipreneuring

10

Making the Transition

Becoming a multipreneur is something you do in your own way. The phrase "in your own way" allows for a range that extends from the relatively simple step of adopting certain attitudes to the more complex task of building a new professional identity. You can move full speed ahead or take a very gradual approach to multipreneuring. Regardless of your multipreneurial goals, you will be pursuing them from your own starting point. Your knowledge, skills, education, employment history, and current situation are uniquely yours and will affect your transition into multipreneuring.

Multipreneuring is both a mind-set and a set of behaviors. To apply any given principle or practice, you must develop the right attitude and take the right action. For example, to manage risk aggressively, you must think clearly about risks and rewards, then pursue the rewards while hedging the risks. To act like a producer, you must first think like one. To take care of business, you must believe that doing so is not only worthwhile, but absolutely essential; only then can you put the pieces in place. So as you make the transition, try to achieve close alignment between attitude and action, between the internal and the external.

The beauty of multipreneuring as a career management strategy is that it enables you to take a methodical, useful approach to inevitable change. If your career has been chaotic or insecure, that is not the real problem. If it were, the solution would be to find a stable career or to somehow make your current career more secure. But there aren't really any stable, secure careers. The problem is environmental. Career chaos and insecurity are symptomatic of the real "problem," which is the fact of continual change in our economy. This situation calls for true adaptation rather than gyrations aimed at preserving the status quo.

General Guidelines for Making the Transition

Before we examine tactics for making the transition to multipreneuring, here are some general guidelines:

- Realize this transition will take months, at least.
- Avoid or minimize debt and negative cash flow.
- Reach out to others and maintain your social life.
- Work with your self and your subconscious to resolve the past and move forward.

Realize this transition will take months, at least, to bear fruit. It can take years to become established as a multipreneur, which is true of other careers as well. In career matters, the long view is the best view. Why will the transition to multipreneuring take months? Because the external work—getting training, setting up a business, soliciting customers—is itself time-consuming and involves trial and error. The internal work, on things such as your identity and approach to risk, by its nature requires thought and reflection over time. We give time to the things we consider priorities. Make restructuring your career a priority.

Avoid or minimize debt and negative cash flow during the transition. You'll recall that cash flow is monthly income minus monthly outgo and that negative cash flow occurs when the latter exceeds the former. Most people who wind up in negative cash flow choose drifting, dreaming, or denial above calculating and planning. In fact, the reason that people don't do financial planning is that the facts discovered in the process would make it more difficult for them to dwell in denial. Like the ill person who avoids lab tests, they don't want to know if anything is wrong. Debt and negative cash flow kill independent careers.

Reach out to others and maintain your social life during the transition. If you are voluntarily leaving a long-standing career for multi-preneuring, you may be criticized. If you are involuntarily unemployed, you may feel depressed. People may avoid you because they think you want them to or because you remind them of unpleasant realities. You must, however, maintain contact with your real friends and others who want to see you succeed, and resist becoming overly withdrawn, if withdrawing is how you cope with loss. Your real friends will be there to encourage you, and just their presence will remind you of your true value. The act of reaching out to others will also give you a sense of social accomplishment. You must, of course, avoid people who are negative or discouraging.

Work with your self and your subconscious to resolve the past and move forward. Learn from your mistakes and move on. Objectify your role in past failures and look for patterns and themes. The reasons for our success and failure are often buried deep within us, and there is no substitute for understanding both. This doesn't happen by itself. Find the gaps between your dreams and your delivery, between your potential and your performance—and address them. There is no other way to grow.

Typical Starting Points in the Transition

Maybe you are happy in your current employment situation. Perhaps you have the perfect setup, with the right mix of challenge and comfort, opportunity and security. But unfortunately your situation will most likely change. No company can guarantee your future, so abandon any sense of conferred security you may still harbor. Some people get blindsided in the workplace because they don't realize that their contribution is not worth their salary, that decades of service do not mean they can rest on their laurels, that when it comes down to you or them, invariably you will be the one to go.

If you've already been thrown overboard, the barrier you face may be anything but a smug sense of security. Instead you may suffer from utter insecurity. You may worry that you'll never recover your professional footing and earning power. If this book has not yet guided you to new hope and aspirations, this chapter will.

Clearly, if you are currently employed in some capacity, you have an advantage in making the transition to multipreneuring. That advantage is financial, to be sure, but it is also psychological. However, being gainfully employed also has two disadvantages aside from the potential for a false sense of security. You may lack the time necessary for serious work on your career, or you may lack the motivation to try a really new approach. If you are unemployed and in negative cash flow, you are at a financial disadvantage, which can mean a psychological disadvantage. However, you do have the advantage of time. You are probably also ready to try something other than a traditional job search or casting about for projects.

The best way to begin the transition into multipreneuring is systematically to use one or more transition tactics geared to helping you maintain your cash flow while learning new skills, getting experience, and establishing new relationships. These transition tactics are not necessarily new forms of employment; what makes them transition tactics is the overarching strategy of fitting them into your vision of a multipreneurial career. Keep that vision in mind as you consider them.

Transition Tactics

Stopgap Employment
If you're unemployed, a stopgap job may not lift you out of debt or depression, but it's a start. If you have a job you dislike and want to pursue a new but risky career, say, in the entertainment business, try a "bread-and-butter job" that will enable you to pay your rent or mortgage but allow you to reserve most of your energy for pursuing your new career. Ideally a stopgap job should also give you enough time or a flexible enough schedule to go on interviews or auditions or to write, study, or conduct the research you need to do.

There are, of course, better and worse stopgap jobs. I've always preferred to be indoors, out of the weather, and in a congenial environment, so I like the restaurant business. Phone work—telemarketing, fund-raising, market research, and collections—tends to be easy to get but tough to do for more than four or five hours a day. Market research is the best form of phone work in terms of wear and tear. Telemarketing pays the best, if you can rack up the sales and, thus, the commissions. Telephone collections is tough. (When I worked in collections in New York during the mid-1970s, I once heard a fellow worker yell into the phone: "Then sell your wheelchair and use the proceeds to pay your bills!") Retail sales offers a nicer environment and the opportunity for commissions, which on the right line of cosmetics, clothing, or appliances can add up.

Volunteer Work or Internship
If you can handle it financially, volunteer work or a low-pay or no-pay internship can be a fine transition tactic. The key is to maximize the knowledge, experience, credentials, and contacts you get and, to the extent possible, to avoid drudge work that precludes your getting knowledge and experience. Credentials come, first, in the form of your being able to say you volunteered or interned. The prestige factor can also play a role here—if you interned at MTV, for example, the world is such that that fact alone can overshadow your having only painted the walls. The second form of credential is a bona fide reference, which you have a right to get from any outfit where you've worked for love or money.

Moonlighting
Moonlighting is the black sheep of career management strategies, but it is a powerful transition tactic. It's worth examining closely.

Many people see having a second job or doing outside projects when you're employed full-time as falling somewhere between conducting a job search on company time and cheating on an expense account. Reflecting this view, a seasoned manager at a brokerage house told me: "We expect people to give at least 100 percent, and nobody with a second job can do that." He's not wrong. The assumption, sometimes explicit but more often implicit, in a full-time job is that you'll forsake all other employment. If you moonlight, it may be difficult to give "at least 100 percent" to your full-time job. But few tactics offer the benefits of moonlighting, some of which can even accrue to your employer.

An architect I know donated over two hundred hours over an eighteen-month period to building a playground in his town. He attended meetings, drew up plans, and educated officials about the state of the art in playgrounds, after learning it himself. He lined up the tools, equipment, and materials and coordinated the on-site work of the parent volunteers (public works employees did the necessary digging). For all this, he got the satisfaction of helping the town's children, gained some new contacts and knowledge about playground design, and learned a bit about how the town works. But he received no money. He donated over two hundred hours of his services, billable at about $20,000, while working full-time at the firm employing him, *but it wasn't moonlighting.*

Now, if pro bono work carries no moral taint (quite the contrary), why should moonlighting? The answer is that it shouldn't. Yet, to many, it does. Moonlighting does place a claim on your time and energy and reduces your emotional commitment to your employer.

An outside job or project always lays claim to some portion of your time, and it's foolish to pretend otherwise. The time you'll need to devote to outside work must come from somewhere: your family time (Can you get your spouse and children to understand?), your personal time (Can you give up the gym or golf?), or your on-the-job time (Can you tell your boss you can't stay late because you have a meeting elsewhere?). Finding the time to moonlight can represent a major hurdle. Family or personal time typically suffers, since a full-time job is generally a full-time job.

Since you will undoubtedly think about the second job or outside project while at your full-time job, this diversion amounts to a forgone resource for your employer, and he or she is not unreasonable to worry about it. On the plus side, however, the things you learn may be useful to your employer.

What about the issue of emotional commitment? Generally, if you are moonlighting, this commitment may be waning anyway, which may be healthy. Many moonlighters find that, in addition to getting the desired skills and experience, having a second source of income is liberating. It liberates you from total financial dependence upon a single entity, which is an important facet of multipreneuring.

Interestingly, one often experiences this sense of liberation even if the money is small. A manager of paralegals for a Washington,

D.C., law firm states that while her piecework job as outside case reviewer for an insurance company "pays only a couple of hundred dollars a case, I like the idea of being an entrepreneur." Working with the insurance company, she's learned about that industry's legal needs and, as a result, realizes that insurance offers her a viable career path.

Moonlighting can be difficult, especially on spouses and other loved ones. You can forget what your kids look like when they're awake. Your friends can stop calling after hearing how often you can't make it that night. Moonlighting is best done for a limited time, with clear goals and the support of others. Workaholics, take note: when moonlighting, you can easily lose sight of something more important than your career.

But, depending upon your goals, your skills, and the market, moonlighting can be among the sharpest tools in the multipreneurial workshop. It can help you develop skills you need but don't have and enable you to try out a new profession in a low-risk environment. It always leads to new contacts. It is a superb job change and career change tactic. It will reduce feelings of dependence on your employer and can represent an escape route if your full-time job is headed for the rocks. And, of course, the money helps.

Project Work or Independent Contractor Status

To undertake a multipreneurial job search when unemployed, you should be prepared to take on project work or independent contractor status in lieu of a full-time job. Like moonlighting, project work is a great way to develop skills you lack or have just acquired or that you need to renew. If you are rearing children full-time, it's a great way to keep in touch with an area, keep skills sharp, and, eventually, reenter your career or start a new one. It gives you the four things you need to get work: knowledge, experience, credentials, and contacts.

You may well be asking, "Why would I be able to get project work, unless I already have those things?" Here's why:

- There is a broad range of opportunities to work on a project basis given the downsizing and outsourcing trends of the 1990s. You have to dig, but they are there.

Five Things to Ask Yourself Before Moonlighting

To get the most from moonlighting, ask yourself the following questions:

1. What is my goal in moonlighting?
    Be clear as to whether you seek money, contacts, a new career path, artistic satisfaction, or some combination. Be very specific: How much money? Whom do you need as contacts? What new career path?

2. What do I have to sell?
    Think in terms of your skills *and* interests in deciding what you have to sell and where you can sell it. Moonlighting can help you break into an area in which you have an interest but need to develop skills.

3. Which should I seek, a part-time job or project work?
    While either arrangement demands time and effort, project work gives you greater control over your time. Although many jobs, such as a chef's, require your presence on site at a certain time, many do not.

4. How will I make the time for outside work?
    Resolve this beforehand rather than risk your marriage or sanity. Also, taking on a project with an unrealistic deadline and thinking, I'll rise to the occasion, tends not to work. Be honest with yourself and others, or you will undercut yourself.

5. How will I handle my employer?
    Honesty may not be the best policy here. Yet while most companies take a dim view of moonlighting, if there is a clear benefit to your employer, or your relationship can accommodate such an arrangement, it may be best to tell. It can make life easier.

- You can price yourself competitively and underprice yourself if necessary to get the work.
- Companies will take a flier more readily on an independent contractor than on a full-time hire. You still have to show you can do the job, but they won't be as wary or as conservative.
- You can and should form a business identity—or at least create project-specific résumés—so you can do mailings and hold yourself out to do this kind of work.
- You can trade on just about any experience you have. I became a corporate trainer as an independent contractor because of skills I acquired doing management presentations in banking and at D&B, plus an audition.

The work is out there, not in every field all the time, but in many fields much of the time. You have to hustle, and you might not make a killing, but this kind of work is another essential tactic for making the transition.

Another transition tactic is asking your employer to move you to independent contractor status. The downside, of course, is the insecurity (unless you also get a long-term, bulletproof contract) and the probable lack of a benefits package. If possible, negotiate a fee that will come close to your total compensation *plus* benefits, at least health care benefits. As a transition strategy, asking your employer for independent contractor status can give you "training wheels" as you move out of the company. You must negotiate a good deal, ideally one that provides a bonus or commission, while giving you time to pursue other interests, other clients, other plans. Many companies are willing to entertain such an offer, but, of course, when you ask for independent contractor status, you reveal your interest in other alternatives, which most managers still view as corporate infidelity. Know your priorities and move carefully in such situations.

Corporate Nomad or Executive/Professional Temp
Both of these terms mean the same thing: an executive, manager, or professional for hire on a temporary basis. The corporate nomad finds his or her own work, while the temp is placed by an agency. The agency may be a regular (that is, nontemporary) employment agency,

a temp agency expanding into the high end of the market or a specialized executive/professional temp agency. Deal with the latter if you can, because it will understand your needs and be focused on clients who need you. Also, executive/professional temp agencies often offer paid benefits (paid by the agency, not its clients). In such arrangements you become an employee of the temp agency.

Professional temping, particularly executive temping, is still new. While companies have long used temps in lower-level positions, they've recently begun using them at higher levels. Rising managerial and professional salaries have been a driver of this, as has the realization that companies often need a higher-level person for a specific task of limited duration.

A temporary position, however you find it, can generate cash and give you time to plan your next move. It may even lead to full-time employment—but don't count on it. Most firms seeking temporary managerial or professional help want exactly that. Although it happens, they are usually not auditioning people for full-time employment. Finally, if you use this tactic, register with several agencies.

Franchise or Purchase a Business
When you run a business, you are an entrepreneur. There is no reason that you can't be an entrepreneur within your portfolio of multipreneurial ventures and projects. But to franchise or purchase a business, you need capital. You must have money—yours or someone else's—for the franchise fee or purchase price. If you have money, great. But if you don't, it may be hard to find a business that will both pay you a good salary and provide your investors a good return. If you want to buy a franchise or business, think about how it fits into your lifetime career plans, since it is a major commitment. The self-analysis phase is key. You must know why you want a business, what your strengths and weaknesses are (and how to deal with the latter), and what kind of business you want. Here are some other guidelines:

- Always exercise due diligence. Check out the financial, credit, legal, and business records of the business and the individuals. Get all the data you can on them. Check references. Talk to customers, suppliers, competitors, and other franchisees—and not just those the other party gives you. Due diligence is *a must*. Never allow yourself to be talked out of exercising it.

- Do the numbers, then do them again. Valuing a business is difficult because you are making judgments about future earnings, future competitive realities, and your ability to manage in the future. The past and current performance of the business is, of course, necessary to know, but the most critical element—its future performance—is unknowable. Yet that is what you are buying. Be conservative when calculating future revenues and earnings.

- Have an attorney and an accountant, paid by you and experienced in business purchases, involved every step of the way. To keep them objective, pay them a fee, not a percentage of the deal. Talk to others who have purchased a franchise or business and ask them what their lawyers and accountants did right and wrong.

- Understand that there are good and bad franchises. The good ones are set up so that if you make money, the franchiser makes money. The bad ones are set up so that the franchiser makes money whether or not you do. Common problems: contractually forcing you to buy equipment or supplies from them at inflated prices, failing to deliver on marketing and advertising promises, intentionally or unintentionally misrepresenting past performance or future plans, encroaching on your territory, withdrawing support, selling out, or otherwise leaving franchisees holding the bag.

- Be sure you have enough capital and then some. To the degree possible, use future cash flow rather than your life savings to finance the purchase price or franchise fee. Get bank credit if possible. The two major reasons businesses fail have long been recognized as lack of capital and lack of managerial skill.

- Regarding the latter point, arrange for and get all the training and coaching you can from those selling you the business. It can be worthwhile to pay someone selling you a business to stick around and show you the

ropes for two or three months (depending upon their
personality and their feelings about selling). Unless
you've run this kind of business before, don't think it's
easy.

Running a real business, with real assets and real employees, is for
many the most satisfying and profitable career of all. But the multipreneur should beware. The commitment is usually (but not always)
long term, the hours can be murder, and much of what you must deal
with is administration unless and until you can get someone competent and trustworthy to run it for you—and that person will not work
for free.

Degree Programs, Continuing Education, Training, Self-Study

Even in this, the Information Age, the Age of the Knowledge
Worker, an astonishing number of people believe that once you are
out of college or graduate school or over the age of thirty (whichever
comes last), your formal education is over. Make no mistake, the
returns from education are among the highest you can get from
anything you can do.

Provided you have the time and money, education and training
represent the best of all transition tactics. You gain knowledge and
credentials and, if you are in a program offering a practicum or
internship, contacts and experience. You tell yourself and the world,
"I am making a change." You get time to think, reflect, and deepen
your perspective. Note that you don't have to undertake a degree
program to get these benefits. You'll get them to some extent even in
a once-a-week continuing ed course.

Moving up, down, or Laterally or Changing Divisions within Your Company

If you are now employed and want to begin a transition to multipreneuring, examine the surrounding territory for routes to your goal.
While everyone likes to move up, it is not going to happen as often as
it did in the past. However, companies are more open to nonpromo-
tional movement by employees than ever before. First, they have an
investment in you, and you are a known quantity. Second, most large
companies have job-posting systems, and many require that hiring

managers consider all interested internals before going outside. Third, in most companies there's an awareness of burnout, boredom, and frustrated ambition and therefore tolerance for those who want to explore in-company options. If you discuss an internal move, there is of course the danger that you are revealing a lack of commitment to your current job, but you may also be revealing it in other, even less positive, ways.

Although internal job postings are a good source of leads, you can also generate leads by mentioning your interest to someone you trust in the area into which you'd like to move or to someone in human resources. Other hints:

- Be prepared to wait. Don't take an internal position just to get out of your present one. You probably won't get more than one additional chance to make an internal move if you screw one up. If you move more often, you'll get a reputation for "bouncing around." Better to wait and prepare for a move to the position, or at least the area, that you really want.

- Understand that preparation has two sides: doing your best in your current position and getting knowledge, experience, and credentials to enable you to move to the new one. You have to make it easy for the person hiring you internally to do so. If you have outstanding performance appraisals and a great reputation, you make it easy. If you've completed coursework or (paid or unpaid) project work in the line you want to move into, again, you make it easy.

- Campaign for the move, but do so quietly and tastefully. The approach is summed up in the phrase "Let your interest be known." Don't express dissatisfaction with your current position. Emphasize your commitment to the company and your interest in the area and in developing along those lines. Try to find an ally—any ally—in the area of interest to you. A good word from a secretary can be gold.

- Be prepared to take a lateral move or even a step backward. Even today, few companies expect you to take a cut in salary in order to effect a career move, and some might doubt your sanity or, worse, your value for doing so. But, again, you have to give the hiring authority every reason to hire you. If you really want to make the move, a lateral should suffice. If you really, really want to make it, a move backward may even make sense.

Combine Transition Tactics

In general, a combination of transition tactics will work better than any single one. Using them in combination boosts their power and reduces the elapsed time needed for the transition. Think about it: if you get some formal training *and* do some moonlighting *and* prepare the way for either a lateral move or a move to independent contractor status, you have multiple supports for your transition, plus potential synergy. If all you do is take a course or take on a project or lobby for a move into your area of interest, you have one support and no synergy. Also, consider the time element. Simultaneous strategies can give you a year of experience in six months.

To make the transition to multipreneuring, start multipreneuring. Send yourself the right message by getting several transition strategies—both long term and short term—going at once.

Multipreneurial Pricing Strategies

Almost everyone who works as an independent finds pricing a tricky issue. Typically, new independent operators err on the side of undercharging because of a hunger to land the business or doubts about their ability to add value. There are reasons to underprice yourself— to increase your value added, to establish competitive advantage, or to get experience, the latter representing realistic pricing rather than underpricing. If you are overcharging, you will quickly find out. You won't get the sale, and if you ask why, your prospects will tell you. For some reason, prospects are not as quick to tell you when you undercharge.

It takes time to learn to price yourself properly. Start with an hourly and a daily rate, developed by looking at your value added, listening to others, and approximating an equivalent level of corporate compensation. Be sure to account for benefits and to allow for nonbillable selling and administrative time. Also, consider the competing costs for which your client could get the job done. You can ask what the prospect has budgeted for the project. Sometimes they'll tell you, sometimes not, reasoning that whatever they tell you will just happen to be what you will charge. To a degree, it's a game.

Almost all clients want a quote for the entire project. Nobody with budget responsibility is crazy enough to let you run the meter and then just pay you for the hours you rack up on a project.

If you properly cost out the job, you will find it easier to explain your pricing in negotiations. When I was a business-writer-for-hire (which I still am, at times), I would explain to clients that I was not charging them $1,200 for the four pages of copy I delivered, but for the sixteen pages I threw away. In market research, clients must often be told how many phone calls it takes to produce one complete survey. You have to tell your clients in a matter-of-fact manner how you work, what you're up against, and what's involved, or they may indeed think that you are overcharging them. To properly cost out a job, you must have a good idea of how long it will take you or your subcontractors to do the work. Think this through carefully.

Once you develop a quote for the job, before you present it to the prospect adjust it up or down in light of the difficulty of the project or client, competitive factors, and your desire for the business (or lack thereof).

If you use subcontractors, always mark up their rates either implicitly in your overall quote for the job or explicitly as a handling charge. Or just mark up each subcontractor's fee: subcontractor charges $250 a day, you pass it through as $300. You have to be compensated for bringing in, overseeing, and managing the subcontractors. If you have pricey subcontractors and mark up their fees, you may price yourself out. Sometimes, to get a job that you want, you can't mark up your "subs" at all. But always try to mark up their fees— or beat them down a bit on theirs (on the grounds that you're bringing them the business and they have no sales costs), then charge through their regular fees.

Always quote jobs as fees plus expenses. Companies vary in their generosity when reimbursing you for project-related expenses. Nobody will put you up at a Ritz-Carlton with an unlimited food and beverage tab. Some clients just give you an allowance or a limit (say, $35 a day for food and $75 for lodging, and you worry about the rest). Forget first-class travel. But structure the proposal so that you pass through all reasonable out-of-pocket expenses, including overnight package delivery services. Telephone and materials charges are generally yours to eat unless the job is telephone or materials intensive (for example, long-distance market research or materials on a print job). Save all receipts.

When in doubt, overprice. It is hard to raise your prices after you've lowered them to buy the business. If you give a client a break, tell him. Tell him that you really want to work with him so you'll adjust to his budgetary constraints this time. Show in the pricing section of your proposal that your normal rate is $500 a day, add up the ten days (or whatever), then show a 20 percent discount since they budgeted only $4,000 for the job. It's a slim reed to cling to when you next price a job for them, but it's better than nothing.

Finally, this discussion about pricing high assumes that you'll deliver what you said you would, when you said you would. If you can't deliver, you're just hosing people. They'll know it, they won't do business with you again, and they'll tell others about their experience. If you cheat yourself out of a few bucks, you'll still have a business. If you cheat your clients, you won't.

Finding a Job in Today's Marketplace

The job search—the search for the full-time, on-staff job on a company's payroll—still exists in the new economy. There will always be a need for full-time jobs in the core of companies, and many people will want one.

The traditional job search centered on responding to want ads, sending out résumés and cover letters, and registering with employment agencies, all with the objective of getting an interview that led to a full-time job. This approach also entailed figuring out what you wanted to do, analyzing the market, deciding where and in what capacity you wanted to work, networking, and interviewing for information.

Many people conducting job searches today ignore the fact that the world has changed. Some still believe that they can readily replace one employer with another who will give them substantially the same job at the same salary or better. But professionals at a certain salary, age, and level of responsibility who have lost their jobs are unlikely to find one at a company similar to the one that let them go. Those functions have been discontinued or consolidated or are being done with cheaper labor. And many companies now need an entirely different type of manager. CPA Larry Elkin points out:

In the corporate environment, there is a sort of adverse selection process that is pushing people out the door while the very same forces that are driving them out of the corporate [job] market are making these people ill suited to be entrepreneurs. When a company becomes flatter and leaner, it is saying to its executive force, "We don't want people who are going to manage in maintenance mode. We want hungry-shark types who are going to grow the business." The people whom the company is inclined to let go are the ones who like to manage something that exists, and those people find it hard to be entrepreneurs. When you're an entrepreneur, you start with nothing or with little. There's nothing to manage.

Again, the essential skill now in demand is the ability to add value, preferably to the essential processes of the business. So the fundamental task in finding work is to create or locate situations where you can add value constantly. This task differs from "finding a job." The multipreneurial job search involves an active, independent approach. Here are the basic principles:

- Market yourself rather than look for a job.
- Stay on "Code Blue."

- Get the right network in place.
- Use the right communications tools.
- Have a portfolio and work samples, if possible.
- Keep good records of all contacts.
- Understand the goal of an interview.

The Myth of Multiple Retainer Relationships

A true retainer is money paid to you by a client at the beginning of the month for services that may be more or less unspecified but within your area of expertise. You then charge hours against this amount and, if necessary, bill for any overage at the end of the month. Many an independent contractor hopes to establish several retainer relationships to replace his corporate income. The reasoning goes, "I'm now earning $70,000. To replace this, all I need is just three clients, each paying me a monthly retainer of only $2,000. That would be $72,000 (= $2,000 × three clients × twelve months)" Unfortunately it tends not to work out this way in practice. Why? Three reasons:

First, clients tend not to see an advantage in agreeing up front to give you money every month for vaguely identified needs. While it's nice that you offer a reduced "retainer rate" because it helps you lock in business and schedule your time, clients tend not to be impressed unless they've actually paid you higher rates in the past. You have a better shot at getting clients to agree to pay you monthly to do a specific ongoing project, such as a newsletter or some kind of repetitive market research. However, that is more in the nature of a monthly fee than a true retainer. While monthly fees for ongoing projects work better than retainers, unless whatever you are working on makes or saves money for your client and your contribution is unique, they are often discontinued or brought in-house during cost-cutting sprees. It can therefore hurt you to become too dependent upon them.

Market Yourself Rather than Look for a Job

In "looking for a job," you seek something that may or may not exist. At any given time there are a limited number of openings in the core of a company for staff workers of a given type, level, and salary range,

---

Second, you have to make sure presold time gets used up. Inventing make-work to burn up a retainer is difficult and quickly becomes apparent to the client. If the work isn't there for you, both you and your client will realize it in a month or so. You may then as a practical matter owe your client money or work.

Third, there is arithmetic. Billing out $6,000 a month for twenty-one workdays a month implies a daily rate of almost $300. That assumes that 100 percent of your time is billable, which it isn't. In reality, the billable percentage will be 50–65 percent due to selling and administrative time. If you bill out twelve days a month at $500 a day, you are doing okay, but not great. A rate of $100 an hour, or about $750 a day, is nice but tough to get month in month out. And it takes talent, credentials, and that thing called "reputation" to *consistently* bill $1,000 to $1,500 or more per day, unless you work for a major consulting firm, which can bill out even junior people at those rates.

Retainer relationships can be terrific for those who can pull them off. Such individuals are most often professors at substantial business schools (who in effect are successful multipreneurs), high-profile executives (who often have "sweetheart deals" with former employers or suppliers), or well-known specialists (such as turnaround artists or those with the latest BBI—big business idea). If your aim is to join their ranks, I'm right behind you (literally). Just be sure you envision the goal clearly and set a true course—but don't quit your job or beat up on yourself as a failure because of the myth of multiple retainer relationships.

in a given geographic area. In contrast, by marketing yourself, you sell something that you know exists: your skills, knowledge, and ability to add value. At a given time there are numerous (perhaps unlimited) opportunities for you to package, position, and present your skills, knowledge, and ability to add value.

If you tell someone you are looking for a full-time job, they will generally respond, "We're hiring," or, "We're not hiring." But if you ask someone for an opportunity to pitch your ability to make or save them money, either they want to make or save money or they do not. Who in business does not want to make or save money?

Relative to the number of qualified people, there are fewer jobs in the managerial and professional ranks in the current marketplace than in the feudal-corporate economy. The economic rationale, the difficulty of terminating people who have been hired, and the trend toward new ways of getting work done all now mitigate against the robust growth of on-staff jobs. And those that do exist are in constant jeopardy because of mergers and acquisitions and other restructurings and the greater number of business and product failures in this competitive environment.

Every multipreneur should have a business that defines his or her professional identity. This "business" includes a d/b/a registered with the town clerk (or a duly formed corporation); a business checking account (or personal account used only for business purposes); an office at home or elsewhere; a database of prospects, customers, and contacts; receipts and other records of business expenditures (invaluable at tax time); and marketing tools, including letterhead, envelopes, business cards, and some kind of collateral material, either a simple brochure or a three-to-five-page description of your business.

In other words, every multipreneur should have a business or (if you have a full-time employer) a side business, one that actually books some revenue and incurs some expenses. Then, as you do business from this platform, if someone wants to hire you or you want to pitch the idea of working on the payroll to someone, you are in a position of strength. This notwithstanding, you can still maintain a résumé and conduct networking efforts geared toward finding an on-staff job and use them when they can be of potential value.

Stay on Code Blue

The true multipreneur is always marketing herself. But even people, multipreneurs or not, who are in full-time jobs should take an ever-ready approach to the job search. As serial executive Hall McKinley believes:

> You have to be in a state of constant readiness, what the Strategic Air Command calls "Code Blue," in today's job market—even if you have a full-time job that you're happy with. Then if something happens, you can move to "Code Pink" and then "Code Red" and shift the job search up to high gear. If you are doing it right, 70 percent of the effort of a job search should be expended before you actually need a job. You should always keep your résumé updated. You should always have a list of companies that you are interested in or that might need you. You should always have your network humming—not just when you need those contacts. You should always be aware of what's up in the job market. You should always, psychologically, be ready to shift into high gear.

In today's market it really doesn't pay to set up an either/or mindset regarding employment situations. There is little point in saying, "I'll never go back to work for someone else," on the one hand or, on the other, saying, "I would never be happy without an employer." Living with the ambiguity that arises when you choose to make neither of these exclusionary statements will help you develop the flexibility necessary in today's job market.

The market is now such that people will be in and out of full-time jobs over the course of their careers. Full-time jobs are here to stay, and there is much to be said for the regular paychecks, the benefit packages, and the learning opportunities that such jobs offer to multipreneurs. But nobody can count on the permanence of any particular full-time job. So "Code Blue" must be the watchwords.

Get the Right Network in Place

Hordes of people seeking jobs, leads, information, and interviews have pounded many helpful people to a pulp. If you are unemployed and actively seeking full-time employment and you want to take a multipreneurial approach, you should be out looking for work as an independent contractor, using the networking methods discussed in chapter 7. If you are on a straight search for a full-time job, the best network will include people who are in the same position you are in. Yes, that's right, other similarly situated job seekers. It is easy to think of the network as comprising only people who are already working and to see them as people who can help you because they either have hiring authority or are in touch with people who have it. However, those who are not working can actually be a better resource. Hall McKinley, the strategic planning executive, points out:

> Career counselors tell you to do networking, but what I did was to get in touch with people who were in the same situation I was. People who were as much like me as I could find. It netted down to about four or five guys. They were looking for jobs. They had worked for IBM. They were encountering a lot of rejection. We were all going through the same thing. And I didn't realize it, but in effect I had created a peer support group. They were the only guys who really had time for me, who had useful suggestions for me. If they were pursuing a job opportunity and the geography or the chemistry was wrong, they would share that with me and I would do the same. For it to work, you've got to find people whom you respect and who respect you. To establish a quid pro quo, you have to be very open with them about what you are doing and about your experiences. You have to establish very strong personal bonds with a relatively small inner network of people who can relate to your situation and problems.
>
> This provides a positive experience in your day-to-day communications. Because if you do regular networking in a job search, a lot of people are too busy to help. In all cases, the people who directed me to the places where I got jobs

were those who were out of work or who had become consultants but were also looking for something full-time. In no
case did I get a valid lead from someone who was employed.
This inner network was more successful than any other
source for me. The peer group not only led to leads, but also
helped me through the negative experiences because I knew
they were good guys and they treated me as a good guy, and it
was very, very helpful.

Remember, there is the world of networking and then there is the
world of genuine relationships.

Use the Right Communications Tools

In the new economy, you can't make it on a résumé and cover letter
alone. Yet neither of these items is about to disappear. People still
want to see them, so get them to work for you. The most common
mistake people make with their résumé and cover letter is to do the
résumé once and redo the cover letter, typically to modify the reader's
understanding of the résumé, to try to explain how they are right for
the job in spite of the résumé.

Here's a better way: Customize the résumé and use a standard
cover letter. To customize the résumé, you need a computer or word
processor (or you will have to pay a service). Each version of the
résumé should announce a different objective, then show the experience and accomplishments that support that objective. At one point
I had six standard versions of my résumé: one for marketing communications, one for product development, one for credit/industry/
competitive analysis, one for sales, one for corporate training, and
one for editor/writer. I was also ready, willing, and able to customize
any of them to fit any new employment situation that attracted me—
or to create an entirely new résumé within two hours. Of course, as a
multipreneur fifteen years into my career, I had enough varied experience and references to support such résumés.

Always use a cover letter, never more than one page long, always
perfect in grammar, layout, and neatness. In my experience cover
letters don't get read as often or as closely as résumés, but many
people do read them. Don't get cute in your cover letter; it backfires

more often than not. If you have personal knowledge or a connection with the outfit you are approaching, by all means cite it, but otherwise tell them briefly that you are interested, why you are interested, and that you appreciate their consideration.

If you are taking the multipreneurial approach of selling your services as an independent contractor rather than just seeking a job on the payroll, do not use a résumé because you will confuse them. Also, if you are at a higher level, don't use a résumé that cites an objective such as "seeking full-time, part-time, or project work," because it smacks of desperation. Use a sales letter, or a sales letter with a brochure, and a business card. Then follow up with a phone call. Remember, you are marketing yourself and your ability to add value.

Have a Portfolio and Work Samples, If Possible

Whether you are selling your services or looking for a job, have a project portfolio, work samples, client lists—any useful proof of the job you can do (unless you are seeking a higher-level post). Do not send these in your initial mailing. Bring them to the interview, but don't offer them unless the prospect is interested. In compiling samples, be sure not to reveal any confidential information to a third party. Pick samples that are relevant and that you can make interesting comments about. Outplacement consultant Charles Cates advises:

> What you need when you are looking for a job has changed. For example, you now should have samples of your work. If you have been in a place for six months and another place for six months, you need some letters and documentation from people you have worked with who have been extremely pleased with your work. These days a job interview is more like an audition. There are important issues involved in how you talk about the fact that you have been in three companies and doing contract work. It's a different way of talking than if you have been in a full-time job in a large company for a while.

When you talk about the companies you've worked for, focus on how you added value. Stress the activities and your role. In the "old way" of talking, the focus was often rendered fuzzy by talk about what you were "responsible for" and what "we were doing at the time in the company." Today, to be convincing, you have to focus on how you got results, who did and didn't do what, what worked and what didn't. When appropriate, work samples act as proof statements and lend verisimilitude to your words.

Don't expect your sample to get read, at least not while you are there. Most people are too busy to do more than skim it and may ask you to leave a copy behind. The important thing is to have samples. In some businesses—publishing, advertising, photography, design, fashion, video, and audio—samples are essential. If you are an actuary or an accountant, it can be impossible or silly to try to compile samples. But think seriously about it if you are a planner, analyst, or even a project manager. In these days of short-term, serial employment, samples are becoming an important means of judging the work you have done.

Keep Good Records of All Contacts

To build networks of contacts, keep track of everyone you meet. This is especially useful in a job search. After you find a job, these contacts can be invaluable to someone else in your network. Also, if you don't have records of your networked contacts, how are you going to call or write to thank them once you've found a job? That rarely performed courtesy marks you as a truly class act.

These contacts become part of your network, the one that you must maintain in order to stay on "Code Blue." These people are in your industry. They may be competitors in some areas, but they are also potential employers, contractors, subcontractors, investors, sponsors, or joint-venturers. Don't throw these names away. Stay in touch, even if only once a year when you see them at a conference or trade show.

Understand the Goal of an Interview

Having interviewed hundreds of candidates as both a hiring manager and as a headhunter, I've learned that many do not fully understand the goal of the process. When you are on any kind of an interview, whether for a full-time job or a small project, there is one major goal: to get an offer. This goal has apparently been obscured in many people's minds by the idea that they should "interview for information." Also, some people have become confused by the notion that "you are interviewing them as much as they are interviewing you." Others seem seriously to believe that they should be courted. (If they approached you, perhaps they will court you, but if you approached them, you're doing the courting.) Sure, you should get information and evaluate the opportunity, but the only useful information is that which helps you get an offer. And only when you have an offer do you have an opportunity to evaluate.

Managing Your Employment Portfolio

In multipreneuring you develop a portfolio of jobs, projects, businesses, and income streams as well as a portfolio of knowledge, skills, contacts, and credentials. Like an investor, you must actively manage your portfolio. This entails balancing risks and returns, desires and obligations, the future and the present. So your employment portfolio should include high-risk/high-return and lower-risk/lower-return opportunities. It should include movement toward your deepest dreams as an artist or athlete or public servant or world traveler, as well as the work that pays the bills (may the two someday be one for you). It should include skill-, contact-, and knowledge-building activities for your next career move and the move after that, as well as activities that add high value in your current situation.

The truly multipreneurial portfolio should, over time, include full-time and project work, managerial and technical skills, large corporate and small company experience, immediate income and future residuals, private enterprise and public service—as well as the full range of principles and practices presented in this book.

Can you build such a rich portfolio in a matter of months or a few years? No. That is why, ultimately, making the transition to multipreneur is a lifelong task. No matter. In the new economy, most of us can count on being in transition for the rest of our working lives. In this career climate, the principles and practices of multipreneuring offer your best route to ever higher levels of freedom, function, and income.

Acknowledgments

Clearly, no one could write a book called *Multipreneuring* on one's own. While the book was taking shape, Paul Miller of the Miller Institute and my colleagues at DRI/McGraw-Hill represented major influences. Paul taught me that among smart people there are varieties of intelligence and that most people can do far more than they imagine to develop professionally. Both our prior work together and methods I learned from Paul made this book possible. My colleagues at DRI, the nation's largest economic forecasting and consulting firm, have achieved a level of excellence in their field such that I couldn't help but be positively influenced.

In the early stages of framing the book and throughout the writing, Peter Lowy of Business Communication Strategies was an invaluable resource and support. Later, Todd Domke of Domke & Associates also generously contributed his knowledge and encouragement.

My agent, Mike Snell, again proved that when it comes to shaping business concepts for the marketplace, he is second to none. Without his faith in the project from day one and, later, that of Marilyn Abraham, this book would not exist. My thanks also go to Trish Todd at Simon & Schuster. Special thanks go to Laureen Connelly Rowland, my editor at Fireside, for her tireless support for the project. Laureen's expert, tasteful editing and her ideas for structural changes truly improved the book.

The multipreneurs who gave of their time, knowledge, and experience in agreeing to be interviewed for this book were most instrumental in bringing it about. My thanks to Tom Cashill, Mark Cohen, Sally Edwards, Arnold Goldstein, Marge and Steve Heiser, Craig Hickman, Hall McKinley, Emmett Murphy, Courtney Nelthropp, Mike Pickowicz, Jim Ryan, David Rye, Mike Silva, Ray Suh, Michèle Van Buren, and John Zemaitis.

Other people were extremely helpful to me in specific areas of multipreneuring. For insights and material on how producers think and work, I am indebted to Todd Domke, Marge Heiser, Roseann Hirsch, Rebecca Miller, and Alexandra Scott. For views on the uses of technology, I thank Steve Childs, Roger Schank, Michael Wolff, and Mary Welch. Special thanks to Larry Elkin and Scott Shires for their advice and insights and the benefit of their experience as financial planners and as multipreneurs. Thank you also to Father William Byron of Georgetown University School of Business for sharing the results of his research on midlife job loss. And thank you to Tom Huf for war stories and support.

Having spent a relatively short time in the formal career management profession as an executive recruiter, and that years ago, I am indebted to the practicing career management and outplacement professionals who gave me their time and insights: Charles Cates, John Challenger, Beverly Kaye, Richard Plazza, and Joanne Pratt.

Many thanks to those who supported my efforts at the logistical level. After working on the book for more than a year during evenings and weekends while employed full-time at DRI/McGraw-Hill, I requested a move to half-time status for four months to finish the book on deadline. Research director and chief financial economist David Wyss, my boss at DRI, graciously granted this request. During that period of half-time status, my staff at DRI, particularly Diane Avery, Donna Laswell, and Rob Ringelstein, covered empty bases efficiently and with good humor. Thanks also to Mary McCaffrey for doing the same. To all of my friends and associates at DRI/McGraw-Hill, I offer my sincerest thanks for your interest, encouragement, and understanding. Thanks also to Bruce Burke and Jack Clancy for office space at reasonable rates and to everyone at the offices of Burclan Productions for their interest in this book.

My deepest thanks go to my wife, Phyllis, health care manager and consultant, certified nurse-midwife, homemaker, and a multi-preneur from way back, and to our children, Danny and Matt, all of whom, with love and faith, endured my absences and my occasional suboptimal responses to stress. Thanks also to both sides of our family, and to all my friends, for your encouragement throughout the effort.

Tom Gorman
Newton, Massachusetts

Index

ABI Inform, 190
accountants, 229
    broad job definition of, 37
acting the part, 125, 127–28
adding value, 10, 24–25, 30, 31, 43–64, 93, 95
    acting like a producer and, 135, 136, 158
    business and household support and, 227–28
    definition of, 43–44
    diagrams for, 57
    enabling factors for, 47–52
    formula for, 43–47, 58, 63
    four tactics for, 58–63
    information technology and, 188, 193
    job hunting and, 249, 257
    marketing and selling yourself and, 161, 162–63
    opportunity analysis and, 63–64
    process and, 55–58
    underpricing and, 57, 58–59, 246–247
    where to apply, 47, 52–58
advertising, 173
affinity groups, 221
Age of Unreason, The (Handy), 26n
American Express, 217

American Management Association, 63
ancillary benefits, 154
answering machines and services, 209
Apple, 130, 202
associations:
    formal networks and, 164, 165–66
    as information sources, 117
attorneys, 142, 227, 228–30
    broad job definition of, 37
automobile industry, 23

back-office (staff) functions, 207–30
    benefits management, 207, 218–27
    business and household support, 207, 227–28
    facilities management, 207–13
    financial management, 207, 213–218
    legal, business insurance, and tax matters, 207, 228–30
bandwidth, 105–6, 108–9
bar code system, 188
beaver farming, 122–23
benefit plans, 69, 207, 241
    corporate reduction of, 11
    personal management of, 11, 218–227
    in value added formula, 44–45

benefits risk, 66, 67, 70–71, 75–76, 86, 87
big business ideas (BBI), 251
Big League Business Thinking (Miller and Gorman), 39n
billable time, 251
binary thinking, 94–95
birds of a feather, core skills application and, 53–54, 64
blue-collar employees, 20, 23
Blue Cross/Blue Shield, 220
books, 61, 63, 116–17, 191, 195
boutique (specialty) shops, 54
buffer time, 101
business and household support, 207, 227–28
business cycles, 18
businesses, purchasing of, 242–44
business insurance, 228, 229
business literacy, 108
business opportunities:
    through information technology, 186, 191–92, 193–99
    plan development and, 197–99
    situational or process analysis and, 194–95
    technological capabilities and, 195–97
"buying the business," 59

calendars, 103
capitalism:
    creative destruction in, 17–18, 19
    individual, 12, 18, 23, 29–30, 65
    intellectual, 135, 137, 158
career management, 12–13, 30, 31–32
car loans, 217
car phones, 209
cash flow:
    negative, 234–35
    schedules for, 217–18
cash value insurance, 223
Cates, Charles, 22, 69–70, 71, 256
CBS, 59
CD-ROMs, 114, 117, 197
chain of command, 27
change:
    handling of, 104–10
    rapid, 22, 23–24, 30

changes and history, researching of, 129, 131
chief executive officers (CEO), 19, 20
Childs, Steve, 185, 193, 201, 204, 205
Cicero, 130
client lists, 172
closing, 176, 183
COBRA (Consolidated Omnibus Budget Reconciliation Act), 221
Code Blue, 249, 253, 257
cold calls, 92, 94, 120, 160, 175–76
collections, telephone, 237
color printing, 203
combinations, new means of, 188–89
companies:
    back-office functions handled by, 207
    benefit plans reduced by, 11
    core capabilities of, 56
    economic rationalizing by, 24–25
    military structure of, 19, 26
    paternal role abandoned by, 19–21, 30, 32, 65
    structure and infrastructure given by, 90–91
    transaction-based relationships and, 25–26
    transformation of, 10–11, 19–22, 26–28
    transitions within, 244–46
    unwritten employment contracts at, 19–20
    virtual, 61, 156–58
    see also corporate feudalism
competition, 22, 23–24, 30, 190–91
competitive advantage, 28, 51–52, 64, 132
compound interest, 224
computer industry, 23, 71, 130
    see also information technology; personal computers
computer literacy, 28, 184, 199–205
    best learning methods for, 200, 204
    overcoming fears and learning rules, 200–201
    proper equipment and service, 200, 203
    using newly-learned skills, 200, 205

your needs and technological limits, 200, 201–3
concept testing, 139
conceptual problems, 150–51
conceptual thinking, 36, 82, 138–39, 143–44
condo office space, 208, 209
conferences, 146–47, 148, 175
Consolidated Omnibus Budget Reconciliation Act (COBRA), 221
consulting firms, 56
contact plans, 171
contacts, keeping record of, 250, 257
contingent pay, 60–61, 64
Continuation Health Law, 221
continuing education, 244
contracts, see employment contracts
contribution, see dollar contribution
control, 110–11
copiers, copy services, 207, 208, 211
core capabilities, corporate, 56
core employees, 26–27
core skills, 47–56, 58, 59, 64, 82, 162–63
corporate feudalism, 12, 18, 19, 26, 29, 43, 65
corporate nomads, 241–42
countercyclicality, 80
cover letters, 248, 255–56
co-workers, 71–72, 90, 98–99
creative destruction, 17–18, 19
creative risk, 11, 67, 74–75, 76, 86, 87, 88
"creatives" vs. "suits," 106
creativity, 125, 193–94
credit approval process audits, 169
credit cards, 217
Creditech Corporation, 162–63, 169, 208

Darwin, Charles, 17
databases, 62, 116–17, 123, 168, 190, 192–93
days off, 226–27
Daytimer, 103
d/b/a ("doing business as"), 157, 158, 252
debt, 216–17, 234–35
defensive investments, 80
deregulation, 23

desktop publishing systems, 202
disability insurance, 219, 223–24
"disaster relief program," 70–71
diversification and portfolio approaches, as risk management tool, 67, 80–82, 84
"doing business as" (d/b/a), 157, 158, 252
dollar contribution:
increasing amount of, 58, 59–60, 64
in value added formula, 43, 45–47
Domke, Todd, 92, 140–41, 153, 154, 166–67, 212–13
door openers, fees charged for, 169–170
downsizing, 24, 104
downward mobility, 12
drivers and transactions, researching of, 129, 130–31
Drucker, Peter, 37

economic rationalization, 22, 24–25, 30, 43
economics, realistic appraisal of, 44
education, 12, 23, 48–49, 116, 244
Edwards, Sally, 32, 36, 50–51, 62, 70, 114
Elkin, Larry, 212, 213–14, 217, 221–222, 225–26, 249
E-mail, 202, 210, 211
emotional risk, 11, 67, 73–74, 75, 76, 86, 87, 88
employees, 10, 25
dollar contribution of, 43, 45–47
inner vs. outer circles of, 26–27
overhead costs created by, 45
part-time, 26, 96, 118, 136
replacement cost of, 45–46
employment contracts:
unwritten, 19–20
written, 82, 228–29
endorsements, 172
engineers, broad job definition of, 37
enjoyment, of work, 92
entitlement, sense of, 44
entrepreneurs, 12
derivation of, 11
Entrup, Bill, 122, 123
escape routes and fallback positions, in risk management, 68, 84–85

evolution, 17–18
Excel, 168, 202
"Executive Computing" column, in
    New York Times, 196
executive/professional temps, 241–42
executives, see management,
    managers
Executive Suites, 208
expectations, managing of, 67, 79–
    80
expenses, 148
    billable, 82
    plus fees, 247–48
    viewed as variable, 20–21, 24
experience, 34–35, 48–49, 241
experts, 174–75
    real vs. instant, 121–22, 127–28
    as sources of information, 116,
        123–24
    see also instant experts
external contractor, see independent
    contractors
external supports, 109–10

facilities management, 207–13
    computer equipment and software,
        207, 211
    copiers or copy services, 207, 211
    office space and basic furniture,
        207, 208–9, 211–13
    sundries, 207, 211
    telephone and fax equipment, 207,
        209–11
faking it, 120–21
families, 82, 213
    interpersonal risk and, 66, 72–73
    managing expectations of, 79–80
    risk sharing and swapping in, 83
    work hours and, 102
fax machines, 209–10
fax modems, 202, 210
feedback, 101
fees:
    based on results, 60–61
    for door openers, 169–70
    expenses, 247–48
    subcontractors', 247
financial management, 207
    ideal budget percentage allocation,
        215
    planning and, 213–18

financial risk, 11, 66, 67, 69–70, 75,
    76, 86, 87
financial skills, 141–42, 145, 148–49
Fleet Feet, 50
flexibility, see working productively
    and flexibly
forums, 175
franchises, 242–44
Franklin, Benjamin, 31
Franklin Quest, 103
freelancers, 12, 20, 21, 161
free money, 226
free trade, 23
front-office (line) functions, 207
fudge factors, 101, 149
"fungibility of resources," 104
furniture, office, 207, 209

Gates, Bill, 130
generalists, 122
Goldstein, Arnold, 81
graphics packages, 202

Handy, Charles, 26n
Harvard Graphics, 202
headhunters, 120
health care costs, 72
health insurance, 219, 220–22
health maintenance organizations
    (HMOs), 219, 220–21
Heiser, Marge, 49, 120
Hickman, Craig, 36, 63, 81–82, 105–
    106
high-return activities, 93–95
High Rollers, 77
high value added situations, 57–58
Hirsch, Roseann, 93–94, 98, 139,
    141, 151
history and changes, researching of,
    129, 131
home offices, 100, 208, 209, 211–13
How to Get Control of Your Time and
    Life (Lakien), 103
HQ Business Centers, 208
human infrastructure, 98–99
"hunter-gatherers," 36

IBM, 23, 51, 71, 202
identity, professional, 24, 47–48, 241,
    252
    broadening of, 36–38, 39

rebuilding of, 35–36, 39
sense of, 30, 31
in-boxes, 90
income:
   as element of financial risk, 69
   multiple sources of, 81, 83
   total dollar income vs. take home
      pay, 214
independent (external) contractors,
      10, 25, 26, 30, 90, 136
   expenses passed on by, 45
   marketing hard and, 161–64
   multiple sources of income for, 81
   as transition tactic, 239–41
index cards, 168, 192–93
individual capitalism, 12, 18, 23, 29–
      30, 65
Industrial Age, 20, 28, 29
Industrial Revolution, 18
inflation, 18
informal networks, 164, 166–68
information:
   definition of, 187
   delivery methods for, 61–63
   dynamics, 192
   see also learning
Information Age, 18, 20, 28, 61
information system, 100
information technology (IT), 12, 30,
      31, 184–205
   business opportunities and, 186,
      191–92, 193–99
   definition of, 187
   effects of, 186–91
   increasing productivity through,
      190–92, 193, 199–205
   primer for exploitation of, 191–
      205
   two types of opportunities created
      by, 186
   see also personal computers
infrastructure, 90–91, 97–100
inputs and outputs (I/O), researching
      of, 129–30
instant experts, 121–32
   business understanding approach
      of, 128–31
   information technology and, 190
   learning techniques for, 123–25
   real experts compared with, 121–
      122, 127–28

skills approach of, 125–28
insurance policies:
   business, 228, 229
   in personal benefits package, 219–
      224
   as risk management tool, 67, 82–
      83
intellectual capitalism, 135, 137, 158
interest, compound, 224
Internal Revenue Service (IRS) 151,
      214
internal supports, 109–10
Internet, 202
internships, 119–20, 237
interpersonal risk, 66, 67, 72–73, 75,
      76, 86, 87, 88
interpersonal skills, 12
interviews, job, 250, 257–58
investing, 225
   diversification and, 80
investor motivation, 141–42
IRS (Internal Revenue Service), 151,
      214
IT, see information technology

Japan, 23
job definitions, see identity,
      professional
job descriptions, 90
job hunting, 248–58
   basic principles of, 249–50
job interviews, 250, 257–58
Jobs, Steven, 130
job sharing, 10–11
joint-venture partners, 27, 136
Jupiter Communications Company,
      72
just-in-time workers, 26–27

Kaye, Beverly, 104
Keogh plans, 225
kill fees, 82
knockoffs, 62
Korea, 23

labor market, globalization of, 23
Lakien, Alan, 103
laser printers, 203
layoffs, 19, 20, 24
learning, 24, 112–32, 244
   as competitive advantage, 132

learning (*continued*)
　formal techniques for, 115–17
　information technology and, 189–190
　instant expertise and, 121–32
　methods of, 113–20
　on-the-job techniques for, 117–20
　two key questions on, 112
legal matters, 228–30
letter agreements, 82, 228
Letterman, David, 59
level playing field, 187–88
leveraging yourself, 58, 61–62, 64
Levitt, Steve, 62
life insurance, 82, 219
line (front-office) functions, 207
loans, 216–17
lone eagles, 53, 54–55, 64
long-term/retirement savings, 224–26
Lotus 1-2-3, 168, 202
low-return activities, 93–95, 101
low value added situations, 57–58
Lowy, Peter, 165, 169, 176
Lucky Ducks, 77

Macintosh, 202
McKinley, Hall, 33, 36, 78, 79–80, 84, 112–13, 253, 254–55
management, managers, 29, 45
　age and career prospects and, 53
　broad job definition of, 37
　increased professional risk for, 71
　as producers, 27–28, 138, 154–56
　producers compared with, 136–38
　team orientation and, 26
　temp work and, 241–42
　as variable expense, 20–21, 24
management information systems (MIS), 106
managerial skills, 142–43, 145–46, 149–50
managing expectations, as risk management tool, 67, 79–80
Manufacturers Hanover Trust, 122
manufacturing, 28, 29
Marino, Jory, 22
marketing, definition of, 161
marketing and selling yourself, 26, 30, 31, 159–83
　hard marketing in, 161–64
　job hunting and, 249, 251–52

offers and, 168–69
　positioning and, 170
　prospects and, 168
　relationship between marketing and selling in, 161
　soft selling in, 176–83
　ten basic tools for, 171–76
　three network types for, 164–68
marketing consultants, 56
marketplace, 22–31
　new characteristics of, 22–31
　transformation of, 19–22
market research, 236–37
marriage, *see* families
Massachusetts Businessperson's Association, 221
MBAs, 108, 114, 116
meetings, closing time for, 102
mentor programs, 99
Mexico, 23
Microsoft, 130
Microsoft Excel, 168, 202
Microsoft Windows, 202–3, 204
Microsoft Word, 202
Miller, Paul, 39n, 62
Miller, Rebecca, 140, 143, 148
Miller Report of Executive Development, The (Miller), 62
modems, 202, 210
moderate value added situations, 57
money:
　as driver, 130–31
　free, 226
　rational thinking about, 69–70
　see also fees; financial management; income
moonlighting, 118, 237–39, 240
mortgages, 216
motivation:
　of investors, 141–42
　of oneself, 95–96
multiple retainers, 250–51
multipreneuring:
　coining of term, 11
　definition of, 10–11
　general guidelines for transition to, 234–35
　practices of, 133–230
　principles of, 41–132
　and response to change, 15–39

starting points in transition to, 235–46
transition to, 231–58
multipreneurs:
  adaptive responses of, 30–31
  broad professional identities of, 36–38
  characteristics of, 18–19, 33–34
  examples of, 12, 32–33
  experts and generalists and, 122
  hypothetical job description for, 90
  learning methods used by, 113–15
  on selling, 160–61
Murphy, Emmett, 36, 52, 73–74, 107–8, 113
"mystery cash," 216

needs assessment, 176, 178–79
negotiations, 176, 180–83
negotiation skills, 141–42, 145, 148–149
Nelthropp, Courtney, 32, 51
networks, 164–68
  formal networks and associations, 164, 165–66
  informal, 164, 166–68
  job hunting and, 250, 254–55
  swap meets, 164–65
newsletters, 173
New York Times, 196
nondisclosure/noncompete provisions, 228

obligations, as elements of financial risk, 69
OEMs (original equipment manufacturers), 198
offers, 168–69
"office noise" background tapes, 210
offices:
  decentralization of, 28–29
  five options for, 208
  home, 100, 208, 209, 211–13
  outside, 100, 208–9
Ogilvy, David, 125
operations consultants, 56
opportunity analysis:
  from risk management perspective, 85–89
  from value added perspective, 63–64

organizational metamorphoses, 22, 26–28, 30
organizational problems, 151–52
Other People's Talent, 135
outsourcing, 11, 24, 57, 61
overhead costs, 45
overpricing, 248

PageMaker, 202
partnerships, 27, 136, 142
part-time employees, 26, 96, 118, 136
pay-for-performance, 60–61, 64
people problems, 152–53
people skills, 140–41, 144–45, 148
personal computers (PCs), 49, 71, 173
  number of, 72
  as office requirement, 211
  technology shift role of, 28–29, 72, 185–86
  two main uses of, 194
  see also computer industry; databases; information technology
physical/systems infrastructure, 98, 100
Pickowicz, Mike, 114
piggybacking, 148
planners, 21, 52, 103, 136
planning and organizational skills, 139–40, 144, 147–48
planning and preparation, as risk management tool, 67, 78
players and teams, 129, 130
playing field, levelling of, 187–88
Plazza, Richard, 22, 52
Polaroid Digital Palette, 203
portfolios, 250, 256–57, 258
positioning, 170
PowerPoint, 202
Pratt, Joanne, 26, 28, 92, 212
preferred provider organizations (PPOs), 219, 220–21
prejudices, 106–7
pricing strategies, 246–48
  see also underpricing
printers:
  color, 203
  laser vs. jet-ink, 203
proactivity, 34
pro bono work, 238

process, added value and, 55–58
producers (producer-intermediaries), 30, 135–58, 233
  five essential roles of, 136
  function of, 27, 135–36
  as individual vs. as team, 136
  managers as, 27–28, 138, 154–56
  problem-avoidance techniques for, 150–54
  project walk-through for, 146–50
  skill assessment for, 143–46
  skills of, 138–43
  traditional managers compared with, 136–38
product and service descriptions, 171–72
productivity:
  personal computers and, 186
  see also working productively and flexibly
professional identity, see identity, professional
professional risk, 11, 66, 67, 71–72, 75, 76, 86, 87, 88
profit, as percentage of sales, 108
profitability problems, 153–54
project work, 239–41
promotional items, 173
proposals, 176, 178–79, 181
proprietary information, 62, 228–29
ProQuest, 190
prospects, 168
public relations, 173–75

Q Score, 62
qualification, 176–78
QuarkXPress, 202

railroad industry, 37
raises, 46
real estate, 46
recent engagements, lists of, 172–73
recessions, 18, 24, 80
references, 172
relationship-based transactions, 21, 25–26
rental office space, 208, 209
replacement cost, 45–46
research:
  organizing for, 129–31
  and writing, 117

see also learning
response capability, 107–9
responsibilities, on-the-job, 117–18
résumés, 241, 248, 255–56
retainers, multiple, 250–51
retirement savings, 224–26
reward systems, 100
RFP (request for proposals), 179
risk, 24, 65–89
  assuming portion of employer's or clients share of, 58, 60–61, 64
  dimensions of, 68–75
  management tools for, 67–68, 76–85, 87–89
  opportunity analysis and, 85–89
  possible benefits of, 67
  recognition of, 66–68, 89
  types of, 11, 66–67
risk profiles, 75–76
risk-return matrix, 77
risk/reward assessment, 85–87
Rule of 72, 224
Rut Walkers, 77
Rye, David, 32–33, 49, 103, 114, 184

salary:
  dollar contribution and, 59–60
  raises in, 46
  in value added formula, 43–47
sales, definition of, 161
sales letters, 172
salespeople, 50
  broad job definition of, 37
  cold calls and, 92, 94, 160, 175–76
  nonsalespeople compared with, 159–60
savings, long-term/retirement, 224–226
savings incentive plan (SIP), 226
Schank, Roger, 189
SCORE, 99
Scott, Alexandra, 151–52
second-order skills, 52
"See one. Do one. Teach one," 121
self-employment tax, 214
self-insight, 34
self-study, 244
selling yourself, see marketing and selling yourself
seminars, 63
service providers, 21, 102–3

service vendors, 197
sharing and swapping, as risk
    management tool, 68, 83–85
Shires, Scott, 216
Short Timers, 77
Shu, Ray, 33, 68, 73, 98, 113–14
SIP (savings incentive plan), 226
skills:
    conceptual thinking, 138–39,
        143–44
    core, 47–56, 58, 59, 64, 82, 162–
        163
    in finance and negotiations, 141–
        142, 145
    instant experts' approach to, 125–
        128
    multiple, 80–82
    people-oriented, 140–41, 144–45,
        148
    planning and organizational, 139–
        140, 144, 147–48
    of producers, 61, 138–46
    second- or third-order, 52
    selling of, 162–63
    software training programs for,
        146–47, 148
    supervisory and managerial, 142–
        143, 145–46, 149–50
Small Business Association, 99
social life, 234, 235
Social Security, 224
soft selling:
    definition of, 161, 176
    see also selling yourself
software training programs, for
    business skills, 146–47, 148
speaking engagements, 175
specialty (boutique) shops, 54
spouses, see families
spreadsheets, 168, 194
staff functions, see back-office
    functions
standing, 118
stopgap jobs, 236–37
strategic alliance partners, 27, 136,
    142
Strategy Game, The, 63
structure, 90–91, 95–97
subconscious, working with, 234, 235
subcontractors, 247
sublet office space, 208

success, identification of, 125–26
"suits" vs. "creatives," 106
supervisors, 21, 52
supervisory skills, 142–43, 145–46,
    149–50
supplier-partners, 27, 136
support systems, 109–10
survival of the fittest, 17–18
swap meets, 164–65

taking care of business, 206–30, 233
    back-office functions, 207–30
    definition of, 207
taxes:
    home offices and, 212
    professional advice on, 229
    self-employment, 214
team and players, 129, 130
techies, 28, 193, 199
technique, in learning skills, 125,
    126–27
technological evolution, 18
technology, see information
    technology
technology consultants, 56
"Technology" pages, in Wall Street
    Journal, 196
technology shift, 23, 28–29, 30, 72,
    185–86
telecommuting, 10, 29
telemarketing, 175, 236–37
telephone collections, 237
telephones, 101, 207, 208
    cold calls, 92, 94, 120, 160, 175–
        176
    as office requirement, 209–11
term insurance, 222–23
third-order skills, 52
ticklers, 103
time:
    billable, 251
    expertise and, 127–28
    structuring of, 95–97, 101, 102,
        103
"to do" lists, 103
touch typing, 200
training, 116, 244
transaction-based relationships, 21,
    22, 25–26, 27, 30
transactions and drivers, researching
    of, 129, 130–31

transportation, 29, 37
travel and entertainment (T&E)
    cards, 217
Trinity Fitness, 50, 51
turnkey offices, 208

underpricing, 241
    added value and, 57, 58–59, 246–
    247
    ancillary benefits and, 154
    benefits and dangers of, 119
understudies, 118

vacation loans, 216–17
vacations, 226–27
value added formula, 43–47, 58, 63
value added tax, 55
Van Buren, Michèle, 33, 99, 114–15,
    163–64, 166
Ventura, 202
virtual companies, 61, 156–58
Visicalc, 194
volunteering, 119–20, 237

Wall Street Journal, 196
wealth, as element of financial risk,
    69
white-collar employees, 20, 23
Windows, 202–3, 204

WNET, 99
Wolff, Michael, 184–85, 187–88,
    191, 192, 195
WordPerfect, 202
word processing, 194, 201–2
working productively and flexibly, 24,
    34, 90–111
    control and, 110–11
    flexibility-related abilities, 104–5
    focusing and, 91–103
    handling change and, 104–10
    high-return vs. low-return
        activities, 93–95
    increasing flexibility, 105–9
    information technology and, 190–
        192, 193, 199–205
    infrastructure and, 90–91, 97–100
    structuring time, 95–97
    ten productivity improvement
        tactics for, 100–103
    three structural questions for, 97
work samples, 172–73, 250, 256–57
World Future Society, 117
Wozniak, Steve, 130
Writer's Digest Books, 174
Writer's Market, 174
writing, 63, 115

Yuba Snowshoes, 50, 51